Teaching Human Rights

ISBN 978-0-87293-147-3

Printed in the United States of America on acid-free paper that meets the American National Standards Institute Z39-48 standard.

Council on Social Work Education, Inc.
1701 Duke Street, Suite 200
Alexandria, VA 22314-3457
www.cswe.org

Teaching Human Rights:
Curriculum Resources for Social Workers

Edited by M. C. "Terry" Hokenstad, Lynne M. Healy, and Uma A. Segal

Alexandria, Virginia

CONTENTS

Teaching Content on Human Rights: Exercises and Supplementary Materials

Teaching Content on Human Rights: Case Vignettes and Discussion Exercises

PREFACE

The Katherine A. Kendall Institute for International Social Work Education is a program unit of the Council on Social Work Education (CSWE) that focuses on global issues and the integration of international content into the social work curriculum. It carries the name of Dr. Katherine Kendall, an international icon in social work education. An advisory board composed of social work educators from the United States along with representatives of international social work organizations serves as the programmatic policy-making and action body.

This book is the result of discussion and action by the Kendall Institute Advisory Board. It was proposed by members of the Advisory Board and unanimously adopted as a major project for the Kendall Institute. The three editors, all members of the Advisory Board, agreed to take responsibility for developing this manual. The proposal was further developed and then approved by the CSWE Council on Publications.

Several people deserve special thanks for their contributions to the manual and help to the editors in the many tasks required to move it from an idea to reality. Dr. Joseph Wronka, a social work educator who is a leading human rights scholar, willingly contributed the first chapter providing a comprehensive overview of human rights as a foundation for the use of the teaching materials in the manual. Andrea Bediako, coordinator of international programs at CSWE, provided consistent support including facilitating the request for contributions to the manual and coordinating the communications between the editors and contributors to the manual. Amy Roberts, doctoral candidate at the Mandel School of Applied Social Sciences, Case Western Reserve University, performed a number of important roles, including coordinating the review of submissions and assembling the final manuscript with both efficiency and effectiveness. Finally, Elizabeth Simon, manager of publications at CSWE, was gracious in response to many questions and helpful in moving the manual forward in the many steps prior to publication.

INTRODUCTION

Social work can rightfully be considered a human rights profession because one major function of social work nationally and internationally is the promotion and protection of human rights for all and specifically for the most socially and economically vulnerable members of the society. Thus, human rights content needs to be fully integrated into social work education in curriculum policy and classroom exercises. Although content about human rights is abundant in the literature, it is not always available in a form that can be readily incorporated into courses in social policy, social and behavioral theory, and social work practice.

The purpose of *Teaching Human Rights* is to provide various types of teaching materials that can be selectively used by educational programs and social work educators to enhance and expand human rights knowledge for their students. The book brings together syllabi, course modules, teaching exercises, and media currently being used by graduate and undergraduate programs throughout the United States. It also provides a bibliography comprised of major websites containing content on human rights and human rights education along with books and articles on social work and human rights. Materials included in the volume have been selected on the basis of their human rights focus and their applicability to classroom teaching and learning. Collectively they provide information and ideas that can be applied across the social work curriculum.

Prefatory articles on human rights and human rights education open the handbook and provide a context for the included teaching materials. Dr. Joseph Wronka, a human rights scholar and social educator, presents an overview of human rights with an examination of the Universal Declaration of Human Rights followed by Guiding Principles and Implementation Mechanisms. His chapter is followed by an editorial article that considers human rights as an essential component of social work education. This second essay provides background information about the World Programme for Human Rights Education and then examines some of the major human rights scholarship by social work educators in the last decade. It also highlights the place of human rights in social work curriculum.

The content of the manual is organized into four sections. In addition to the introductory material in Part 1, they include (1) syllabi from undergraduate and graduate social work programs; (2) human rights exercises; and (3) media on human rights, including a brief human rights bibliography. Introductory summaries of the sections are provided to help the reader locate the most useful teaching materials.

These teaching resources have been shared by a range of educational programs, including those that offer human rights specializations and those that have integrated human rights content into individual foundation and elective courses. It is our hope that sharing these resources will facilitate additional inclusion of human rights in social work education; foster collaboration among social work educators; and ultimately, inspire students to be professionally active in promoting and protecting human rights.

The Editors

PART 1
BACKGROUND

An Overview of Human Rights

Joseph Wronka

The day before he died, the Reverend Dr. Martin Luther King spoke about the urgency of implementing what he called "the human rights revolution" (1968, p. 1) echoing his feelings that the real issues of the time were not civil rights, but rather human rights. Other luminaries such as Malcolm X urged oppressed peoples of the world to see their issues as a "struggle for human rights...and use United Nations avenues, its Human Rights Commission as a way of garnering "the moral support of the world" (King, 1992, as cited in Wronka, 2008a, p. 33). The term *human rights*, ultimately the legal mandate to fulfill human need, was officially coined by the United Nations (UN) in 1945. Echoing the wisdom of Victor Hugo, author of *Les Miserables,* it is a powerful idea whose time has come. Indeed, Eleanor Roosevelt (1963), a prime leader in the earlier days of the human rights movement, saw the importance of ideas when she said that "the force of ideas, rather than material goods ... [and] ... only the power of ideas and enduring values, can keep us ... great. ... For where there is not vision, the people perish" (p. 6).

Today no government or professional organization would dare say that it is against human rights, a powerful idea that arose from the ashes of World War II. Indeed, the International Federation of Social Workers (IFSW) has stated: "From its inception, social work has been a human rights profession, having as its basic tenet the intrinsic value of every human being" (United Nations, 1994, p. 3). Although social justice is essential to social work theory and praxis, it is often an amorphous concept (Reichert, 2011). Viewing human rights as its bedrock, however, should help clarify its contours and move us more readily toward socially just actions and policies.

But the question is: What exactly are human rights? More accurately, what is a human right, for as we will discuss, human rights are interdependent, indivisible, and interrelated. It is customary in the United States, for example, to speak of civil rights such as freedoms of speech and the press. But what is freedom of speech to a person who is homeless, lacks health care, and lives in a world at war? Adequate shelter, health care, and peace, to be discussed, are human rights.

Toward the Creation of a Human Rights Culture

Ultimately, we are talking about the creation of a human rights culture, which is a lived awareness of human rights principles in our minds and hearts that is dragged into our everyday lives (Wronka, 2013a). But that journey from the mind to the heart is a long one. If we view education as from the Latin *educare* meaning to grow, nourish, and strengthen, teaching and learning about human rights in this Second World Decade for Human Rights Education and Training, not only in formalized settings like schools, but also informal venues such as the media, the family, and the community both local and global, can play a pivotal role in moving us toward a socially just world where every person everywhere has her or his human rights realized.

Only chosen values endure. Thus, human rights education, broadly defined, must come from a nonelitist approach, having essentially an interdisciplinary, if not phenomenological orientation, and from the perspective of the educated layperson, as Eleanor Roosevelt wanted it. A phenomenological approach would take seriously, for example, the dictum of its founder Edmund Husserl, who spoke of the importance to "go back to the things themselves" (*Internet Encyclopedia of Philosophy*, 2013, p. 6);

and later, Gabriel Marcel, who talked about the inner strivings in the human species for a decent world that always rise up when confronted with social injustice. Thus, education ought to tap deeply into such strivings, the things themselves that speak to the core of our individual and collective well-being. Knowing about one's human rights, therefore, and feeling deeply about them in educated layperson's terms appears the best way to engage in a creative dialogue individually and collectively, yet across disciplines, to choose one's values and affect public sentiment (Wronka, 2013a).

To be sure, if we seriously consider the words of former Supreme Court Justice Louis Brandeis that "Government teaches the whole people by example" (Brainy Quote, 2013) then we can easily see how the choices that governments have made through their constitutions and policies in general can also serve as conduits for values clarification and formation. But so, too, we must now consider the role that corporations, businesses in general, and other nongovernmental organizations (NGOs) serve as teachers (Robinson, 2013).

In the final analysis, human rights represent a crystallization of values, which can, in turn, further influence values and vice-versa. But in both instances what we are speaking about is the fulfillment of human needs. Whereas knowledge of needs is imperfect, Gil (1992, 2013) has defined them roughly as biological–material (e.g., food, water), social–psychological (kinship, family), productive–creative (work, artistic expression), security (peace, privacy), self-actualization (education, living to one's potential), and spiritual (religion, human dignity). However, the point is that speaking about values, needs, or for that matter, social justice, although important, does not have the urgency and power to move people in positive directions as do the words *human rights* (Ife, 2008; Reichert, 2007, 2011; Wronka, 1995, 2008, 2012). The formation of the United Nations can easily be seen as a major attempt by the world community to help the human species survive given the atrocities of the Second World War, including the possibility of total nuclear global annihilation. Given that the human condition is moved toward altruism in times of disaster, if not urgency, the clarion call to create a human rights culture may indeed be the key to the creation of a socially just world.

A Brief History of the Idea

Because human rights discussions cannot take place in a historical–philosophical vacuum, it is necessary to briefly sketch select antecedents. In 1938, with pressure from a number of NGOs, President Roosevelt called the Conference of Evian to stop the ever increasing abuses of the Third Reich. The German representative there appealed to domestic sovereignty and the hypocrisy of nations, making note of other nations' abuses. The conference ended in failure because other countries did not want to bring attention to their own atrocities, such as public lynchings in the United States, the Soviet Union's own Gulag, and France's policies of torture in Africa (Buergenthal, Sheldon, & Stewart, 2009) A 1943 conference in Bermuda had a similar fate.

Certainly, such conferences were late in coming given the trans-Atlantic slave trade, genocide against indigenous peoples, and already centuries of oppression by European and other powers in Africa, Asia, and elsewhere. Yet what ensued was the killing of 10 million innocents, primarily Jews, but also others such as homosexuals, Jehovah's Witnesses, one-fourth of Poland, and Roma in a pogrom commonly known as the Holocaust. With increased sophisticated weaponry, as evidenced in part by so-called carpet bombings of cities such as Dresden and Tokyo and the nuclear bombings of Hiroshima and Nagasaki, overall an estimated 92 million people were killed.

To help assure that such atrocities never to happen again, the United Nations was formed on October 24, 1945. Although governments were initially reluctant to draft a human rights document "for lack of time" (UN Information Organization, 1945, p. 456) according to official recordings, NGOs, called in primarily by President Roosevelt, put pressure on them. They formed a committee, which elected Eleanor Roosevelt as chair, to come up with a document that was at least hortatory, urging governments to abide by human rights standards.

On December 10, 1948, the Universal Declaration of Human Rights was endorsed by the General Assembly with no dissent. In short, the Universal Declaration was an historical–philosophical compromise, or what may be called a dignified compromise (a phrase often used by Mahatma Gandhi) among various historical epochs and philosophical and religious traditions. After its drafting and in anticipation of further and stronger developments, Eleanor Roosevelt said it was a "good document.... Not a perfect document" (cited in Wronka, 2008a, p. 33).

Five Crucial Notions of the Universal Declaration of Human Rights

In short, the Universal Declaration consists of five crucial notions. Indeed, some human rights activists, such as the late Pope John Paul II, viewed that document as the foundation for a "culture of human rights" and the "responsibility of all" (Pope John Paul II, 1999, sec. 12, p. 10). As such, human rights can be viewed as a way of life, requiring major character transformation from the personal to the societal and the local to the global. For example, the first two crucial notions are human dignity and nondiscrimination (in Articles 1 and 2, respectively). These reflect essential strands of some of the world's major religions, largely the Judaic–Christian–Islamic tradition (reflective of the preponderance of western countries at the time at the United Nations), but also others such as Hinduism and Buddhism. The substance of the first two articles also can be found in the U.S. Declaration of Independence with its emphasis on equality. Thus, the only criterion to have one's rights is one's humanity, not one's gender, national or social origin, religion, language, circumstances of birth, or other status. Therefore, we must constantly be on guard not to treat others in discriminatory or prejudicial ways, but rather as human beings with rights to dignity and potential for growth, beyond our preconceived notions, to perceive them as possibilities, rather than actualities.

The third notion is civil and political rights (Articles 3–21), such as the freedoms of speech, the press, peaceful assembly, religion, and expression in general, largely mirroring values that emerged during the Age of Enlightenment and that are found in such documents as the U.S. Bill of Rights. Also referred to as negative freedoms or first generation rights, they mandate that governments not interfere with basic human needs for free access to information or the free exercise of religion, which had been extensively violated during centuries of religious and nationalistic wars in Europe.

The fourth crucial notion is economic, social, and cultural rights (Articles 22–27), such as rights to socially useful work at reasonable wages and in safe working conditions that contribute to the development of the human personality; rest and leisure; adequate shelter, clothing, food medical care, security in old age; family protections; education urging peace, tolerance, and friendship; and participation in culture. Such rights are also called positive freedoms, or second generation rights, and mandate that government provide for certain human needs to be productive or creative, rest, protect oneself from the elements, bond with friends and family, be cured from disease, and have a sense of social inclusion in general. They came about largely as a response to problems wrought by the Age of Industrialization with its growing, long, and monotonous assembly lines; poor working conditions; unremunerated work; and the increasing poverty such conditions engendered. Although the U.S. delegation to the UN at that time was a strong proponent of such rights, they also can be found in the Soviet Constitution of 1923.

The fifth crucial notion is solidarity, or third generation rights (Articles 28–30). Although still in the process of conceptual elaboration, these rights are the product of Post-Modernism, reflecting not only the failure of domestic sovereignty to solve global conflicts, but also concerns that blind trust in scientific knowledge and technological expertise will alone rescue humanity from contemporary scourges such as imperialism war, hunger, and thirst. A case in point is the invention of the airplane, raising the world's hopes that the sick would be more easily escorted to hospitals and food transported to the Third World. Rather, commodities were more easily extracted from places like Northern Africa, fitting the bill for the so-called Roaring Twenties in the United States (Zinn, 1990). The first explosive device also was dropped from an airplane by the Italian government in Ethiopia (Engelhardt, 2010).

Third generation rights get their substance largely from Articles 28–29 then, the former emphasizing the right to a socially just international order and the latter urging duties to the community. Together these have come to mean the rights to a clean environment, humanitarian disaster relief, global distributive justice (Wronka, 2007), self-determination (Kly, Kly, &d Falk, 2001), development, protection of the cultural and common heritages of humanity (such as places of worship, the oceans, mountains, and space), peace, and cultivating a sense of world citizenship. The right to a clean environment, for example, necessitates that one does not litter, but also the duties of governments to cooperate so that our seas and oceans are not polluted (Wronka, 1998, 2008).

Those above crucial notions also echo, if not substantively borrow, from President Roosevelt's famous Four Freedoms Speech (1941), in which he spoke about "freedom of speech and expression" and "the right of every person to worship God" (negative freedoms); "freedom from want" (positive freedoms); and "freedom from fear" (solidarity rights). The legacy of Roosevelt's speech is also indicative of the U.S. influence in the early days of the formation of the UN. To be sure, the UN has also asserted that all human rights are interdependent and indivisible. This was recently reaffirmed in the Vienna Declaration (1993), more specifically Article 5: "All human rights are universal, indivisible and interdependent and interrelated. The international community must treat human rights globally in a fair and equitable manner."

It should now be more readily apparent how human rights are interdependent and challenge us to live together in socially just ways, realizing the Beloved Community that the Reverend Dr. Martin Luther King often spoke about and the need to praise the peacemaker rather than the warrior as enunciated by the late President John F. Kennedy. Our educational system, the media, and society in general may tend to view such values as idealistic and encourage consumerism, competition, and violence to solve conflicts. But the right to food, for example, means also the duty not to overconsume and a socially just world that distributes food equitably, imposing obligations on the global community to make that happen. To meet the challenge, the modern world must overcome socialization that may have dulled us into blindly accepting a socially unjust order of *haves* and *have nots*, more colloquially known in these times as the 1% and the 99% (Gil, 2013; Wronka, 2011). Success cannot be realized if one can express the right to food, but never receive it or be in constant threat of food insecurity.

It is noteworthy, finally, to acknowledge that the Universal Declaration is considered customary international law, by international legal authorities (Steiner & Alston, 2000; Weissbrodt, Aolain, Fitzpatrick, & Newman, 2009) and by a U.S. federal court in the Second Circuit in *Filartiga v. Pena-Irala* (1980), which ruled against a torturer for an act committed in Paraguay. As justices Feinberg, Kaufmann, and Kearse stated: "This prohibition [against torture] has become part of customary international law as defined by the Universal Declaration of Human Rights (630 F.2d 884-885)." Known as the Filartiga Principle, to this day it has not been overturned, and also is viewed as a viable way to argue for one's human rights (Weiss, 2011).

Table 1 summarizes the above discussion with particular attention to the articles of the Universal Declaration that correspond with the five crucial notions. The table provides examples and notes their philosophic–historical legacies.

Table 1. Five Core Notions of the Universal Declaration of Human Rights (UDHR)

Articles of the UDHR	Crucial Notion	Examples	Philosophic–Historical Legacy
Article 1	Human dignity	Equality, freedom, the duty to act in a spirit of brotherhood and sisterhood	Judaic–Christian–Islamic tradition; the U.S. Declaration of Independence
Article 2	Nondiscrimination	Based on race, color, sex, language, religion, political opinion, national or social origin, property, birth, or other status	Judaic–Christian–Islamic Tradition; the U.S. Declaration of Independence
Articles 3–21	Civil and political (or first-generation or negative rights)	Freedoms of thought, religion, expression in oral and written form, and access to information; rights to privacy and a fair and public hearing	The U.S. Constitution's Bill of Rights; Franklin D. Roosevelt's Four Freedoms speech
Articles 22–27	Economic, social, and cultural rights (or second-generation or positive rights)	Rights to meaningful and gainful employment, rest and leisure, health care, food, housing, education, participation in the cultural life of the community; special care and assistance for motherhood and childhood	The Soviet Constitution of 1923; Roosevelt's Four Freedoms speech
Articles 28–30	Solidarity rights[a] (or third-generation rights)	Rights to a just social and international order, self-determination, peace, preservation of the common and cultural heritages of humanity, development, humanitarian disaster relief, and international distributive justice	The failure of domestic sovereignty, a reawakening of Third World nationalism, and increasing maldistribution of wealth; Roosevelt's Four Freedoms speech

Note. All rights are interdependent and indivisible. The UDHR is increasingly referred to as customary international law, by which all countries must abide. (Source: Wronka, 2008a, p. 23)

[a] Solidarity rights are still in the process of conceptual elaboration and are based on Articles 28 to 30, which emphasize rights to a just social and international order and that rights have corresponding duties and limitations.

The Human Rights Triptych

René Cassin, often referred to as the father of human rights, felt that human rights could be best understood as a triptych with the Universal Declaration of Human Rights, the authoritative definition of human rights standards, as the center panel. The other panels amplify the meaning of the center panel. On the right panel are the documents following the Universal Declaration, such as guiding principles, declarations, and conventions, which generally are developed in that order. The left panel is implementation measures, such as human rights reports to UN monitoring committees, special rapporteurs on specific countries and thematic issues, world conferences, and most recently the Universal Periodic Review of the Human Rights Council.

Such demarcations, however, are reminiscent of Cartesian dualism of the *res extensa*, or the world "out there, the environment," and the *res cogitans*, the world "inside, the mind." It may be important to reject such a *Weltanschauung* (worldview), which seems to espouse the idea that thinking is distinct from doing. Thinking is doing. Thus, it must be emphasized that knowing one's rights and living them are what is most important and directly consistent with the notion that social work is a human rights profession aligned with a phenomenological framework that operates on the assumption that a human is a being-in-the-world—that is, integral to a social environment—and emphasizes faithfulness to phenomenon in this case the creation of a human rights culture.

The Right Panel: Guiding Principles, Declarations, and Conventions

The right panel then consists of documents such as the Guiding Principles to Eradicate Extreme Poverty (2012), Declarations on the Rights of Indigenous Peoples (2007), Principles for the Protection of Persons With Mental Illness and the Improvement of Mental Health Care (1991), and conventions discussed below. In brief, those documents, reflective of years of work by governments and NGOs and thus representative of much of the world's collective wisdom, also consist of essential themes, generally elaborating on the principles of the Universal Declaration. The document on extreme poverty authored by special rapporteur Magdalena Sepulveda Carmona, for example, views poverty as a multidimensional phenomenon that ought to take into consideration income, human development, and social inclusion; a moral outrage and legal obligation to eradicate; a vicious and mutually enforcing cycle of powerlessness, stigmatization, discrimination, exclusion, and material deprivation; a matter of human choice; created by structural inequities and injustices; and the accumulation of indignities against the poor who are not passive recipients of government aid, but rather rights holders (Carmona, 2012).

The document on indigenous peoples urges *inter alia* the right to self-determination; full guarantees against genocide; redress for deprivation of cultural values and ethnic identities; special protections in periods of armed conflict; the right to control the education of indigenous children; the right to establish media; the right to traditional medicines and health practices; the right to maintain and strengthen distinctive spiritual and material relationship with lands, waters, seas, sea ice, flora, and fauna; and full recognition of cultural and intellectual property (cited in Wronka, 2008a, pp. 83–84).

The document pertaining to mental illness asserts that the determination of mental illness should be based on internationally accepted standards, not on membership in a cultural, racial, or religious group or nonconformity with moral standards prevailing in the person's community; that the right to life, work, and treatment shall be in the least restricted environment; that treatment shall be based on an individually prescribed plan, reviewed regularly by qualified personnel, and designed to enhance autonomy; that medication shall be administered for the health needs of the patient, not the convenience of others; that informed consent must be obtained without threat or improper inducement; and that appropriate disclosure of treatment must be given in language understood by the patient (cited in Wronka, 2008a, pp. 181–182).

The Nine Major Conventions or International Treaties

Documents with stronger judicial force are generally called conventions or covenants, which have the status of international treaties. Generally, such documents are written after international bodies first discuss the guiding principles, which can eventually evolve into declarations, later becoming conventions, or treaties, sometimes also referred to as covenants. Some countries, such as the United States in its Supremacy Clause, have statements in their constitutions that state that treaties when ratified shall "become the Supreme Law of the Land. … And the judges bound thereby" (Article VI), thus trumping domestic laws and policies. Unfortunately, not many policy makers are aware of that important clause. The inability to implement that clause led former Attorney General Ramsey Clarke, in a brief discussion after a side event on peace and democracy at the Human Rights Council meeting, to call it "a total failure of our legal system" (personal communication, March 2012) Implementing that clause can become a powerful tool for social change.

Presently, there are nine major covenants, which are often also referred to as conventions (Alston & Goodman, 2013): (1) International Covenant on Civil and Political Rights (ICCPR); (2) International Covenant on Economic, Social, and Cultural Rights; (3) International Convention on the Elimination of All Forms of Racial Discrimination (CERD); (4) Convention on the Elimination of All Forms of Discrimination against Women (CEDAW); (5) Convention Against Torture and Other Cruel, Inhuman or Degrading Treatment or Punishment (CAT); (6) Convention on the Rights of the Child (CRC); (7) International Convention on the Protection of the Rights of All Migrant Workers and Members of Their Families (CMW); (8) Convention on the Rights of Persons with Disabilities; and (9) International Convention for the Protection of all Persons from Enforced Disappearance (ICPPED).[1] Also, there are occasional additional optional protocols to the above conventions, such as the protocols on the prohibition of child soldiers, child pornography, and sex trafficking.

Generally, they further elucidate the principles of the Universal Declaration. Whereas, for instance, the Universal Declaration speaks of special protections for motherhood and children, CEDAW further discusses what this might mean, such as maternity leave with pay without loss of former employment or seniority; encouragement of the provision of necessary social services to enable parents to combine family obligations with work responsibility, such as the promotion of good quality day care; and the right to decide freely and responsibly the number and spacing of children. CRC recognizes the highest attainable standard of health for all children; the provision of adequate nutritious foods and clean drinking water; the advantages of breastfeeding, hygiene, and environmental sanitation; and the abolition of traditional practices prejudicial to the health of children.

Signing a document means that a government will consider it for ratification in its legislative bodies. As Table 2 below illustrates, as of July 2013 the United States has signed all of those conventions except the CMW and the ICPPED. The United States has ratified only the ICCPR, CERD, and CAT, even then with the stipulation that they be "non self-executing," that is, not

---

[1] For a summary of basic themes with corresponding articles for the first six conventions, and other select documents, please see Wronka (2008), pp. 68–84 and pp. 181–182.

enforceable in U.S. courts (Buergenthal, Shelton, & Stewart, 2009, p. 439). Ratification thus was actually symbolic. Such a shameful caveat ought to be stricken. However, symbols can move people to action, such that U.S. ratification, however weak, can serve as a relatively stronger means than signing alone of moving toward the creation of a human rights culture. It is important to note here that lack of seriousness behind these conventions by governments has been a factor in mobilizing shame against them, thus pressuring them to make their policies consistent with human rights principles. As President Obama said about the failure of the United States to ratify the CRC, the other country being Somalia, which does not appear to have the governmental capacity to do so, this failure is indeed "shameful."

Table 2 depicts the years the conventions were opened for signature, their entry into force, and U.S. signature and ratification.

Table 2. Nine Major United Nations Human Rights Conventions

Convention[a]	Opened for Signature	Entered Into Force	United States Signature	United States Ratification
ICCPR	1966	1979	1977	1992
CESCR	1966	1976	1977	
CERD	1966	1969	1966	1994
CEDAW	1979	1981	1980	
CAT	1984	1987	1988	1994
CRC	1989	1990	1995	
CMW	1990	2003		
CRPD	2006	2008	2009	
ICPPED	2006	2010		

NOTE: Although ratification means that conventions must be implemented according to the Supremacy Clause (Article VI of the U.S. Constitution), "the judges bound thereby," the United States has ratified these conventions with the condition that they not be self-executing, thereby giving the conventions largely a symbolic rather than practical significance. The link to these conventions, optional protocols, and other human rights documents, as well as select governments' concerns about them, can be found at http://treaties.un.org/pages/Treaties.aspx?id=4&subid=A&lang=en.

[a] ICCPR=International Covenant on Civil and Political Rights; CESCR=International Covenant on Economic, Social, and Cultural Rights; CERD=International Convention on the Elimination of All Forms of Racial Discrimination; CEDAW=Convention on the Elimination of All Forms of Discrimination Against Women; CAT=Convention Against Torture and Other Cruel, Inhuman or Degrading Treatment or Punishment; CRC=Convention on the Rights of the Child; CMW=International Convention on the Protection of the Rights of All Migrant Workers and Members of Their Families; CRPD=Convention on the Rights of Persons with Disabilities; ICPPED=International Convention for the Protection of all Persons from Enforced Disappearance.

Toward an International Convention to Abolish Extreme Poverty

The International Association of Schools of Social Work (IASSW) and IFSW issued their first joint statement before the Human Rights Council in Geneva in September 2007, acknowledging that close to 1 billion people go to bed starving each night. IASSW and IFSW called on all governments to endorse the Final Draft of the Guiding Principles on Extreme Poverty and Human Rights with an eye toward an internationally legally binding convention (Wronka, 2012, 2013b; Wronka & Staub-Bernasconi, 2012). Now called the Convention to Abolish Extreme Poverty (CAEP), nearly every year since the joint statement this convention has been brought up before the Human Rights Council, receiving support from the Indigenous Peoples Coalition, the International Human Rights Association of American Minorities, and the Kaoni Foundation. Most recently, in 2013 the Special Rapporteur on Peace and an Equitable Democratic Order, Alfred Zayas, stated that such a convention was a "great idea" (personal communication, March 2013) and in his recent report on the Promotion of a Democratic and Equitable Social Order (2013) urging governments and supranational bodies like the World Bank and the World Trade Organization to develop structures and mechanisms so that those "living in extreme poverty, who lack the possibility to effectively participate in decision–making" (p. 8) can participate in policy making. Obviously, more coalition building is necessary.

The Left Panel: Implementation Mechanisms

The left panel, historically the weakest part of the triptych, consists of implementation mechanisms such as (a) human rights education, (b) country reports to human rights conventions' monitoring committees, (c) special rapporteurs on thematic issues and specific countries, (d) the Universal Periodic Review, (e) general debate, and (f) world conferences (Wronka, 2008a, 2012).

Human Rights Education

Therefore, education should take into consideration formal sectors such as educational and training institutions from pre- and grammar school to postgraduate settings and also informal ones, such as the media, religious, spiritual, and even secular venues dedicated to ethical decision making, as well as the family and intergenerational teaching in general.

Research repeatedly indicates that when values are inculcated before adulthood it is very difficult to change them. It is imperative, therefore, that educators teach human rights principles in age appropriate ways. Some examples are (a) asking children which animal or flower they would like to be and why, an exercise acknowledging differences and similarities, or unity in diversity; (b) playing "washing machine," in which each child goes through two lines of other children who are to say just good things about that child; (c) engaging in "giraffe projects," in which they discuss situations when people stuck their necks out for others who were not as fortunate; (d) writing human rights documents in ways that children and adolescents understand; and (e) using the CRC as a way to influence school policies.

Teaching children about such basic rights as human dignity and nondiscrimination has not only been shown to significantly cut down on bullying (Greene, 2006), but it can also develop adult commitment to social justice. In college and postgraduate settings more attention should be given to integrating principles of human rights documents into not just social work, but also the social sciences, medicine, and other curricula. In part, this would underscore their importance, but it also would show that such guiding principles ought to undergird policies. Thus, scientific advancement, which should be shared globally as stated in Article 27 of the Universal Declaration, should unequivocally serve as the basis for equitable access to medicines. In professional settings such as social work, the principles of human rights documents can be used to assess the profession's policies and to monitor itself—an important mandate of the profession (Staub-Bernasconi, 2012)—vis à vis such documents as the Protection of Persons with Mental Illness.[2]

The media also has a strong educative function. Whereas only a few countries allow advertising on children's television on ethical grounds, the United States is replete with advertising urging consumption of foods and products of questionable value; programs glorifying violence as a means to resolve conflict; the promotion of gender bias; and a blame-the-victim mentality. Ronald McDonald encourages children to eat fast food; the cartoon character Road Runner accepts violence as a given; many of the antics of the cartoon character Pepé le Pew can easily be described as rape; and subtly, *Sesame Street's* Oscar the Grouch, who lives in a garbage can, is blamed for his temperament.

Realizing the importance of human rights principles, countries have commemorated international days such as International Women's Day (March 8) on primetime television (Switzerland); discussed an article from the CRC between cartoons, rather than approving fast foods (Norway); and had MTV skits on human dignity, emphasizing Article 1 of the Universal Declaration (France). The arts, with the proliferation of songs and music such as "Strange Fruit," "We Shall Overcome," and Beethoven's "Turkish March" and "Ode to Joy" are also ways to change people's consciousness regarding public lynchings, civil rights, and Judaic-Christian-Islamic dialogue.

Often the Golden Rule, which ultimately is what human rights is all about—to treat others like we would like to be treated—is found in almost all of the world's religions. As Rabbi Hillel stated: "The rest is just commentary" (*Judaism 101*, 2013). That rule ought to be taught literally more religiously and has the potential to unite us all. Norman Rockwell's painting *The Golden Rule*, depicting people of different religions, ethnicities, and ages, displayed in the hall of the United Nations in New York, obviously has teaching potential.

Country Reports to Human Rights Monitoring Committees

In addition to human rights education, after ratifying a human rights treaty, countries must file a report to the UN treaty monitoring committee every 5 years concerning compliance with the treaty's provisions. The committee then makes positive comments, expresses concerns, and offers recommendations. In response to the U.S. report on CERD (2008) the committee commended the United States for launching the E-Race initiative aimed at raising awareness of discrimination in the workplace and the National Partnership for Action to End Health Disparities for Ethnic and Racial Minority Populations, as well as for various programs adopted by the U.S. Department of Health and Human Services to address the persistent health disparities affecting low-income persons belonging to racial, ethnic, and national minorities.

Select concerns were various legislation that was not intended to be discriminatory, but resulted in de facto discriminatory policies, such as racial segregation in the schools; the increase in racial profiling against Arabs, Muslims, and South Asians in the wake of the September 11, 2001, attack; and the development of the National Entry and Exit Registration System (NEERS) for nationals of 25 countries, all located in the Middle East, South Asia, or North Africa; the disproportionate

---

[2] An excellent resource for teaching and training materials can be found on the Internet at http://www.ohchr.org/en/publicationsresources/pages/trainingeducation.aspx.

concentration of Latino and African American persons in poor residential areas characterized by substandard housing conditions, limited employment opportunities, inadequate access to health care facilities, under-resourced schools, and high exposure to crime and violence; and the disproportionate number of racial and ethnic minorities in prison.

Select recommendations were to review all laws and practices that were allegedly nondiscriminatory, but were discriminatory in effect; to repeal NEERS and end racial profiling; and to eliminate obstacles limiting affordable housing and the phenomenon of "steering" by the private sector; to end life imprisonment without parole for children; to ensure that reports of rape and sexual violence against women belonging to minorities and in particular Native American women are promptly and thoroughly investigated; and for the United States to organize public awareness and education programs on the CERD and its provisions and step up efforts to make government officials, the judiciary, federal and state law enforcement officials, teachers, social workers and the public in general aware of the responsibilities of the state party under the Convention, as well as the mechanisms and procedures provided for by the CERD in the field of racial discrimination and intolerance. The monitoring committee recommended that the next report be comprehensive and address all points raised in the present concluding observations. The expansion by President Obama of the Violence Against Women Act (2013) to include Native American women may be a direct result of this report. (These country reports can be found on the Internet at http://www.unhchr.ch/tbs/doc.nsf/ newhvdocsbytreaty?OpenView.)

NGOs have also filed shadow reports with the human rights committees that address matters they feel the official government has omitted. Following are examples of such reports:

- Shadow Report on Older Women's Rights in the United Kingdom (2012)
- Older Women's Network (Europe and the National Alliance of Women's Organizations)
- Shadow Report on Racial Injustice and Crimes Against Humanity (2007, Indigenous Peoples and Nations Coalition)
- A Shadow Report on the Violation of Human Rights on Native Hawaiians and the Hawaiian Archipelago (2006, Kaoni Foundation)
- Shadow Report on Forced Drugging, Electroshock and Mental Health Screening of Children (2006, New York Organization Against Psychiatric Assault, Mind Freedom, Law Project International)

They can be effective. At least in one instance, with pressure from the Indigenous Peoples Coalition and the Koani Foundation, the UN monitoring committee for the CERD asked the United States to apologize for what it did to the indigenous peoples of Hawaii.

Special Rapporteurs

Special rapporteurs assess and make recommendations concerning various human rights thematic issues, which have risen in the global consciousness. Some examples are rapporteurs on reparations and the promotion of truth, justice, and nonrecurrence (2012); the protection of human rights while countering terrorism (2005); international solidarity (2005); trafficking in persons, especially women and children (2004); internally displaced persons (2004); highest attainable standard of physical and mental health (2002); migrants (1999); extreme poverty (1996); and violence against women, its causes and consequences (1994). Apart from these issues there are also country mandates, such as situations in Belarus and Eritrea (2012); Iran, Syria, and Cote d'Ivoire (2011); Cuba (2007); Sudan (2005); Democratic Republic of Korea and the Congo (2004); Liberia (2003); and Somalia and the Palestinian

Territories (1993). Various state parity laws regarding payment for physical and mental health issues and the President Obama's recent mandating of insurance companies to grant parity may be a result of at least one of those reports. It is important to acknowledge here the confidential 1503 procedure, which examines serious and gross violations in countries such as genocide, apartheid, torture, mass imprisonment, and exterminations. The confidential nature of the 1503 procedure appears to have led to the resolutions of many of the conflicts of the "dirty wars" in Latin and South America in the 1970s and 1980s (Steiner & Alston, 2000).

The Universal Periodic Review

The Universal Periodic Review is a relatively recent development in human rights implementation mechanisms, having begun in 2008. Every 4 years a country must submit a report, assisted by troikas, that is, other countries chosen by lot, before the Human Rights Council to assess its progress toward complying with fundamental human rights principles as found in the Universal Declaration and the conventions, whether or not the country is a signatory. As a general rule, countries tend to emphasize their strong points and other countries relate their weaknesses. A case in point is the report by the United States in November 2010 that extolled the U.S. commitment to the freedoms of expression and the press by noting that each day Americans wake up to a broad cacophony of viewpoints in the media. In reply, Cuba, which states in its constitution that health care is a human right, pointed out the lack of health care in the United States and its failure to ratify CEDAW.

General Debate

In open debate before the Human Rights Council, which meets generally 10 weeks throughout the year in March, June, and September, governments and NGOs have the opportunity to respond to a variety of topics, such as extreme poverty, and comment on issues that need the attention of the Council. Over the years IFSW and IASSW have urged governments to endorse the Guiding Principles to Eradicate Extreme Poverty with an eye toward an internationally binding convention; include the eradication of extreme poverty in their constitutions; integrate human rights language into the millennium development goals; and to recall the words of President Eisenhower that "every gun that is made, every warship launched… signifies, in the final sense, a theft from those who hunger and are not fed" (Eisenhower, 1953). Live and archived webcasts of Human Rights Council meetings can be found on the Internet at http://www.unmultimedia.org/tv/webcast/c/un-human-rights-council.html.

World Conferences

World conferences are excellent ways to bring attention to social problems. Often under UN auspices with various follow-up conferences, they tend to deal with specific human rights violations, though their basic thrusts are acknowledgment that social justice is a struggle and that the world should not rest until every person everywhere has his or her rights realized. Examples are the Conference on Water Cooperation (Zaragoza, 2013); the Conference on Sustainable Development Twenty Years Later (Rio, 2012); the Conference on Climate Change (Copenhagen, 2009); the Durban Review Conference on Racism (Geneva, 2009); the World Food Conference (Rome, 2008); the World Conference on Disaster Reduction (Hyogo, 2005); the Conference on the Information Society (Geneva, 2003), and the Conference Against Racism, Xenophobia, and Related Intolerance (Durban, 2001). Thus, world conferences can play a major role in harnessing world opinion about the need to guarantee human rights for every person, everywhere.

Certainly, any individual either alone or collectively can write books, letters to the editor, provide input into human rights reports, or even file complaints. The possibilities are endless it seems. Thus, if the standards are human rights principles one can easily examine, for instance, executive, judicial, legislative, and public discourse movements toward compliance. For example, a reading of the Universal Declaration in comparison with the U.S. federal and 50 state constitutions revealed serious gaps regarding economic, social, cultural, and solidarity rights; and nothing on rights to employment, rest and leisure, health care, shelter, food, security in old age, or education, for instance (Wronka, 1998). States, which ought to act as "laboratories of democracy" (Brandeis, 2013, p. 1) in the words of Justice Brandeis, barely do any better. The only right they generally further is the right to education, although it is still questionable whether the educational systems encourage "peace, tolerance, and friendship among nations" as stated in Article 26 the Universal Declaration.

Regional Developments

Often referred to as human rights regimes, these expansions of human rights bodies globally consist of the African Union (AU), the Organization of American States (OAS), and the Council of Europe (CE), each with its own human rights triptychs. The AU has at its center the African Charter on Human and Peoples' Rights, followed by such documents as the Convention Concerning Specific Aspects of Refugee Problems, the Charter on the Rights and Welfare of the Child, the Protocol of the Rights of Women in Africa, and various reporting mechanisms for implementation. The African Charter (2013) speaks *inter alia* about the "unquestionable and inalienable right to self-determination;" (Article 20) that "colonized and oppressed people shall have the right to free themselves from the bonds of domination" (Article 20); and calls up states to "eliminate all forms of foreign economic exploitation particularly that practiced by international monopolies" (Article 21).

The OAS has the American Convention on Human Rights, followed by such documents as the Convention to Prevent and Punish Torture and the Convention on the Prevention, Punishment, and Eradication of Violence Against Women. The Council of Europe has the most extensively developed human rights machinery, the most poignant document being the European Social Charter of 1999, which strongly supports second generation rights, delineating approximately 40 of them in such areas as social welfare services, dignity through work, and protections against poverty and social exclusion. The challenge now is to develop similar human rights mechanisms in Asia, the Middle East, and Oceania. A step in the right direction is the formation in 2007 of the Association of South East Asian Nations, which has expressed strong support for human rights principles.

The UN and those regional developments have a vast array of bodies, such as a General Assembly, Secretariat, Economic and Social Council, Trusteeship, International World Court, and the like. Arguably, from an internationally legal standpoint it is important to know about their functions and interrelationships. But as a newly decorated banquet can frighten away the beggar, so too can this somewhat confusing labyrinth be intimidating. The human rights/social justice advocate perhaps more appropriately might be called *un hombre (or mujer) sincero,* as popularized by Pete Seeger the song "Guantanamera" when referring to the poet and activist José Marti. As mentioned, such an advocate should sincerely keep in mind the words of Eleanor Roosevelt, who, when drawing up the Universal Declaration, wanted a document not for the doctorate of jurisprudence, but for the educated layperson. Thus, the real substance of the UN and other organizations are the human rights documents the values of which should become the basis for a general global consensus to create social change.

Implications for Social Work Theory and Praxis

Chief Joseph's wisdom that "good words do not last long unless they amount to something" (New Perspectives, 2013, p. 2) is directly relevant to social work theory and praxis, which are interrelated, constantly nourishing each other. The guiding principles asserted in the human rights triptych are those that could inform practice for this human rights profession; likewise, practice can provide insight into strengthening and expanding on those principles. More than half a century after the endorsement of the Universal Declaration, this powerful idea is nearly ubiquitous, strongly suggesting that human rights, simply because it makes sense to so many, is a people's movement.

Select examples from the advanced generalist social work model that address the relevance of human rights are first the meta-macro level (Wronka, 2008a) which, echoing the words of Martin Luther King (1963) that "injustice anywhere is a threat injustice everywhere" necessitates a lived awareness of global interventions. The United Nations Charter, for example, which also has the status of a treaty and must be implemented according to the U.S. Constitution's Supremacy Clause, commits member states to promoting full employment and the development of conditions favorable to economic and social progress, thereby becoming an instrument to eradicate extreme poverty.

Human rights education from the grammar school to the professional levels is a perfectly reasonable intervention on the macro level to deal with whole populations. Having discussions in all echelons of learning about teaching the importance of nondiscrimination and tolerance and friendly relations among nations as asserted in the Universal Declaration can easily create an attitude among the general populace that no person should live in poverty. An example of working with at-risk populations might be organizing workers for their collective interests, as stated in human rights documents, so that the workers would have due process before possibly losing their jobs. Interventions at the micro level generally consist of dealing with individuals who have become almost entirely victims of an unjust order. Thus, the other levels of intervention simply did not work and now the person may be living in dire poverty and homeless. Here, one must build homeless shelters, assist in helping the homeless find employment, and help them deal with some of the stresses of poverty. Thus, the symptoms of an unjust order have become particularly apparent, necessitating at times emergency interventions. It should be fully evident here how clients should be treated with human dignity, as they need assistance in transitioning back to the formal workforce, a fundamental human rights value. At the meta-micro level (Wronka, 2008a), at times referred to as the level of everyday life, structures that support peer group and significant others in helping can be further developed and encouraged. Self-help groups for those looking for work or support groups for those with disabilities are cases in point. Finally, research, both quantitative and qualitative can constantly provide input into best practice models.

Obviously, the demarcation among levels is blurred. Despite that ambiguity, yet with an awareness of social justice as struggle, it is important to be aware of multipronged interventions to eradicate social and individual malaises and fulfill human needs and promote well-being. Such interventions—from the global to everyday life—with human rights at their core, that is, a human rights culture, ought to result in a socially just world.[3]

---

[3] My website, www.humanrightsculture.org, has numerous links, videos, public service announcements, and literature that should be helpful to the social justice/human rights activist, particularly those in the social work profession.

Calling for the Spirit of Crazy Horse: Vision, Courage, Humility, and Everlasting Love

In conclusion, perhaps this entire overview can be summed up in what may be called the Spirit of Crazy Horse, an indigenous leader committed to the self-determination of peoples. Indeed, the true spirit of self-determination can be defined in Mohawk simply as "living together nicely" (Daes, 2001, p. 58). Yet Crazy Horse was stabbed in the back by a soldier while protesting against a breach of promise by the U.S. government that his nation could live wherever they wanted after surrender. That spirit calls for the vision and courage of the eagle, a bird notorious for going right into the storm while it hunts for prey for its young, and "peace, humility, and everlasting love" (Matthiessen, 1992; Wronka, 2008b, p. 427).)

References

African Charter on Human and Peoples' Rights. (2013). Retrieved from http://www1.umn.edu/humanrts/instree/z1afchar.htm

Alston, P., & Goodman, R. (2013). *International human rights: The successor to international human rights in context: Law, politics and morals*. Oxford, UK: Oxford University Press.

Brandeis, L. (2013). Laboratories of democracy. Retrieved from http://en.wikipedia.org/wiki/Laboratories_of_democracy

Brainy Quote. (2013). *Louis D. Brandeis quotes*. Retrieved from http://www.brainyquote.com/quotes/authors/l/louis_d_brandeis.html

Buergenthal, T., Sheldon, D., & Stewart, D. (2009). *International human rights law in a nutshell*. St. Paul, MN: West Publishing.

Carmona, M. (2012). Final draft of the Guiding Principles to Eradicate Extreme Poverty. Retrieved from http://daccess-dds-ny.un.org/doc/UNDOC/GEN/G12/154/60/PDF/G1215460.pdf?OpenElement

Daes, E. (2001). Striving for self-determination of indigenous peoples. In Y. Kly & D. Kly (Eds.), *In pursuit of the right to self-determination* (pp. 50–62). Atlanta, GA: Clarity.

Eisenhower, D. D. (1953, April 16). Speech Before the American Society of Newspaper Editors, April 16, 1953. Retrieved from http://www.edchange.org/multicultural/speeches/ike_chance_for_peace.html

Engelhardt, T. (2010). *The American way of war: How Bush's wars became Obama's*. Chicago, IL: Haymarket.

Filartiga v. Pena-Irala. (1980). 630 F2nd. 876 (2nd Circuit 1980), 30 June 1980.

Gil, D. (1992). *Unravelling social policy*. (rev. 5th ed.). Rochester, VT: Schenkman.

Gil, D. (2013). *Confronting Injustice and oppression: Concepts and strategies for social workers*. New York, NY: Columbia University Press.

Greene, M. (2006). Bullying in schools: A plea for a measure of human rights. *Journal of Social Issues, 62*(1), 63–79.

Ife, J. (2008). *Human rights and social work*. New York, NY: Cambridge University Press.

Internet Encyclopedia of Philosophy. (2013). Phenomenology. Retrieved from http://www.iep.utm.edu/phenom/

Judaism 101. (2013). Love and brotherhood in Jewish sources. Retrieved from http://www.jewfaq.org/brother.htm

King, M. L., Jr. (1963, April 16). Letter from a Birmingham jail. Retrieved from http://www.africa.upenn.edu/Articles_Gen/Letter_Birmingham.html

King, M. L., Jr. (1968). I've been to the mountaintop. Retrieved from http://www.afscme.org/union/history/mlk/ive-been-to-the-mountaintop-by-dr-martin-luther-king-jr

King, W. (Director). (1992). *Malcolm X: Death of a prophet* (Video). United States: Sterling Entertainment Group.

Kly, Y., Kly, D., & Falk, R. (2001). *In pursuit of the right to self-determination.* Atlanta, GA: Clarity.

Matthiessen, P. (1992). *In the spirit of Crazy Horse.* New York, NY: Penguin.

New Perspectives on the West. (2013). Chief Joseph speaks. Retrieved from http://www.pbs.org/weta/thewest/resources/archives/six/jospeak.htm

Pope John Paul II. (1999). Message of His Holiness for the World Day of Peace, January 1. Retrieved from: http://www.vatican.va/holy_father/john_paul_ii/messages/peace/documents/hf_jp-ii_mes_14121998_xxxii-world-day-for-peace_en.html

Reichert, E. (2007). *Challenges in human rights: A social work perspective.* NY: Columbia University Press.

Reichert, E. (2011). *Social work and human rights.* New York, NY: Columbia University Press.

Robinson, M. (2013). *Everybody matters: My life giving voice.* New York, NY: Walker.

Roosevelt, E. (1963). Tomorrow is now. Retrieved from http://www.gwu.edu/~erpapers/abouteleanor/er-quotes/

Roosevelt, F. (1941). "Four Freedoms" Speech, 87-I Cong. Rec. 4, 46–47. Available at http://voicesofdemocracy.umd.edu/fdr-the-four-freedoms-speech-text/

Staub-Bernasconi, S. (2012). Human rights and their relevance for social work as theory and practice. In L. Healy & R. Link (Eds.). *Handbook of international social work: Human rights, development, and the global profession* (pp. 30–36). New York, NY: Oxford University Press.

Steiner, H., & Alston, P. (2000). *International human rights in context: Laws, politics, morals.* New York, NY: Oxford University Press.

United Nations. (1994). *Human rights and social work: A manual for schools of social work and the social work profession.* New York, NY: Author.

United Nations Information Organization. (1945). *Documents of the United Nations Conference on international organization at San Francisco, 1945* (Vol. 6). Published in cooperation with the Library of Congress.

Weiss, P. (2011). On the thirty-fifth anniversary of his death Filartiga lives! *The Guardian.* Retrieved from http://www.guardian.co.uk/commentisfree/cifamerica/2011/apr/04/us-constitution-and-civil-liberties-us-supreme-court

Weissbrodt, D., Aolain, F. N., Fitzpatrick, J., & Newman, F. (Eds.). (2009). *International human rights: Law, policy, and process.* Newark, NJ: Lexis/Nexis.

Wronka, J. (1995). Human rights. In R. Edwards (Ed.), *Encyclopedia of social work* (1404-1418). Washington, DC: National Association of Social Workers.

Wronka, J. (1998). *Human rights and social policy in the 21st century: A history of the idea of human rights and comparison of the United Nations Universal Declaration of Human Rights with United States federal and state constitutions* (rev. ed.). Lanham, MD: University Press of America.

Wronka, J. (2007). Global distributive justice as a human right: Implications for the creation of a human rights culture. In E. Reichert (Ed.). *Challenges in human rights: A social work perspective.* (pp. 44–75). New York, NY: Columbia University Press.

Wronka, J. (2008a) *Human rights and social justice: Social action and service for the helping and health professions.* Los Angeles, CA: SAGE.

Wronka, J. (2008b). Human rights. In T. Mizrahi & L. Davis. (Eds.). *Encyclopedia of Social Work* (pp. 425-429). Washington, DC: NASW Press.

Wronka, J. (2012). Overview of Human Rights: The UN Conventions and Machinery (pp. 439-446) In L. Healy and R. Link, *Handbook of International Social Work.* London: Oxford University Press.

Wronka, J. (2013a). Creating a human rights culture. Retrieved from www.humanrightsculture.org

Wronka, J. (2013b). Written statement by IASSW on eradicating extreme poverty submitted to the 24th session of the Human Rights Council under agenda item 3. Retrieved from http://www.ohchr.org/EN/HRBodies/HRC/Pages/HRCIndex.aspx

Wronka, J., & Staub-Bernasconi, S. (2012) Human rights. In K. Lyons, M. Hokenstad, S. Pawar, N. Huegler, & N. Hall (Eds.), *The SAGE handbook of international social work.* Los Angeles, CA: SAGE.

Zayas, A. (2013, July). Report of the independent expert on the promotion of a democratic and equitable international order. Retrieved from http://www.ohchr.org/Documents/Issues/IntOrder/A-HRC-24-38_en.pdf

Zinn, H. (1990). *A people's history of the United States.* New York, NY: Harper & Row.

Human Rights: An Essential Component of Social Work Education

M. C. "Terry" Hokenstad and Amy Restorick Roberts

Human rights education should be an integral part of the educational system at all levels of learning and in countries around the globe. Recognition of this mandate led the United Nations to establish the World Programme for Human Rights Education in 2005. The overall goal of this programme is to build knowledge about and skills in supporting and maintaining human rights. A first phase of the World Programme (2005–2009) focused on elementary and secondary education. The second phase now underway (2010–2014) focuses on higher education. A major goal is to integrate human rights education effectively into the higher education systems of member countries. The Office of the United Nations High Commissioner for Human Rights and the United Nations Educational, Scientific, and Cultural Organization are the lead agencies for the implementation of the World Programme (United Nations, 2012).

Human rights education in social work can be considered an important component of the United Nations World Programme. Social work's international organizations have worked closely with the United Nations in the past in the development of human rights teaching materials. In 1994 the United Nations published *Human Rights and Social Work: A Manual for Schools of Social Work and the Social Work Profession*. The International Federation of Social Workers (IFSW) and the International Association of Schools of Social Work (IASSW) collaborated on this publication, which detailed a process for social workers to learn about human rights, including recognizing human rights issues and responding to violations. Intervention strategies at the micro, mezzo, and macro levels of practice were discussed. Case studies that could be used as classroom exercises were arguably the most valuable learning tool in the volume. In the intervening years they have been used in many social work courses (United Nations, 1994).

Another social work human rights training manual, this time published by IFSW, followed a decade later. *Social Work and the Rights of the Child: A Professional Training Manual on the UN Convention* provides information specific to the human rights of children, with guidance on how to translate the ideals of the United Nations convention into everyday social work practice. The manual contains practical examples designed to develop critical thinking skills that can be used as classroom exercises. The manual has proven useful for professional development programs directed at child welfare social workers as well as degree based educational programs (IFSW, 2002).

This IFSW has also given attention to teaching and learning about human rights in its *Social Work Around the World* series. It emphasizes that social workers in all countries should be knowledgeable not only about human rights declarations and conventions, but also about the implications of the documents for social work practice. This includes an understanding of human rights dilemmas that must be addressed in either case work or social development situations. Thinking in a human rights framework is emphasized as an important outcome of social work education (IFSW, 2013).

Leading social work organizations have demonstrated commitment to human rights in response to an increasing awareness of the challenges social workers face around the world. The IFSW and IASSW have recently formed a joint Human Rights Commission to give attention to human rights action and education. Their joint *Statement of Ethical Principles* forms a basis for human rights in social work and provides social workers with guidance on how to make ethical decisions framed through the unifying principles of human rights, dignity, and social justice (IFSW & IASSW, 2004). In

addition, the IASSW has established a Human Rights Committee to promote human rights education of social workers.

Human Rights Books by Social Work Educators

In the past several years there has been a considerable increase in human rights information and teaching materials particularly appropriate for both undergraduate and graduate social work education. Recent human rights books by social work educators provide an in-depth examination of human rights instruments and their general implementation but also focus on social work roles and responsibilities in promoting and protecting human rights. Some of these significant contributions to the human rights literature are briefly reviewed here.

Human Rights and Social Justice: Social Action for the Helping and Health Professions by Joseph Wronka (2008) discusses the importance of creating a human rights culture to promote social justice in the world. Drawing from the core principles of the Universal Declaration of Human Rights, Wronka discusses social work practice strategies to ensure human rights at various levels of intervention. This model of five levels of intervention includes the macro level (described as the whole-population approach), the mezzo level (intervening with groups at risk), the micro level (clinical interventions with individuals or small groups), the meta-macro level (global), and the meta-micro level (the healing power in everyday life). Wronka offers a comprehensive approach to examining social issues through applying all five levels of intervention together to address common individual and social problems. He argues that social workers need to use human rights as a guiding principle to develop interventions that are effective with whole populations, at-risk groups, and individuals. The book also suggests ways for students to become involved in research and social action.

Elisabeth Reichert has contributed three books to the human rights literature. In 2006 she authored *Understanding Human Rights: An Exercise Book*, which emphasizes how human rights are embedded into social work practice through explicating principles in the NASW Code of Ethics. In the book she connects social work interventions with human rights principles. Case studies with discussion questions are provided as tools to help students identify human rights issues, appropriate social work interventions, and ethical practice issues within the principles of human rights. Exercises are also provided to help students understand human rights and social work at an international level.

Reichert's next book, *Challenges in Human Rights: A Social Work Perspective* (2007), is an edited volume with chapters written by educators and professionals from around the globe. The primary theme is human rights within a social work context with a focus on economic, social, and cultural rights. Attention is given to differing perspectives on human rights issues in different parts of the world.

In 2011 the second edition of Reichert's book *Social Work and Human Rights: A Foundation for Policy and Practice* was published. The book covers a broad range of areas in which human rights apply to the social work profession and social work practice. One major area of emphasis is Reichert's application of guidelines from the NASW Code of Ethics along with the IFSW Statement of Ethical Principles to practice-oriented case studies of human rights issues that have implications for ethical dilemmas.

The third edition of a book by James Ife titled *Human Rights and Social Work: Toward a Rights-Based Practice* (2012) places emphasis on the link between social work ethics and human rights. He argues that human rights discourse provides a base of action for social workers facing ethical dilemmas in practice.

In a section of the book on social work education attention is given to field education in addition to classroom learning and curriculum design. Student roles in collaborative learning also receive attention as one dimension of incorporating human rights into the educational program.

Human Rights in the Social Work Curriculum

These books, along with numerous other contributions to the social work literature listed in the bibliography at the end of this manual, give evidence of considerable interest in human rights by social work educators and scholars. However, available information suggests that this literature and the subject of human rights in general have yet to be fully incorporated into the social work curriculum. Although there is no current data, a recent study by Steen and Mathiesen (2008) found that 91% of the 135 social work programs they reviewed had no identifiable human rights content, based on course titles and descriptions. It is possible that human rights content could have been infused within some of these courses, but if so it was not prominent enough to be mentioned in the course description. The authors concluded that much more attention is given to human rights in law schools than in schools of social work.

The Educational Policy and Accreditation Standards (EPAS) of the Council on Social Work Education (CSWE) do include "advocate for human rights and social and economic justice" as a required competency for social work students graduating from a CSWE accredited program (CSWE, 2010, p. 5). This adds incentive for social work programs to include some human rights content in the curriculum. Dewes and Roche (2001) propose a multimethod four-part pedagogy for social work teaching about human rights. They include course readings, case vignettes, multimedia and videos, and direct involvement in a human rights action event to achieve various types of learning. Certainly, experiential learning in the field along with cognitive learning in the classroom are important objectives of human rights education for social workers.

This manual is designed to provide a variety of resources for educators who are committed to adding or expanding human rights content in the social work curriculum. The manual provides sample syllabi from undergraduate and graduate programs that offer either courses or modules focused on human rights. It also presents a variety of learning tools ranging from skill building exercises to videos and other media that have been instrumental in human rights education. Introductory summaries by the editors precede each section of the resource manual and highlight areas of the curriculum that can be enriched by human rights content.

As evidenced by the United Nations World Programme, human rights education in social work is a part of a larger movement to incorporate human rights into all levels of learning. Social work education can and should be a leader in this movement to reinforce the fact that social work is a human rights profession. This resource manual on teaching human rights is designed to facilitate that outcome.

References

Council on Social Work Education. (2010). *Educational policy and accreditation standards.* Retrieved from http://www.cswe.org/File.aspx?id=13780

Dewes, M., & Roche, S. E. (2001). Teaching about human rights in social work. *Journal of Teaching in Social Work, 21*(1–2), 137–155.

Ife, J. (2012). *Human rights and social work: Towards rights-based practice* (3rd ed.). Cambridge, UK: Cambridge University Press.

International Association of Schools of Social Work. (n.d.). *About IASSW.* Retrieved from http://www.iassw-aiets.org/about-iassw

International Federation of Social Workers. (n.d.). *About IFSW.* Retrieved from http://ifsw.org/

International Federation of Social Workers. (2004). *Social work and the rights of the child: A professional training manual on the UN Convention.* Retrieved from http://cdn.ifsw.org/assets/ifsw_124952-4.pdf

International Federation of Social Workers. (2013). *Teaching and learning about human rights.* Retrieved from http://ifsw.org/resources/publications/human-rights/teaching-and-learning-about-human-rights/

International Federation of Social Workers & International Association of Schools of Social Work. (2004). *Ethics in social work, statement of principles.* Adelaide, Australia: IFSW. Retrieved from http://ifsw.org/policies/statement-of-ethical-principles/

Office of the High Commissioner on Human Rights at the United Nations. (2012). *World programme for human rights education: Second phase plan of action.* New York, NY: United Nations.

Reichert, E. (2006). *Understanding human rights: An exercise book.* Thousand Oaks, CA: SAGE Publications.

Reichert, E. (2007). *Challenges in human rights: A social work perspective.* New York, NY: Columbia University Press.

Reichert, E. (2011). *Social work and human rights: A foundation for policy and practice* (2nd ed.). New York, NY: Columbia University Press.

Steen, J. A., & Mathiesen, S. (2008). Human rights education: Is social work behind the curve? *Journal of Teaching in Social Work, 25,* 143–156.

United Nations. (1994). *Human rights and social work: A manual for schools of social work and the social work profession.* (Professional Training Series No. 1). New York, NY: Author.

Wronka, J. (2008). *Human rights and social justice: Social action and service for the helping and health professions.* Thousand Oaks, CA: SAGE Publications.

PART 2
TEACHING CONTENT ON HUMAN RIGHTS

Undergraduate Syllabi

Introduction to Undergraduate Syllabi

Uma A. Segal

In the United States, social work curricula at the baccalaureate level pays particular heed to issues of oppression, marginalization, and diversity; however, in general, baccalaureate social work programs have been slow to incorporate language on human rights or recognize the extent of human rights abuses in the country. Despite data provided by Amnesty International and publications of a small cadre of social work academics in the United States, human rights violations are generally perceived as occurring outside the nation, and interest in integrating content on this important concern into social work education is still in a nascent stage. It is important that social work education and the profession of social work recognize that human rights violations are often integral components in oppression and marginalization, and inclusion of a human rights perspective in discussions by academics, researchers, students, and practitioners can provide a wider lens through which to view the experience of many groups and communities. Furthermore, mainstream social work education in the United States has tended to focus primarily on intracountry issues, and despite the Council of Social Work Education's international arms—the Commission on Global Social Work Education and the Katherine A. Kendall Institute for International Social Work Education—has had a fairly incidental interest in cross-border and global issues. The BSW syllabi included in this publication will help broaden student understanding of our global connectedness.

The undergraduate syllabi presented here reflect a range of approaches to offer insight into the relevance of discussions on human rights for the profession of social work. Several provide an introduction to human rights and the history of its development, integrating theoretical material and making human rights issues pertinent to students and their learning by including, for example, hands-on exercises, assignments that engage them with communities and individuals whose rights have been denied, and personal reflection papers and portfolios. Other syllabi that are more specialized also include some of these elements but add dimensions such as an exploration of global differences in society and culture and implications for human rights discussions, inspection of primary legal statutes on human rights, and concern with the rights of women and children.

A few syllabi are somewhat less traditional or include unique elements. One syllabus involves a cross-national assignment that requires students to pair themselves with counterparts in a second country, another is entirely Web-based and addresses global social justice issues in developing countries, and a third is a travel course that allows students a firsthand glimpse into topics covered by the course. Thus, this combination of syllabi allows academics to include traditional courses on human rights in their curricula that provide a foundation for students on the subject as well as more creative courses that can be alternative ways of engaging students on an important topic that has received relatively limited attention in the BSW curriculum in the United States.

Society and Human Rights

Lacey Sloan
College of Staten Island, The City University of New York

Course Description

Human rights represent one of the most important concepts in society today. Human rights are particularly important for social workers. Indeed, social work can be described as a human rights profession, providing a moral basis for social work practice. Human rights can help link micro practice to macro practice and connect the varying roles of the social worker. This course will examine human rights, social work as a human rights profession, and in particular, vulnerable populations.

Course Objectives

At the end of this course students will

    A.   understand human rights concepts and terms,

    B.   understand the evolution of human rights,

    C.   understand ethical dilemmas presented by human rights and culture,

    D.   understand human rights abuses,

    E.   identify vulnerable populations and the special rights afforded to them,

    F.   understand international human rights conventions, declarations and covenants, and

    G.   understand human rights principles as they apply to social work practice.

At the end of this course students will be able to

    A.   participate in human rights discourse;

    B.   describe the evolution of human rights;

    C.   identify and analyze ethical dilemmas presented by human rights and culture;

    D.   identify and analyze human rights abuses;

    E.   identify vulnerable populations and the special rights afforded to them;

    F.   identify and describe international human rights conventions, declarations, and covenants; and

    G.   begin to apply human rights principles to social work practice.

Teaching Methods

This course will use a variety of teaching methods including lecture, group and class discussion, experiential exercises in and out of the classroom, assigned readings, individual research, Internet and e-mail communication, and audiovisual materials. The textbook for this course is Elisabeth Reichert, *Understanding Human Rights: An Exercise Book* (Thousand Oaks, CA: SAGE Publications, 2006).

Assessment Tools

Students will be graded on a variety of assignments to earn points for this class. Each assignment is described below. All assignments are to be submitted electronically.

Midterm exam (20 points) and final exam (30 points): The exams are cumulative and will cover all material from the readings, class discussion and lectures, assignments, and individual student research.

International exchange (10 points): Students will engage in semistructured electronic communication with social work students in the United States. Each student will be (a) paired with another student in a social work practice course at the University of North Carolina at Greensboro or (b) participate in two polycom sessions. See further description in the appendix.

Written assignments (10 points each): Each student will write three 3-page papers (see appendix for further details) on the following topics.

1. Personal human rights or standing up for human rights
2. Biography of a human rights activist
3. Local problem

Participation (10 points): Each student is expected to have completed all assigned reading prior to coming to class and should be prepared to participate fully in class. Class assignments will be used to determine participation grade.

Assessment Policies/Grading Criteria

- Written assignments, 30 points
- International exchange, 10 points
- Participation, 10 points
- Midterm exam, 20 points
- Final exam, 30 points

Course Schedule

Date	Topic	Reading	Assignments
Week 1	Human Rights in a Globalized World	Reichert, Intro	
Week 2	What Are Human Rights?	Reichert, Chapter 1	
Week 3	History of Human Rights	Reichert, Chapters 2 & 3	
Week 4	Culture and Human Rights	Reichert, Chapter 6	
Week 5	Human Rights and Human Needs		Assignment 1 due
Week 6	Human Rights and Obligations		
Week 7	Ethics and Human Rights	Reichert, Chapter 7	Midterm exam
Week 8	Participation in the Human Rights Discourse		
Week 9	Constructing Human Rights for Social Work Practice		
Week 10	Achieving Human Rights Through Social Work Practice		Assignment 2 due
Week 11	Respecting Human Rights in Social Work Practice		
Week 12	Social Work With Vulnerable Populations	Reichert, Chapter 5	
Week 13	Prospects for Human Rights Practice	Reichert, Chapter 8	Assignment 3 due
Week 14		Final exam review	

Reference List/Additional Resources

Appleby, G. A., Colon, E., & Hamilton, J. (2001). *Diversity, oppression and social functioning: Person in environment assessment and intervention*. Boston, MA: Allyn & Bacon.

Bettcher, T. M. (2007). Evil deceivers and make-believers: On transphobic violence and the politics of illusion. *Hypatia: A Journal of Feminist Philosophy, 22*(3), 43–65.

Daniel, R. G. (2002). *More than Black: Multiracial identity and the new racial order*. Philadelphia, PA: Temple University Press.

Freire, P. (1993). *Pedagogy of the oppressed* (M. B. Ramos, Trans.). New York, NY: Continuum.

Healey, J. F. (2003). *Race, ethnicity, gender, and class: The sociology of group conflict and change* (3rd ed.). Thousand Oaks, CA: Pine Forge Press.

Ife, J. (2008).*Human rights and social work: Towards rights-based practice*. New York, NY: Cambridge Press.

Lie, G.-Y., & Lowery, C. T. (2003). Cultural competence with women of color. In D. Lum (Ed.), *Culturally competent practice: A framework for understanding diverse groups and justice issues* (2nd ed., pp. 282–309). Pacific Grove, CA: Brooks/Cole.

Liu, W. M., Soleck, G., Hopps, J., Dunston, K., & Pickett, T., Jr. (2004). A new framework to understand social class in counseling: The social class worldview model and modern classism theory. *Journal of Multicultural Counseling and Development, 32*(2), 95–123.

Lum, D. (Ed.). (2003). *Culturally competent practice: A framework for understanding diverse groups and justice issues* (2nd ed.). Pacific Grove, CA: Brooks/Cole.

Marsh, J. C. (2004). Social work in a multicultural society. *Social Work, 49*, 5–6.

Mullaly, B. (2002). *Challenging oppression: A critical social work approach.* Toronto, ON: Oxford University Press.

Parks, C. A., Hughes, T. L., & Matthews, A. K. (2004). Race/ethnicity and sexual orientation: Intersecting identities. *Cultural Diversity and Ethnic Minority Psychology, 10*(3), 241–254.

Potok, A. (2002). *A matter of dignity: Changing the world of the disabled.* New York, NY: Bantam.

Priestly, M. (2001). Introduction: The global context of disability. In M. Priestly (Ed.), *Disability and the life course: Global perspectives* (pp. 3–15). New York, NY: Cambridge University Press.

Rothman, J. C. (2003). *Social work practice: Across disability.* Boston, MA: Allyn & Bacon.

Saulnier, C. F. (2000). Incorporating feminist theory into social work practice: Group work examples. *Social Work with Groups, 23*(1), 5–29.

Schmitz, C. L., Stakeman, C., & Sisneros, J. (2001). Educating professionals for practice in a multicultural society: Understanding oppression and valuing diversity. *Families in Society, 82*, 612–622.

Schmitz, C. L., Vazquez Jacobus, M., Stakeman, C., Valenzuela, G., & Sprankel, J. (2003). Immigrant and refugee communities: Resiliency, trauma, and social work practice. *Social Thought, 22*(2/3), 135–158.

Stroman, D. F. (2003). *The disability rights movement: From deinstitutionalization to self-determination.* New York, NY: University Press of America.

van Wormer, K. (1994). A society without poverty: The Norwegian experience. *Social Work, 39*, 324–327.

Wildman, S. M., & Davis, A. D. (2002). Making systems of privilege visible. In P. Rothenberg (Ed.), *White privilege essential readings on the other side of racism* (pp. 85–95). New York, NY: Worth.

Appendices

Assignment 1: Standing Up for Rights

The paper should be approximately three pages long. The goal is to reflect on a time you stood up for your rights, or the rights of another person.

Specifics: Remember a time when you stood up for your rights, or the rights of another person.

- Describe what happened
- Where did it happen?
- Why did I stand up?
- Who or what were my sources of support?
- Was this a positive experience? Why or why not?
- How did this experience relate to human rights?

Grading for Each Specific Point of Assignment 1

- Excellent description: 1.5 points
- Average description: 1 point
- Little or no clear description: 0 points

Alternative Assignment 1: Personal Human Rights

The paper should be approximately three pages long. The goal is to identify the human rights that are most important to you.

Specifics: Using the Universal Declaration of Human Rights, select three rights that are most important to you. In the paper, address the following:

- Why are these three rights the most important to you?

- Are there any special circumstances in your community that relate to these rights being most important to you?

- Are the rights you chose in the category of civil/political or social/economic/cultural? Discuss why.

Grading for Each Specific Point of Alternative Assignment 1

- Excellent description: 3 points

- Average description: 2 points

- Poor description: 1 point

- No description: 0 points

- Excellent organization: 1 point

- Average organization: .5 point

- Poor organization: 0 points

Assignment 2: Biography of a Human Rights Activist

The paper should be approximately three pages long. The goal is to understand the life of a human rights activist.

Specifics: Identify a human rights activist. Conduct research on the selected historical figure. In addition to basic biographical information, analyze the following:

- Causes for which the person worked

- Obstacles encountered and to be overcome

- Accomplishments and influence on others

Grading for Each Specific Point of Assignment 2

- Excellent description: 3 points

- Average description: 2 points

- Poor description: 1 point

- No description: 0 points

- Excellent organization: 1 point

- Average organization: .5 point

- Poor organization: 0 points

Assignment 3: Local Human Rights Problem

The paper should be approximately three pages long. The goal is to develop skills in analyzing a local human rights problem through a human rights lens.

Specifics: Select a human rights problem in Qatar for analysis. Identify sources to address the following points, including interviewing service providers.

- Describe the problem.

- What agencies address this problem?

- Is there a particular group that is more affected by this problem (i.e., women, children, immigrants, etc.)?

- What are the government policies related to this problem?

These are only sample questions and they may differ depending on the problem you choose. The goal is to describe a local human rights problem, the resources devoted to this problem, and efforts being made to address the problem.

Grading for Each Specific Point of Assignment 3

- Excellent description: 2 points

- Average description: 1 point

- Poor description: 0 points

- Excellent organization: 2 points

- Good to fair organization: 1 point

- Poor organization: 0 points

International Exchange

To help promote cultural competence among students in the Qatar University social work course Society and Human Rights, students will engage in semistructured electronic communication with social work students in the United States. You will receive 1 point each week for participation and 0 to 1 point for the quality of your contribution. To guide the discussion and optimize the experience, topics for discussion have been selected for each week:

- Week of 2/22: Introductions

- Week of 3/1: Gender

- Week of 4/5: Culture

- Week of 4/26: Human rights

- Week of 5/10: Wrap up and conclusion

You may want to review the following links prior to your Moodle sessions.

Human Development Index: http://hdr.undp.org/en/statistics/

Global Gender Gap Report 2010: http://www.youtube.com/watch?v=GdGMz8gN_Pk

Integrative Methods in Social Action and Social Change: Community-Building for Human Rights

Dennis Ritchie
Cathy Thompkins
Emily Ihara
George Mason University

Course Description

The course uses generalist social work practice concepts with large systems and provides students with a hands-on opportunity to apply concepts and principles of intervention with large systems. Students will work with organizations and communities on a local, national, or global level to promote social action and social change. The course will also focus on evaluating interventions addressing the social justice needs of diverse, at-risk, and oppressed populations.

Research and Scholarship (RS) Designation

This class is designated as an RS intensive course, which means that students are given the opportunity to actively participate in the process of scholarship and will make a significant contribution to the creation of a disciplinary-appropriate product. Thus, in this class you will be partnering with organizations, agencies, or groups to identify human rights issues, engage in the process of problem identification, gather data, and disseminate the findings. Through this kind of authentic inquiry into the discipline, you will become a more critical consumer and generator of knowledge and a more skillful change agent in the field of social work.

RS Student Learning Outcomes

In this RS course students will demonstrate an advanced level of competence in scholarly inquiry and the creation of scholarship.

Students will engage in scholarly inquiry by

A. choosing an appropriate discovery process for scholarly inquiry with a faculty member and students about the state of human rights education at the university,

B. gathering appropriate evidence to describe the state of human rights education at this university, and

C. situating the scholarly inquiry within a broader context by developing an event focused on engaging the university community in human rights education on campus.

Students will participate in the creation of scholarship by

A. creating an original scholarly or creative project by working as a coalition to research and describe the state of human rights education at this university, and

B. communicating knowledge from an original scholarly or creative project through the dissemination of the data that is gathered and analyzed for the project via the final course capstone event, the Web page that will be developed for this class, and/or through a formal conference presentation at the community, state, or national level.

Course Format

This course is designed so that students work together as one community coalition to advance human rights education even though (for university logistics) there are three sections. We expect each participant to act responsibly and professionally. Therefore, any issues with work distribution, group dynamics, conflicts, and so forth should be worked out within each group/committee. Instructors are available to assist with this process if necessary. Students should complete all readings prior to the class session to maximize participation.

BSW Program Competencies

- Identify as a professional social worker and conduct oneself accordingly.

- Apply social work ethical principles to guide professional practice.

- Apply critical thinking to inform and communicate professional judgments.

- Engage diversity and difference in practice.

- Advance human rights and social and economic justice.

- Engage in research-informed practice and practice-informed research.

- Apply knowledge of human behavior and the social environment.

- Engage in policy practice to advance social and economic well-being and to deliver effective social work services.

- Respond to contexts that shape practice.

- Engage, assess, intervene, and evaluate with individuals, families, groups, organizations, and communities.

Educational Policy and Accreditation Standards Competencies and Operational Practice Behaviors (CSWE, 2008)

Competency		Operational Practice Behaviors
2.1.3	Apply critical thinking to inform and communicate professional judgments	• Demonstrate information literacy by distinguishing, appraising, and integrating multiple sources of knowledge, including research-based knowledge and practice wisdom.
2.1.4	Engage diversity and difference in practice	• Recognize the extent to which a culture's structures and values may oppress, marginalize, alienate, or create or enhance privilege and power. • Recognize and communicate their understanding of the importance of difference in shaping life experiences.
2.1.5	Advance human rights and social and economic justice	• Advocate for human rights and social and economic justice. • Engage in practices that advance social and economic justice.
2.1.6	Engage in research-informed practice and practice-informed research	• Use research evidence to inform practice.
2.1.8	Engage in policy practice to advance social and economic well-being and to deliver effective social work services	• Analyze, formulate, and advocate for policies that advance social well-being. • Collaborate with colleagues and clients for effective policy action.
2.1.9	Respond to contexts that shape practice	• Continuously discover, appraise, and attend to changing locales, populations, scientific and technological developments, and emerging societal trends to provide relevant services. • Provide leadership in promoting sustainable changes in service delivery and practice to improve the quality of social services.
2.1.10	Engage, assess, intervene, and evaluate with individuals, families, groups, organizations, and communities	• Engagement – substantively and effectively prepare for action with individuals, families, groups, organizations, and communities.

Course Expectations

- The use of "person-first language" (e.g., *people with disabilities* rather than *the disabled*) and nonsexist language (e.g., *one's* and/or *her or his* and/or *his/her* rather than only *his*) in all written and verbal aspects of the class is mandatory.

- Students are expected to complete all assigned readings and assignments before coming to class and be prepared to participate fully in the discussion.

- All written work should use the style and format specified in the *Publication Manual of the American Psychological Association* (6th edition), particularly for in-text citations and the reference page.

- Good writing skills and the ability to organize thoughts clearly using proper English are critical for students and future professionals.

- When conducting research for an assignment, particularly for online sources, students should scrutinize the source carefully. This link provides a guide for how to evaluate Internet sources: http://www.lib.berkeley.edu/TeachingLib/Guides/Internet/Evaluate.html. *NOTE:* Wikipedia should not be used as a resource.

Assignments

Student learning and achievement will be assessed as follows:

Assignments	Percentage of Final Grade	Due Dates
Class participation	10	Ongoing
Scholarly inquiry logs	25	Submit weekly; graded randomly
Perceptions of human rights	20	February 26
Final course capstone event/human rights educational project (including the integrative reflective summary paper of the project and the class)	45	Date of project Integrative paper due on May 2

Class Participation (10%)

For many class assignments and projects students will work in teams. Professional behavior involves attending team meetings (during class and specific meetings that may be arranged outside of class) so that you can be a good team player! Please note that all three instructors will be making observations about your participation throughout the semester. You may also be asked to assess your peers' participation on the teams.

Scholarly Inquiry Logs (25%)

The journal consists of weekly critical reflections on assigned readings, class sessions, and the personal scholarly inquiry process required of this RS course. You are expected to demonstrate that you have completed all readings and are attempting to integrate this material and content from class sessions into your developing understanding of human rights, generalist social work for community practice and macro level intervention, and personal–professional perspective as a social worker. The weekly scholarly inquiry log/journal entry should be submitted through Blackboard before 12:00 noon every Tuesday. Late entries will not be graded. Weekly entries are expected to be a minimum of 2 double-spaced pages in length and should include the content and process of the previous week's class sessions and the current week's readings.

The weekly scholarly inquiry log/journal entries should identify key concepts and issues presented in each assigned reading and provide critical reflections on and discussion of them. It should also include critical reflections on each class session and course committee meeting and its content and process. Each weekly journal entry should also end with one or more student-generated question that the student would like to discuss with classmates and the professor during a class session.

You are expected to demonstrate that you have completed all readings and are attempting to integrate this material and content from class sessions into your developing understanding of human rights, generalist social work for community practice and macro level intervention, and personal–professional perspective as a social worker. Reflections on readings should focus on major concepts/learning and questions from the reading and how it relates to your developing understanding of the course content. This journaling will also include an ongoing descriptive log (listing of activities and time allotted each week toward the project) and personal critical reflections on the research and scholarly inquiry process. This should include any successes, obstacles, questions, and identification of themes and explanations of the data that need to be further verified and refined with additional data. Individual journal entries when compared and contrasted with others will enable the instructors to focus class sessions, discussions, and the project planning process to achieve the course objectives.

Hopefully, the journal will be more than a purely descriptive experience: rather, it should be a more personal and meaningful reflection, analysis, and synthesis of the course content and experience. A final integrative summary of the journal experience will be required at the end of the course.

Scholarly inquiry log/journal entries should be submitted weekly and will be graded randomly a minimum of four times with letter grades and written feedback. Students are also invited to specify any particular entries on which they desire feedback. Final grades for the scholarly inquiry log will average the graded weekly entries and consider the quality of the final integrative summary and the comprehensiveness of all weekly journal entries. Guidelines for the journals/logs and grading are based on the following expectations.

- **A/A-:** High quality journal entries incorporating critical reflections on each assigned reading and each class session (minimum of 2 double-spaced typed pages per week). High quality integrative reflective summary (minimum of 2 double-spaced typed pages) at end of course.

- **B+/B/B-:** Quality critical reflections each week, but falling short of the quality and/or minimum requirement for A-level work. Integrative reflective summary (minimum of 2 double-spaced typed pages) at end of course.

- **C+/C:** Incomplete and/or low quality entries regarding content of each assigned reading and class session. Integrative summary at end of course.

- **D:** Poor quality and/or incomplete journal. Journal summary at end of course.

- **F:** Failure to do the above.

Perception of Human Rights and Poverty (20%)

The poverty simulation experience is designed to help participants begin to understand what it might be like to live in a typical low-income family trying to survive from month to month. In the simulation 40–80 participants assume the roles of up to 26 different families facing poverty. Staff from the county Department of Family Services will be providing an orientation to the poverty simulation. Participation in the training and the event is mandatory.

The perception of human rights and poverty paper should be a minimum of 4 double-spaced typed pages and should include at least 2 pages of critical reflection on the actual training and experience of the simulation, as well as the reasons the Department of Family Services invests time and resources into this type of activity. The remaining 2 pages should focus on synthesizing the assigned readings on poverty and human rights.

Once we have all experienced the poverty simulation, the class will work together as a group to organize, plan, and implement a final course capstone event (which should include a version of the poverty simulation and how poverty is connected to human rights and human rights education) for the university community. Details of the event will be determined by the class as a whole.

Final Course Capstone Event/Human Rights Education Project (45%)

This project has several components. All three instructors will be assessing participation and quality of work throughout the semester and soliciting feedback from committee members for your grade.

There will be three overarching committees, each of which will be responsible for collecting data, analyzing data, and creating a dissemination plan for the results of the data analysis. The committees will be responsible for organizing themselves and creating appropriate task groups. One member of each task group will serve on the Steering Committee with the instructors.

Each committee will be responsible for answering the following questions (other questions can be added if the committees decide to do so):

- What is the state of human rights education for undergraduates at this university?
- Why is human rights education important or needed in undergraduate education?
- What resources exist for promoting human rights education at this university?
- How can students promote human rights education at this university and in surrounding communities?
- What are possible ways to infuse human rights education in a large undergraduate university?

Assessing Campus Resources Committee

This committee will have the responsibility of identifying appropriate faculty/staff members and campus resources. Members will interview campus librarians; individuals from the Office of Diversity, Inclusion, and Multicultural Education; faculty/staff members from each college with curricula about human rights resources; and other campus resources. This committee will assess at least 10 resources on campus using a rubric that they develop.

Assessing Student Opinion Committee

This committee will identify student groups and find a way to collect information from students about their opinions of human rights education. This may be accomplished by conducting individual interviews and running focus groups with students and student organizations.

Assessing Community Agencies and Organizations Committee

This committee will identify and interview staff members from local or national agencies or organizations that focus on human rights. Before interviewing staff, students must thoroughly understand what the agencies' missions and goals are.

Final Course Capstone Event

The class as a whole will work closely together throughout the semester to organize, plan, and implement a final course capstone event (which should include a version of the poverty simulation and how poverty is connected to human rights and human rights education) for the university community.

Details of the event will be determined by the class as a whole, and work will be organized through the Steering Committee.

The requirements for the final course capstone event include dissemination of the results of each of the three committees' work (via Photovoice, videos, posters, podcasts, presentations, etc.) and an experiential component for participants (e.g., the poverty simulation). Outreach and messaging will be key components to make this event successful. The dissemination of the results should be transferrable to a website that will be developed for this class. The instructors are open to hearing other ideas from students about various ways to create a sustainable product to advance human rights education.

Integrative Reflective Summary Paper

We hope that you have been challenged in this course to think and act outside your comfort zone. We are interested in your reflections on the content and process of both the research project (including the dissemination event) and the course overall. Please submit a well-written and organized reflective summary paper (4–5 double-spaced pages not including title page) and submit on Blackboard as an attachment by the due date. Be sure to think about the various components of the course (readings, scholarly inquiry logs, poverty simulation, the IRB process, data collection, coding and analyzing the data, creating the posters, organizing the event, and putting on the event itself) and integrate these into your paper. Headings are not necessary, but if used, please be sure your headings are descriptive (e.g., do not use headings such as *content* or *process*).

Content

- Describe and reflect on your learning process about human rights. Try to remember what knowledge you began the class with and how the course has contributed to your understanding of human rights and human rights education.

- Answer the five research questions that you set out to explore (this should be in narrative form and complete sentences and could be part of your introduction or conclusion):

    1. What is the state of human rights education for undergraduates at this university?

    2. Why is human rights education important or needed in undergraduate education?

    3. What resources exist for promoting human rights education at this university?

    4. How can students promote human rights education at this university and in surrounding communities?

    5. What are possible ways to infuse human rights education in a large undergraduate university?

Process

- Describe and reflect on the process of creating an original scholarly project (your research), including how to articulate your research questions and engage in key elements of the research process.

- Describe and reflect on the process of organizing the dissemination event, including your efforts to situate the concepts, practices, and results of the project within a broader societal context.

- In the last section of your paper, please describe your postgraduation plans and how you plan to integrate what you have learned into your identity and practice as a social worker.

Course Schedule

Class Meetings	Topics	Readings	Assignments Due
Week 1	• All three sections meet together • Overview of the course • Introduction to Human Rights • Meaning of Human Rights		
Week 2	• All three sections meet together • Human Rights: Categories, Principles, and Issues • Universal Declaration of Human Rights	• United Nations. (2000). *Human rights and human development.* 2000 UN Human Development Report. • United Nations. (2003). *Millennium Development Goals: A compact among nations to end human poverty.* UN Human Development Report (p. x, pp. 1–25).	Scholarly Inquiry Log due by Tuesday at noon
Week 3	• Social Work and Human Rights • UN World Program for Human Rights and Human Rights Education • Helping tell stories – gathering data, working with community agencies	• Healy, L. M. (2008). Exploring the history of social work as a human rights profession. *International Social Work, 51,* 735–748. • Resources include 　◦ WITNESS Video Advocacy Planning Toolkit: See It, Film It, Change It (www.ushrnetwork.org/resources-media/witness-video-advocacy-planning-toolkit) 　◦ Articles on photovoice at http://heb.sagepub.com/content/24/3/369.short	Scholarly Inquiry Log due by Tuesday at noon
Week 4	• Poverty and Human Rights • Project Organization • Small groups meet to formulate plan for gathering data	• Go to http://www.amnesty.org/en/poverty to read about poverty and human rights and then follow link to read "New youth website will enhance understanding of human rights and poverty." • Evans, J., & Klasing, A. (2012). Discrimination, inequality, and poverty—A human rights perspective. Human Rights Watch. • Pogge, T. (2005). World poverty and human rights. *Ethics & International Affairs, 19*(1), 1–7. Retrieved from http://www.carnegiecouncil.org/publications/journal/19_1/symposium/5109.html/_res/id=sa_File1/5109_eia19-1_pogge01.pdf	Scholarly Inquiry Log due by Tuesday at noon

table continues

Class Meetings	Topics	Readings	Assignments Due
Week 5	• Poverty Simulation Training • Poverty Simulation	• Nickols, S. Y., & Nielsen, R. B. (2011). So many people are struggling: Developing social empathy through a poverty simulation. *Journal of Poverty, 15,* 22-42. doi:10.1080/10875549.2011.539400 • Life in the state of poverty: Fairfax County, Virginia, 2013 http://www.fairfaxcounty.gov/dfs/caab/povertysimulation.htm • Community Action Advisory Board (CAAB): Updated for 2012 Fairfax County, Virginia http://www.fairfaxcounty.gov/dfs/caab/ • The poverty simulation is run by CAAB. Please read and learn about CAAB. Be sure to click on the following links on the CAAB website: • What are Community Action Programs? • What population is served by Community Action Programs? • Community Action in Fairfax County: An overview – history • Community Services Block Grants Programs	Scholarly Inquiry Log due by Tuesday at noon
Week 6	• Process Poverty Simulation • Data Collection	• The Purdue Online Writing Lab (OWL) [1995-2011] http://owl.english.purdue.edu/ • This is a good website to explore. Be sure to review the Creating Good Interview and Survey Questions (Interview and Survey Questions) section as well as the Interviewing section. • Research Observatory: Designing Interview Questions http://ro.uwe.ac.uk/RenderPages/RenderLearningObject.aspx?Context=7&Area=1&Room=3&Constellation=25&LearningObject=120 • Please review the university Institutional Review Board (IRB) website. The IRB has confirmed that we do not need formal approval to begin our data collection. However, if you are going to publish from any data collection that you do involving human subjects, you need to receive the approval. During the semester we will seek to gain this approval in anticipation of a published article on our work together. Please begin to review the policies and procedures on the website.	Perceptions of Human Rights and Poverty paper due

table continues

Class Meetings	Topics	Readings	Assignments Due
Week 6 (continued)		• Creswell, J. W. (1998). Data collection. In *Qualitative inquiry and research design: Choosing among five traditions* (3rd ed., pp. 109–137). Thousand Oaks, CA: SAGE. • Creswell, J. W. (2009). Research questions and hypotheses. In *Research design: Qualitative, quantitative, and mixed methods approaches* (pp. 129–142). Thousand Oaks, CA: SAGE.	
Week 7	• All three sections meet together • How to Analyze Data	• Sandelowski, M. (1995). Qualitative analysis: What it is and how to begin. *Research in Nursing & Health, 18,* 371–375. • Read examples to see how individual interviews are coded and focus group data are summarized.	Scholarly Inquiry Log due by Tuesday at noon

Week 8	• Data Collection (cont.)
	• Begin data analysis and presentation of results
		• Please be sure to reflect on the group process that has been occurring in your committee and on your committee's plan (be sure to reflect on the plan and not describe it in detail here). This should make up most of the content for your scholarly logs this week. You also have two newspaper articles to read and reflect on.
		
		• Readings:
		
		  ◦ Reilly, C. Finding homes for the homeless in Fairfax County. *The Washington Post,* March 4, 2013, Retrieved from http://www.washingtonpost.com/local/virginia-politics/finding-homes-for-the-homeless-in-fairfax-county/2013/03/04/1307ba60-81ce-11e2-a350-49866afab584_story.html
		
		  ◦ This is a *Washington Post* story on the 1,000 Homes Campaign. As we are focused on the class project relative to human rights education, it is important to stay current on the human rights issues, interventions and advocacy that is occurring within and outside of our own country everyday (in this case, our own county).
		
		  ◦ Luck, T. As Syrian refugee population nears 1 million, relief agencies cannot keep up. *The Washington Post,* March 4, 2013, Retrieved from http://www.washingtonpost.com/world/middle_east/as-syrian-refugee-population-nears-1-million-relief-agencies-cannot-keep-up/2013/03/04/1f0bf5f2-80f6-11e2-a350-49866afab584_story.html
			Scholarly Inquiry Log due by Tuesday at noon

table continues

Class Meetings	Topics	Readings	Assignments Due
Week 9	• All three sections meet together • Data Analysis and Presentation of Results (cont.)	• Sandretto, S. (2007). *Discussion paper: Action research for social justice.* Retrieved from http://www.tlri.org.nz/sites/default/files/pages/action-research.pdf	Scholarly Inquiry Log due by Tuesday at noon
Week 10	• Data Analysis and Presentation of Results (cont.) • Event Planning	• Please explore the toolbox on community-based participatory action research and reflect on that as it applies to the research you are doing in your committees. Don't forget to reflect on the process that is occurring in your committees. • Community Toolbox of the Workgroup on Community Health and Development of the University of Kansas. (2013). Retrieved from http://tb.ku.edu/default.aspx	Scholarly Inquiry Log due by Tuesday at noon
Week 11	• All three sections meet together • Event Planning (cont.)	• Please continue to read and explore the links on the website, Community Toolbox: Bringing Solutions to Light: http://ctb.ku.edu/en/default.aspx	Scholarly Inquiry Log due by Tuesday at noon
Week 12	• Event Planning (Final)	• Anderson, C. (2010). Presenting and evaluating qualitative research. *American Journal of Pharmaceutical Education, 74*(8), 1–7.	Scholarly Inquiry Log due by Tuesday at noon
Week 13	• Course Capstone Project/Human Rights Education Event	• Ryan, G. W., & Bernard, H. R. (2003). Techniques to identify themes. *Field Methods, 15,* 85–109. doi:10.1177/1525822X02239569	Scholarly Inquiry Log due by Tuesday at noon
Week 14	• All three sections meet together	• Prepare for final capstone event.	Integrative reflective summary paper of the project and the class

Recommended Readings

Beverly, C. J., McAtee, R., Costello, J., Chernoff, R., Casteel, J. (2005). Needs assessment of rural communities: A focus on older adults. *Journal of Community Health, 30*(3), 197–212. doi:10.1007/s10900-004-1958-y

Community Services Center, School of Social Work, University of Texas at Arlington. (2006). *Client-centered community needs assessment for homeless residents of Tarrant County.* Retrieved from http://wweb.uta.edu/ssw/csdc/documents/Client%20Centered%20Community%20Needs%20Assessment%20-%20Tarrant%20County.pdf

Council on Social Work Education. (2008). *Educational policy and accreditation standards.* Retrieved from http://www.cswe.org/File.aspx?id=41861

Healy, L. (2008). Exploring the history of social work as a human rights profession. *International Social Work, 51*, 735–748.

Hymans, D. J. (2000). Teaching BSW students community practice using an interdisciplinary neighborhood needs assessment project. *Journal of Baccalaureate Social Work, 5*(2), 81–92.

Jones, A. (2011). *Genocide: A comprehensive introduction* (2nd ed.). New York, NY: Routledge.

Langwith, J. (Ed.). (2008). *Human rights: Opposing viewpoints*. Farmington Hills, MI: Greenhaven Press.

Reichert, E. (Ed.). (2007). *Challenges in human rights: A social work perspective*. New York, NY: Columbia University Press.

Sharma, A., Lanum, M., & Suarez-Balcazar, Y. (2000). *A community needs assessment guide: a brief guide on how to conduct a needs assessment*. Center for Urban Research and Learning and the Department of Psychology, Loyola University Chicago. Retrieved from http://www.luc.edu/curl/pdfs/A_Community_Needs_Assessment_Guide_.pdf

Stanton, G. H. (1998). *The 8 stages of genocide*. Retrieved from the Genocide Watch website: http://www.genocidewatch.org/genocide/8stagesofgenocide.html

United Nations Centre for Human Rights. (1994). *Human rights and social work: A manual for schools of social work and the social work profession*. New York, NY: United Nations.

Wang, C., & Burris, M. A. (1997). Photovoice: Concept, methodology, and use for participatory needs assessment. *Health Education & Behavior, 24*(3), 369–387.

Wronka, J. (2008). *Human rights and social justice: Social action and service for the helping and health professions*. Thousand Oaks, CA: SAGE.

Global Human Rights (Web-Based)

Khadija Khaja
Indiana University

Course Description

This course will predominantly cover issues related to human rights, and cross-cultural practice. Social work practice in different continents will be also discussed. Global social justice issues faced by developing countries will be examined. A large part of the course will focus on our own assumptions and biases about cultures different from ours.

The Council on Social Work Education (CSWE), the accrediting body for schools of social work in the United States, requires social work programs to demonstrate how each course in the curriculum helps students develop competencies expected of all who seek entry into the profession. Programs must document a match between course content and CSWE competencies defined in the Educational Policy and Accreditation Standards (EPAS). This elective course in the BSW curriculum draws on basic knowledge and understanding of global human rights. Course content contributes to building knowledge and skills for students to demonstrate EPAS (CSWE, 2008) Competencies 2.1.5 (advance human rights and social and economic justice), 2.1.2 (apply social work ethical principles to guide professional practice), 2.1.4 (engage diversity and difference in practice), and 2.1.3 (apply critical thinking to inform and communicate professional judgments).

Course Objectives

Through active participation in the learning experiences and completion of the readings, assignments, and learning projects offered throughout this course, students are expected to demonstrate the ability to

- understand global interdependence and international social work (Educational Policy [EP] 2.1.5 and 2.1.4),

- understand the global issues of human rights (EP 2.1.5),

- analyze the global inequalities of women (EP 2.1.5 and 2.1.3,

- explain the importance of eastern and western paradigms when working with diverse cultures around the world,

- examine social work practice in selected countries (EP 2.1.5),

- discuss values and ethics in cross-cultural practice (EP 2.1.2 and 2.1.3),

- explain ethical and value dilemmas when intervening in a culturally sensitive manner (EP 2.1.2., 2.1.4, and 2.1.3), and

- demonstrate increased understanding of cultural competency skills (EP 2.1.4).

Content Outline and Reading Assignments

Module 1 Unit 1

- Orientation to the classroom
- Introduction/expectations/course objectives
- Recommended technology requirements
- Learning in a virtual classroom

Reading: Oncourse Interactive Notes for Module 1-Unit 1 Orientation to classroom

- What Are Global Human Rights?
  - Why Human Rights and Social Work?
  - Definition of Human Rights
  - Human Rights Terms
  - Enforcement of Human Rights

Reading: Chapter 1, Reichert: What Are Human Rights?

Module 2 Unit 1 Overview of Human Rights: Diverse Paradigms

- Global human rights issues
- Diverse ways to view the world & solving problems
- Eastern and western paradigms
- Bridging cultures
- Global human rights in social work

Reading:

- Oncourse Interactive Notes for Module 2 Unit 1, Global Human Rights
- Khaja & Queiro-Tajalli, PDF file in Oncourse Module 2 Unit 1, Bridging Eastern and Western Paradigms: Transforming How We Teach Diversity

Module 2 Unit 1 Beginning of Human Rights

- Evolution of the human rights framework
- The Universal Declaration of Human Rights
- Social workers and development of human rights

Reading: Chapter 2, Reichert, Beginning of Human Rights

Module 2 Unit 2 Introduction to Cross-Cultural Counseling

- Eastern and Western paradigms
- Cultural sensitivity
- Cultural diversity
- Diverse values
- Global social work
- Social work practice in the United States and Canada
- Multicultural counseling techniques
- Counseling Muslim families
- Caste systems in India

Reading:

- Oncourse Interactive Notes for Module 2, Unit 2, Introduction to Cross-Cultural Counseling
- Oncourse Interactive Notes for Module 2, Unit 2: Powerpoint video presentation on social work practice in the world with a focus on the United States and Canada
- Khandare, PDF File in Oncourse Module 2, Unit 2: *Hidden Apartheid in India: The ContinuedPractice of Untouchability*
- Khaja, PDF File in Oncourse Module 2, Unit 2: *Reflections on Teaching Effective Social Work Practice with Muslims*

Module 2 Unit 2 Universal Declaration of Human Rights

- Why is it important?
- What are the controversies about it?
- Can human rights truly be universal?

Reading: Chapter 3, Reichert, Building the Foundation: Universal Declaration of Human Rights

Module 2 Unit 3 Global Women's Movements

- Globalization
- International social work
- Gender inequalities
- Jata rituals in India
- Social work practice in Latin-America

Reading:

- Hokenstad & Midgley PDF File in Oncourse Module 2, Unit 3: *Globalization and Gender Inequalities*
- Oncourse Interactive Notes for Module 2, Unit 3: *Global Social Work and Global Women's Movements*
- Oncourse Interactive Notes for Module 2, Unit 3: Powerpoint video presentation on social work practice in Latin America
- Queiro-Tajalli and Campbell PDF
- Resilience and violence at the macro level

Due: Midterm Paper

Module 2 Unit 3 Other Types of Rights

- International covenant on civil and political rights
- International covenant on economic rights
- Global social and cultural rights

Reading: Chapter 4, Reichert, Beyond the Universal Declaration of Human Rights

Module 2 Unit 4 Case Study of Female Circumcision

- Global interventions with female circumcision
- Universal human rights complexities
- Clinical practice with circumcised women

Reading:

- Oncourse Interactive Notes for Module 2, Unit 4 Case Study of Female Circumcision: Human Rights Complexities
- Khaja PDF File in Oncourse Module 2, Unit 4 Omar Family: A Case Study of Female Circumcision with Couple Intervention
- Oncourse Interactive Notes for Module 2, Unit 4 Powerpoint video presentation: *Female Circumcision: We See it as Power Not Oppression*

Module 2 Unit 4 Human Rights and Vulnerable Groups

- Who is vulnerable?
- Women as vulnerable
- Children as vulnerable
- Victims of racism
- Persons with disabilities
- Persons with HIV/AIDS
- Older persons
- Gays and lesbians

Reading: Chapter 5, Reichert, Human Rights and Vulnerable Groups

Module 2 Unit 5 Ethical and Value Dilemmas in Counseling

- Cultural value conflicts
- Imposing values on clients
- Value case studies
- Personal belief systems
- Social work and Human Rights: Do they fit?
- Social work practice in Europe

Reading:

- Corey, Corey, & Callanan PDF File in Oncourse Module 2, Unit 5, Issues and Ethics in the Helping Profession
- Ife PDF File in Oncourse Module 2, Unit 5, Local and global practice: Relocating social work as a human rights profession in the new global order
- Oncourse Interactive Notes for Module 2, Unit 5 PowerPoint video presentation
- *Social Work Practice in Europe*

Module 2 Unit 5 Cultural Relativism and Global Human Rights

- What is cultural relativism?
- Why should we care?
- How does it affect global social work practice?

Reading: Chapter 6, Reichert, Cultural Relativism

Module 2 Unit 6 Global Poverty

- Developing countries and poverty
- Developed countries and poverty
- Inequalities of wealth
- Social work practice in Africa
- Challenge of social work practice in Africa
- Children of war
- Nongovernmental organizations to help children

Reading:

- Oncourse Interactive Notes for Module 2, Unit 6, Global Poverty and Inequality
- Oncourse Interactive Notes for Module 2, Unit 6 PowerPoint video presentation, *Social Work Practice in Africa*
- Hwedie PDF File in Oncourse Module 2, Unit 6, *The Challenge of Social Work in Africa: Starting the Indigenisation Process*
- Burke & Ngonyani PDF File in Oncourse Module 2, Unit 6, *A Social Work Vision for Tanzania*
- Noyoo PDF File in Oncourse Module 2, Unit 6, *Social Development in Sub-Saharan Africa: Lessons for Social Work practice in South Africa*

Module 2 Unit 6 Global Human Rights and Ethics

- NASW code of ethics
- IFSW code of ethics
- Human rights and ethics
- Social work practice and human rights
- International side of human rights and social work

Reading:

- Chapter 7, 8, 9, Reichert, Human Rights and Ethics, Social Work Practice and Human Rights, The International Side of Human Rights and Social Work

Module 2 Unit 7

- Social work practice in the Middle East
- Southeast Asia: Lessons from Indonesia
- Demographics of refuges around the world
- United Nations High Commission for Refugees
- Cultural sensitivity working with refugees
- Social work practice in Asia and the Middle East
- Non–social work practitioners serving vulnerable populations: The Indonesia case
- Benefits of international field placements, independent studies, and service learning

Reading:

- Special presentation about Indonesia and human service providers
- UNHCR PDF file in Oncourse Module 2, Unit 7, *The State of the World's Refugees*
- UNHCR PDF file in Oncourse Module 2, Unit 7, at http://www.unhcr.org/cgi-bin/texis/vtx/ home
- Oncourse Interactive Notes for Module 2, Unit 7, PowerPoint video presentation, *Study Abroad: A Social Work Student in Afghanistan*
- Oncourse Interactive Notes for Module 2, Unit 7, PowerPoint video presentation, *Social Work Practice in the Middle East and Asia*

Due: Final Paper

Module 2 Unit 7

Final Class; Web-based evaluation of course

Required and Recommended Texts and Journal Articles

Required Text

Reichert, E. (2006). *Understanding human rights: An exercise book*. Thousand Oak, CA: SAGE Publications.

Recommended

American Psychological Association. (2010). *Publication Manual of the American Psychological Association* (6th ed.). Washington, DC: Author.

Websites related to APA style

- http://www.apastyle.org/
- http://webster.comment.edu/apa/apa_index.htm
- http://owl.english.purdue.edu/ (online writing laboratory at Purdue University)

Assignments

Structured Critical Reflection on Human Rights Paper (40 Points; EPAS 2.1.2., 2.1.3., 2.1.3., and 2.1.5)

The National Association of Social Workers states that the primary mission of social work is to enhance human well-being and help meet the basic human needs of all people, with particular attention to the needs of those people who are oppressed, vulnerable, and live in poverty. This first paper requires you to write a 5-page essay in APA format with five references from text and three references from materials outside of the course that address the following questions. Reflect on a time when you stood up or did not stand for your own human rights or the human rights of other people and address the questions below.

- What happened?
- Where did it happen?
- The motive: Why did you stand up or not stand up for your human rights or someone else's?
- Who were or were not your sources of support in this instance to influence how you acted?
- What does this tell you about how to be an effective helper?
- What does this tell you about your own ethics and values?
- How do you define *human rights*?
- What are challenges to addressing human rights at a global level?
- In your view how does culture affect the perception of human rights?

Human Rights and Cultural Competency Final Research Paper (60 points; EPAS 2.1.2., 2.1.3., 2.1.3., and 2.1.5)

This final paper should be 12–15 pages long, written in APA style with at least five references from interdisciplinary peer-reviewed journals and five references from text; other references can come from websites/books, and so forth. The paper should be organized under the following headings.

History of the Human Rights Problem (20 points)

Identify a human rights problem from a country other than the United States and why it is relevant to us as social workers. Provide demographic, political, social, and economic contexts of the human rights problem. State its relevance to the international social work profession. Some examples of human rights problems are genocide, ethnic conflict, mass violence, child and or human trafficking, honor killing, female circumcision, children of war, refugees, child soldiers, food and water famine, rape, and victims of torture.

Global Human Rights Policies (20 Points)

Identify what global human rights policies exist under the International Declaration of Human Rights and/or other international laws, agreements, codes, or enactments that address this human rights violation.

Cultural Competency Issues (15 Points)

Identify the cultural challenges that you may face as a social worker when trying to work with this population. As you conceptualize working with this culturally diverse population, how will you address these challenges? Be specific.

Scholarly Writing, Organization, Professional References (5 Points)

Peer-reviewed journals are used and references are cited in correct APA style. Paper is professionally written with correct grammatical structure and is well-organized. Paper demonstrates academic rigor.

Bibliography

Corey, G., Schneider-Corey, M., & Callanan, P. (2003). Values and the helping relationship. In G. Corey, M. Schneider-Corey, & P. Callanan (Eds.). *Issues and ethics in the helping professions*. Pacific Grove, CA: Brooks/Cole.

Christian, J. (2009). Examining the intersection of race, gender, and mass imprisonment. *Journal of Ethnicity in Criminal Justice, 7*(1), 69–84.

Council on Social Work Education. (2008). Educational policy and accreditation standards. Retrieved from http://www.cswe.org/File.aspx?id=41861

Healy, L. M., & Link, R. J. (2012). *Handbook of international social work: Human rights, development, and the global profession*. New York, NY: Oxford University Press.

Ife, J. (2001). *Human rights and social work: Towards rights-based practice*. Cambridge, UK: Cambridge University Press.

Khaja, K. (2005). Omar family: A case study of couple intervention with female circumcision. In B. Compton, B. Galaway, & B. R. Cournoyer (Eds.). *Social work processes* (7th ed.). Pacific Grove, CA: Brooks/Cole.

Khaja, K. (2007). Teaching lessons learned by entering the world of female circumcision. *Reflections Narratives of Professional Helping, 13*(4), 39–43.

Khaja, K., & Frederick, C. (2008). Reflection on teaching effective social work practice for working with Muslim communities. *Advances in Social Work, 9*(1), 1–7.

Lum, D. (2011). *Culturally competent practice: A framework for understanding diverse groups and justice issues*. Belmont, CA: Brooks/Cole.

Marsiglia, F. F., & Kulis, S. (2009). *Culturally grounded social work: Diversity, oppression and change*. Chicago, IL: Lyceum Books.

Semati, M. (2010). Islamophobia, culture, and race in the age of empire. *Cultural Studies, 24*(2), 256–275.

Sheets, R. H. (2005). *Diversity pedagogy: Examining the role of culture in the teaching-learning process*. Boston, MA: Pearson Education.

Steiner, H. J., & Alston, P. (2000). *International human rights in context: Law, politics and morals*. New York, NY: Oxford University Press.

Tumlin, K. (2004). Suspect first: How terrorism policy is reshaping immigration policy. *California Law Review, 92*, 1173–1239.

Welch, C. E. (2001). *Ngo's and human rights: Promise and performance*. Philadelphia, PA: University of Pennsylvania Press.

Internet Resources

List of United Nations accredited NGOs: http://www.unpan.org/NGO-Global.asp; (United States, pp. 311–396)

Miscellaneous sites

Academy for Educational Development: http://www.aed.org/Gender/

American Association of University Women: http://www.aauw.org/

Amnesty International USA: http://www.amnestyusa.org/

Amnesty International Women's Human Rights Network: http://www.amnestyusa.org/women/index.do

Asha for Education (India): http://www.ashanet.org/index.php?page=home

Association for Women's Rights in Development: http://www.awid.org/

Association of International Women of Indianapolis: http://www.aiwindy.org/

Center for American Women and Politics: http://www.cawp.rutgers.edu/

Center for Women Policy Studies: http://www.centerwomenpolicy.org/

Center for Women's Global Leadership (Rutgers University) http://www.cwgl.rutgers.edu/

Center for Media Literacy: http://www.medialit.org/

Centre for Leadership for Women (Australia): http://www.leadershipforwomen.com.au/

Center for Women, the Earth, the Divine: http://www.cwed.org/

Coalition Against Trafficking in Women: http://www.catwinternational.org/

Corporate Alliance to End Partner Violence: http://www.caepv.org/

Domestic Violence Network of Greater Indianapolis: http://www.domesticviolencenetwork.org/

Ecofeminism News: http://www.ecofem.org/

Faith Trust Institute (against sexual and domestic violence): http://www.faithtrustinstitute.org/

Family Violence Prevention Fund: http://endabuse.org/

Feminist Majority Foundation: http://www.feminist.org/

Feminist Sexual Ethics Project (Brandeis University): http://www.brandeis.edu/projects/fse/about/about-index.html

Girls Inc.: http://www.girlsinc.com/ic/page.php?id=1

Center for the Study of Global Change (Indiana Univ.): http://www.indiana.edu/~global/

Gender and Food Security (UN): http://www.fao.org/gender/

Global Alliance for Women's Health: http://www.gawh.org/

Global Fund for Women: http://www.globalfundforwomen.org/cms/

Global Women's Leadership Network (Santa Clara Univ.): http://www.scu.edu/business/gwln/

Grassroots Organizations Operating Together in Sisterhood: http://www.groots.org/

Hot Peach Pages (International Domestic Violence and Abuse agencies list): http://www.hotpeachpages.net/

Indiana Coalition Against Sexual Assault: http://www.incasa.org/

Center for International Business Education and Research (IU) : http://www.kelley.iu.edu/CIBER/

Institute for Women and Work (Cornell Univ.): http://www.ilr.cornell.edu/iww/

Institute for Women's Policy Research: http://www.iwpr.org/index.cfm

International Center of Indianapolis: http://www.icenterindy.org/

International Center for Research on Women: http://www.icrw.org/html/issues/violence.htm

International Network on Gender and Sustainable Energy: http://www.energia.org/

International Lactation Consultants Association: http://www.ilca.org/

International Leadership Association: http://www.ila-net.org/index.htm

International Planned Parenthood Federation: http://www.ippfwhr.org/

Office of International Affairs (IUPUI) : http://www.iupui.edu/~oia/

Journal of Gender, Social Policy and Law (American Univ.) (list of other journals and resources): http://www.wcl.american.edu/journal/genderlaw/links.cfm

Women's Studies Internet Resources (IUPUI Library): http://www.ulib.iupui.edu/subjectareas/women/history.html

League of Women Voters (US): http://www.lwv.org/AM/Template.cfm?Section=Home

Ms. Foundation for Women: http://www.ms.foundation.org/

National Association for Multicultural Education: http://www.nameorg.org/

The National Archives-Women's Suffrage (US): http://www.archives.gov/education/lessons/woman-suffrage/kaiser-wilson.html

National Center on Domestic and Sexual Violence (US) : http://www.ncdsv.org/

National Coalition Against Domestic Violence (US): http://www.ncadv.org/

Nationalities Council of Indiana: http://nationalitiescouncil.org/

The Julian Center for Women (Indianapolis): http://www.juliancenter.org/

The National Council for Research on Women (US): http://www.ncrw.org/

The National Domestic Violence Hotline (US): http://www.ndvh.org/

National Organization for Women (US): http://www.now.org/index.html

National Sexual Violence Resource Center (US): http://www.nsvrc.org/

National Women's Law Center (US): http://www.nwlc.org/index.cfm

National Women's Studies Association (US): http://www.nwsa.org/

Office of International Women's Issues, The US Department of State: http://www.state.gov/g/wi/

Our Shared History, African-American Heritage: http://www.cr.nps.gov/aahistory/

School for International Training: http://www.sit.edu/index.html

Sloan Work and Family Research Network (Boston College): http://wfnetwork.bc.edu/activities. php?area=academics

The Center for Public Integrity, Investigative Journalism in the Public Interest: http://www. publicintegrity.org/default.aspx

United Nations Development Programme: http://www.undp.org/equatorinitiative/

United Nations Development Fund for Women: http://www.unifem.org/

United Nations Inter-agency Network on Women and Gender Equality (WomenWatch):

http://www.un.org/womenwatch/

White Violet Center for Eco-Justice (St. Mary of the Woods): http://www.spsmw.org/cgi-bin/site. pl?3208&dwContent_contentID=1

Women's Development and Environment Organization: http://www.wedo.org/

Women's Global Education Project: http://womensglobal.org/

Women of Color websites: http://research.umbc.edu/~korenman/wmst/links_wc.html

Women's Institute for Leadership Development in Human Rights: http://www.wildforhumanrights. org/about/index.html

Women's Law: http://www.womenslaw.org/

World Resources Institute: http://population.wri.org//pubs_description.cfm?PubID=4073

Special Topics: International Social Work

Catherine A. Hawkins
Texas State University

Course Description

This special topics elective course presents an overview of international social work, including theoretical and practical approaches. A values-based orientation will focus on an exploration of empowerment, social and economic justice, and human rights. Particular cultures and specific global problems will be examined in depth so that students can achieve an international worldview and contribute to humane global change through informed practice.

Course Learning Aims

After students complete this course, they will be able to do the following:

- Explain a global perspective on human rights with special consideration for the variable effects on vulnerable and marginalized populations

- Identify theoretical models of empowerment and social development and how they variably influence social work approaches to global human problems

- Articulate how our own cultural backgrounds influence our belief systems about other countries and people, and demonstrate an appreciation of cultural competency

- Critically examine the underlying causes of social and economic differences around the world and describe appropriate interventions, practice models, and roles for effective social work practice as well as values, ethical issues, and laws pertinent to service provision

- Identify and critically assess contemporary trends and issues in international social work and consider a personal belief system regarding social change

Textbook

Mapp, S. C. (2008). *Human rights and social justice in a global perspective: An introduction to international social work.* New York, NY: Oxford University Press.

Additional readings posted online or placed on reserve in the library.

Student Competencies Focused on in This Course

Educational Policy (EP) 2.1.4, Engage diversity and difference in practice (Council on Social Work Education, 2008)

Social workers understand how diversity characterizes and shapes the human experience and is critical to the formation of identity. The dimensions of diversity are understood as the intersection of multiple factors including age, class, color, culture, differential ability, ethnicity, gender, gender identity, immigration status, political ideology, race, religion, and sexual orientation. Social workers

appreciate that, as a consequence of difference, a person's life experiences may include oppression, poverty, marginalization, and alienation as well as privilege, power, and acclaim.

Student Practice Behaviors

- Recognize how a culture's structure and values may affect privilege and power

- Gain self-awareness to eliminate the influence of personal biases and values in working with diverse groups

- Recognize and communicate understanding of the importance of difference in shaping life experiences

- View selves as learners and engage those with whom they work as informants

  - Curriculum location: autobiography, weekly activity assignments and reaction papers, self-evaluation

EP 2.1.5, Advance human rights and social economic justice

Social workers are informed, resourceful, and proactive in responding to evolving organizational, community, and societal contexts at all levels of practice. Social workers recognize that the context of practice is dynamic and use knowledge and skill to respond proactively.

Student Practice Behaviors

- Understand the forms and mechanisms of oppression and discrimination

- Advocate for human rights and social and economic justice

- Engage in practices that advance social and economic justice

  - Curriculum location: Interviews, weekly activity assignments and reaction papers, group action-step project

Student Competencies Supported in This Course

- EP 2.1.2 Apply social work ethical principles to guide professional practice

- EP 2.1.5 Advance human rights and social and economic justice

- EP 2.1.9 Respond to contexts that shape practice

Teaching Methods

Students will learn the material in this course through a combination of class lectures and discussions, outside readings, in-class group exercises, audio-visual material, Web-based resources, guest speakers, case studies, reflective writing assignments, weekly activities, and an individual project that culminates in a class presentation.

Student Outcome Measures

Practices behaviors are measured by three to six methods at different times during enrollment in the program. Methods include a self-efficacy survey, field evaluation, grades, focus groups, poster presentations, and an alumni survey. Please see the school website for further details on how we measure practice behaviors and ensure that all students achieve social work competencies.

How Students Demonstrate They Have Achieved Course Aims

The goal of this course is to encourage and support students in expanding their knowledge, empathy, and responsibility for universal human rights and social justice through both scholarship and self-reflection. I strive to make the course as experiential as possible. I assume that you are in this course because you are motivated to pursue this journey. Therefore, although I do not require exams or research papers, the major assignments demand thought and reflection at a level that should be both challenging and rewarding.

Autobiography

At the beginning of the semester, you will write a brief history of your individual and cultural development, reflect on how it has influenced you to date, and speculate on how it might shape your future growth. You will explore your own thoughts and feelings regarding the difficult questions posed by local and global human inequality and injustice. This is an unstructured personal paper, and I will give you considerable flexibility regarding the format. You will be graded on the quality of the writing as well as the thoroughness and thoughtfulness of the content. This paper is worth 5% of your final grade.

Activities

This course is designed to be as experiential as possible, and you must engage in 10 out-of-class activities. This assignment will give you a broader perspective across many human rights issues. You are required to prepare a brief (one page) reaction to what you did and what you learned. We will take some class time for students to share their activities and then you will submit your paper to me. This is essentially a credit or no-credit assignment in that I will not evaluate your activity per se; you will receive points for a genuine effort (1% per week). This ongoing assignment is worth 10% of your final grade.

Interviews

During the course of the semester you will conduct two interviews, one with a person who is actively advocating for human rights and working to redress injustice. There are many local agencies in the central Texas region or you may contact someone by phone or Internet. Also, you will interview an individual (or find an equivalent resource such as a website or video) who has experienced a human rights violation or who has recently arrive in the United States. The interviews are intended to assist you in developing a broader worldview and deepening your empathy through a more personal format. I will assist you in identifying subjects to interview, if needed. You will write a summary of and reaction to both interviews (3–5 pages each), that is, not a transcript. We will discuss the interviews in class to broaden the perspective for all of us. Each interview is worth 10% of your final grade (a total of 20% together).

Project

Students will work in groups to identify a specific human rights concern and engage in an in-depth exploration of the problem and solutions, including community-based advocacy and/or action steps toward redressing the problem. There are many agencies, both locally and globally, that are available

either directly or online. I will assist you throughout the semester, and you are encouraged to get input from your classmates, faculty members, or other interested persons. This is a unique assignment that requires hands-on effort, so I am quite open to possibilities and to your creativity. You will create a brief packet containing an executive summary of the problem (10 points) and real or proposed solutions (10 points), human interest story, description of your action step(s) and future directions, and an annotated bibliography of at least 10 current scholarly resources. You will give a 20-minute presentation of your project to the class at the end of the semester. This is a major semester-long assignment, so it is worth the most points (40%) and includes credit for effort. It is expected that all group members will make equal and substantial contributions to the project, and you will have the opportunity to evaluate each member's input. Additional instructions will be provided for the presentation and paper.

Self-Assessment

You will engage in a critical analysis of your own growth and development over the semester. In this paper you will specifically consider how your thinking and feeling has evolved over the semester as you learned more about universal human rights from a personal, cultural, and global perspective. A helpful way to enhance your self-assessment is to keep a weekly journal throughout the semester. Occasional class time will be used for you to share your growth and changes with your peers. This paper is an inner exploration on the process of your journey. The more thoughtful your journal and activities, the more insightful will be your paper. It is worth 10% of your final grade.

NOTE: Your final grade may be lowered due to lack of adherence to course policies (see below). All assignments must be successfully completed to pass the course (i.e., you may not opt out of any assignment even if you have enough points for a desired grade).

Evaluation of Student Learning

- Autobiography: 10%
- Weekly activity (10): 10%
- Interviews (2 x 15%): 30%
- Self-assessment: 10%
- Group project: 40%

Course Overview

Course Sequence: Week 1

Learning Theme and Concepts

- Introduction and course overview
- Review of course requirements and activities
- Introduction to universal human rights
- Developing an international perspective for the global 21st century
- Distinguishing the arguments (e.g., universalism vs. cultural relativism, globalism vs. exceptionalism, nationalism vs. globalism)

Learning Opportunities

- Survey of student characteristics and course-related interests
- Discussion of global awareness
- In-class exercise on universal human rights

Course Sequence: Week 2

Learning Theme and Concepts

- History of international social work
- Understanding the world (geography, maps, cartography)
- Demographics and current global trends
- Realities of poverty, oppression, and inequality
- Social, cultural, and religious/spiritual diversity (similarities/differences)

Assigned Readings

- Mapp (2008), Preface and Chapter 1: International social development; Chapter 9: A call to action
- Healey (2008), Milestones in the history of international social work (handout posted on TRACS)
- Hawkins (2009), Global citizenship (posted on TRACS)
- List of major UN human rights documents (handout)

Learning Opportunities

- Complete maps of the world
- Class discussion on major global trends
- Identify selected problem or issue for individual project
- Weekly activity 1 due

Course Sequence: Week 3

Learning Theme and Concepts

- Overview of universal human rights (history, basic tenets, philosophical foundations)
- Multivariable approach (social, cultural, historical, legal, economic, political, etc.)

Assigned Readings

- Mapp (2008), Ch. 2: Human Rights
- Timeline of human rights (Hawkins handout posted on TRACS)
- Kristof & WuDunn (2009) (posted on TRACS)
- United Nations Universal Declaration of Human Rights (1948)
- What are Human Rights? video (available from HumanRights.com)

Learning Opportunities

- In-class examination of women's rights case study

- Watch video and discuss history of human rights

- Work on developing proposal for group projects

Course Sequence: Week 4

Learning Theme and Concepts

- 30 videos—30 rights video (available from http://www.humanrights.com/home.html)

- Social work values and ethics on an international stage

- Social work as advocacy and empowerment of vulnerable populations

- Developing empathy in an unfair world and facing compassion fatigue

- Connecting the global, national, and local and cultural, familial, and personal levels

Assigned Readings

- Ramathan & Link (2004), Global social work values and ethics (handout)

- International Federation of Social Workers Statement of Ethical Principles (handout)

Learning Opportunities

- Discussion of various aspects of values and generating empathy

- Sharing of personal stories, professional experiences, and career goals

- Autobiography Paper Due

Course Sequence: Week 5

Learning Theme and Concepts

- United Nations: additional treaties and conventions

- Critical analysis of human rights, Universal Declaration of Human Rights, and additional documents

- Millennium Development Goals (MDGs)

- Focus on environmental sustainability

Assigned Readings

- Mapp (2008), Chapter 8: MDGs

- UN Millennium Development Report (2012) (posted on TRACS)

- Hawkins (2010), Sustainability (posted on TRACS)

Learning Opportunities

- Open class discussion of MDGs

- Small group exercise on sustainability

Course Sequence: Week 6

Learning Theme and Concepts

Forced labor and human slavery

Assigned Readings

Mapp (2008), Chapter 3, Forced labor

Learning Opportunities

- Discussion of forced labor reading and Web searches
- Plan or group project due

Course Sequence: Week 7

Learning Theme and Concepts

- Forced labor and human slavery (cont.)

Assigned Readings

Swartz (2010), *Lost Girls* (posted on TRACS)

Learning Opportunities

- Guest speaker: Dottie Laster, MA, human trafficking advocate, Laster Global Associates
- Current status of human trafficking legislation in the United States and Texas
- Interview 1 due

Course Sequence: Week 8

Learning Theme and Concepts

International child welfare

Assigned Readings

- Mapp (2008), Chapter 4, International child welfare
- UN Convention on the Rights of the Child

Learning Opportunities

- Discussion of basic rights and examples of violations
- Round table of weekly assignments
- Social indicators of development

Course Sequence: Week 10

Learning Theme and Concepts

International child welfare (cont.)

Assigned Readings

Blanchfield (2012), UN CRC Background & Policy Issues (posted on TRACS)

Learning Opportunities

Integrating knowledge, values, and skills for effective action

Course Sequence: Week 11

Learning Theme and Concepts

War and conflict

Assigned Readings

Mapp (2008), Chapter 5, War and conflict

Learning Opportunities

- Discussion of invisible children and child soldiers
- Update on group project due

Course Sequence: Week 12

Learning Theme and Concepts

- War and conflict (cont.)
- Religion and spirituality as global conflict
- Global economic patterns underlying conflict
- Grameen Bank (see http://www.grameen-info.org)

Assigned Readings

- Guari & Gloppen (2012), *Human Rights Based Approaches to Development* (posted on TRACS)
- Healey (2008), Appendix B: UN Summit for Social Development—10 Commandments

Learning Opportunities

- Exercise: How to live on $2/day (http://www.globalpovertyproject.com)
- Second interview due

Course Sequence: Week 13

Learning Theme and Concepts

- AIDS and major global health problems
- Overpopulation

Assigned Readings

- Mapp (2008), Chapter 6, AIDS

- Kunzig (2011), 7 Billion (posted on TRACS)
- UN Population Report Executive Summary (posted on TRACS)

Learning Opportunities

- Class discussion of population trends
- Case examples from UN Population Reports

Course Sequence: Week 14

Learning Theme and Concepts

Women's issues

Assigned Readings

- Mapp (2008), Chapter 7, Issues particularly affecting women
- Hawkins (2012), Women's human rights (posted on TRACS)

Learning Opportunities

Discussion of women's issues

Course Sequence: Week 15

Learning Theme and Concepts

- Other groups: LGBTQ rights, disability rights, indigenous peoples rights
- Applying course content to one's own worldview
- Future directions

Assigned Readings

Mapp (2008), Appendix B: Opportunities in international social work

Learning Opportunities

- Graduate student book reports
- Reflection on personal and global self-awareness
- Course evaluation
- Self-assessment due

Course Sequence: Final exam

Student Group Presentations

Resource Materials and Bibliography

Books and Articles

Agosin, M. (Ed.). (2001). *Women, gender, and human rights: A global perspective.* New Brunswick, NJ: Rutgers.

Ahmadi, N. (2003). Globalization of consciousness and new challenges for international social work. *International Social Work, 12,* 14–23.

Blanchfield, L. (2012, July 2). The United Nations convention on the Rights of the Child: Background and policy issues. *Congressional Research Service, R44048.*

Caragata, A., & Sanchez, M. (2002). Globalization and global need: New imperatives for expanding international social work education in North America. *International Social Work, 45*(2), 217–238.

Council on Social Work Education. (2008). *Educational policy and accreditation standards.* Alexandria, VA: Author. Available at http://www.cswe.org/Accreditation/2008EPASDescription.aspx

Cox, D., & Pawar, M. (2006). *International Social Work: Issues, strategies, and programs.* Thousand Oaks, CA: SAGE.

Donnelly, J. (1989). *Universal human rights in theory and practice.* Ithaca, NY: Cornell University Press.

Ehrenreich, B., & Hochschild, A. R. (Eds.). (2002). *Global woman.* New York, NY: Holt.

Facing History and Ourselves. (2010). *Fundamental freedoms: Eleanor Roosevelt and the Universal Declaration of Human Rights.* Brookline, MA: Author.

Gauri, V., & Gloppen, S. (2012). Human rights-based approaches to development: Concepts, evidence, and policy. *Polity, 44,* 485–503.

George, J. (1999). Conceptual muddle, practical dilemma: Human rights, social development, and social work education. *International Social Work, 42*(1), 15–26.

Gray, M., & Fook, J. (2004). The quest for universal social work: Some issues and implications. *Social Work Education, 23,* 625–644.

Grief, G. L. (2004). How international is the social work knowledge base? *Social Work, 49,* 514–517.

Hare, I. (2004). Defining social work for the 21st century: The International Federation of Social Workers' revised definition of social work. *International Journal of Social Work, 47,* 407–424.

Hawkins, C. (2009). Global citizenship: A model for teaching universal human rights in social work education. *Critical Social Work, 10*(1). Retrieved from http://www1.uwindsor.ca/criticalsocialwork/global-citizenship-a-model-for-teaching-universal-human-rights-in-social-work-education

Hawkins, C. (2010). Sustainability, human rights, and environmental justice: Critical connections for contemporary social work. *Critical Social Work. 11*(3), 68–81.

Hawkins, C. (2012). Women's human rights: The global intersection of gender inequality, sexual and reproductive justice, and healthcare. *Journal of Research on Women and Gender, 4,* 159–184.

Healy, L. (2008). *International social work: Professional action in an interdependent world.* New York, NY: Oxford.

Hokenstad, M. C., & Midgley, J. (Eds.). (1997). *Issues in international social work: Global challenges for a new century.* Washington, DC: NASW Press.

Ife, J., & Fiske, L. (2006). Human rights and community work. *International Social Work, 49,* 297–308.

Kristof, N. D., & WuDunn, S. (2009, August 17). The women's crusade. *New York Times Magazine,* pp. 28–29.

Kunzig, R. (2011, January). Population 7 billion. *National Geographic.* Retrieved from http://ngm.nationalgeographic.com/2011/01/seven-billion/kunzig-text

Mapp, S. (2010). *Global child welfare and well-being.* New York, NY: Oxford.

Midgley, J. (1997). *Social welfare in global context.* Thousand Oaks, CA: SAGE.

Ramathan, C. S., & Link, R. J. (2004). *All our futures: Social work practice in a global era.* Belmont, CA: Brooks/Cole.

Reichert, E. (2003). *Social work and human rights: A foundation for policy and practice*. New York, NY: Columbia University Press.

Rothenberg, P. S. (Ed.). (2005). *Beyond borders: Thinking critically about global issues*. New York, NY: Worth.

Schriver, J. M. (2001). *Global perspectives and theories. Human behavior and the social environment: Shifting paradigms in essential knowledge for social work practice*. Boston, MA: Allyn & Bacon.

Skegg, A. (2005). Human rights and social work: A western imposition or empowerment to the people? *International Social Work, 48*, 667–672.

Swartz, M. (2010, April). The lost girls. *Texas Monthly*. Retrieved from http://www.texasmonthly.com/story/lost-girls

Tripodi, T., & Potocky-Tripodi, M. (2007). *International social work research: Issues and prospects*. New York, NY: Oxford.

United Nations. (2012, July 2). *Millennium Development Goals report*. New York, NY: Author.

United Nations. (2012, November 12). State of the world population. New York, NY: UN Population Fund.

Van Soest, D., & Crosby, J. (1997). *Challenges of violence worldwide*. Washington, DC: NASW Press.

van Worner, K. (1997). *Social welfare: A world view*. Chicago, IL: Nelson-Hall.

Williams, J. (2004). *50 facts that should change the world*. Cambridge, UK: Icon.

Journals

Gender and Development

Gender Issues

International Journal of Politics, Culture & Society

International Social Welfare

International Social Work

Journal of Ethnic and Cultural Diversity in Social Work

Journal of Social Service Research

Journal of Social Work Education

Multinational Monitor

Social Development Issues

Social Service Research

Social Work

Social Work Education

Websites

Amnesty International: http://www.amnestyusa.org/get-involved/take-action-now

Association for Women's Rights in Development: http://www.awid.org/

Council on Social Work Education: http://www.cswe.org

Doctors Without Borders: http://www.doctorswithoutborders.org/

Earth Institute (Columbia University): http://www.earth.columbia.edu/sections/view/9

Human Rights Resource Center (University of Minnesota): http://www.hrusa.org/

Human Rights Watch: http://www.hrw.org/

International Federation of Social Workers: http://ifsw.org/

International Committee of the Red Cross: www.icrc.org

Disability Rights International: http://www.disabilityrightsintl.org/

National Geographic: http://www.nationalgeographic.com

Oxfam International: http://www.oxfam.org/

Refugees International: http://refugeesinternational.org/

Social Watch: http://www.socialwatch.org/

UNICEF: http://www.unicef.org/

United Nations: http://www.un.org/en/

U.S. Department of State: http://www.state.gov/

PRAXIS (University of Pennsylvania): http://www.sp2.upenn.edu/restes/praxis.html

Save the Children: http://www.savethechildren.org/site/c.8rKLIXMGIpI4E/b.6115947/k.8D6E/Official_Site.htm

World Bank: http://www.worldbank.org/

World Fact Book (CIA): https://www.cia.gov/library/publications/the-world-factbook/

World Health Organization: http://www.who.int/en/

Human Rights and Global Justice

Donald D. Mowry
University of Wisconsin—Eau Claire

Course Description

This course seeks to provide students with a basic understanding of two pressing social issues: the challenges that confront individuals and families who are not being accorded basic, universal human rights, and the effect that this has on their lives and liberties, on societies, and an understanding of the social policy options that have been used or might be used to redress their injustices; and the notion of social justice and its relationship to the values of universal human rights.

Human Rights and Global Justice will give students an understanding of the importance of tackling social issues from different perspectives by bringing together resources from a number of disciplines.

This course will also expose students to service-learning opportunities in the greater community and challenge them to generate ideas and actions that will contribute to more effective ways of fighting poverty and social injustice locally and globally. Each week lab time will be devoted to exploring the greater community.

This course seeks to introduce students to a liberal education and awaken their intellectual curiosity by engaging them in an interdisciplinary study and analysis of poverty and social justice. In addition to the interdisciplinary course content, a variety of teaching methods will be used to actively engage students in the topic. Students will be expected to engage in a minimum of two out-of-class experiences from a list of several opportunities, and they will also be expected to gain exposure through service activities to a variety of community efforts that are relevant to poverty and social justice, homelessness, and hunger prevention.

In the realm of personal and social responsibility/accountability, by the end of the course students will be required to formulate their own personal philosophy of social justice.

Students will learn the difference between charity and working for justice through systemic change, and they will be asked to reflect on the tensions between their individual beliefs and personal interests, political realities, and the common good in local and global communities.

Students also will gain knowledge and skills as civic action leaders by being exposed to and learning tools of community organization around shared interests and needs such as one-to-ones, power mapping, values exploration in groups, advocacy, lobbying, and media campaigns.

Course Competencies, Practice Behaviors, and Assignments

Successful completion of this course implies that students will have progressed toward achieving some of the core social work competencies (as expressed in the Educational Policy and Accreditation Standards of the Council on Social Work Education [2008]) by demonstrating the following practice behaviors.

Competencies Addressed In Course	Practice Behaviors Addressed in Course	Assignments Measuring Behavior
Educational Policy (EP) 2.1.1: Identify as a social worker and conduct oneself accordingly.	• Advocate for client access to the services of social work. • Attend to professional roles and boundaries. • Demonstrate professional demeanor in behavior, appearance and communication.	2, 3, 6
EP 2.1.2: Apply social work ethical principles to guide professional practice	• Recognize and manage personal values in a way that allows professional values to guide practice. • Make ethical decisions by applying standards of the NASW. • Apply strategies of ethical reasoning to arrive at principled decisions.	2, 3, 4, 5, 6
EP 2.1.5: Advance human rights and social and economic justice	• Understand the mechanisms of oppression and discrimination. • Advocate for human rights and social and economic justice. • Engage in practices that advance social and economic justice.	3
EP 2.1.6: Engage in research-informed practice and practice-informed research	• Use research evidence to inform practice.	3
EP 2.1.9: Respond to contexts that shape practice	• Provide leadership in promoting sustainable changes in service delivery and practice to improve the quality of social services.	7
EP 2.1.10a: Engage with individuals, families, groups, organizations and communities	• Develop a mutually agreed-on focus of work and desired outcomes.	2
EP 2.1.10b: Assess individuals, families, groups, organizations and communities	• Develop mutually agreed-on intervention goals and objectives. • Select appropriate intervention strategies.	3
EP 2.1.10.c: Intervene with individuals, families, groups, organizations and communities	• Initiate actions to achieve organizational goals.	2

Liberal Education Learning Goals

This course will touch on all of the Liberal Education Learning Goals, including the following.

Knowledge of Human Culture and the Natural World

Poverty and social justice will be considered from a global perspective and dimensions considered will include basic human rights, individual human dynamics, and systemic issues and structural components.

Creative and Critical Thinking

Simple explanations and solutions to the very intractable problems of poverty, social justice, and social injustice are not very useful. Students will be encouraged to think very creatively and critically.

Effective Communication

Learning how to establish and maintain a dialogue that includes a diversity of disciplines, perspectives, opinions, and values is a critical component of addressing big picture issues confronting our world.

Individual and Social Responsibility

This will be the central learning outcome addressed across all aspects of the course.

Respect for Diversity Among People

Persons who are living in poverty and facing social injustice are most likely to be diverse and belong to ethnic and racial minority groups. They are also likely to have lower class status and lack power to change their lives and their situations.

Course Content, Teaching Methods/Course Schedule

Tentative Class Schedule

The instructor reserves the right to make minor adjustments to the schedule as the term progresses, but due dates will not be moved up, but may be moved back at times.

Week	Topic	Reading, Online Reading, and Assignments
Week 1	Introduction to course and topic, 7 Revolutions	Read: Reichert forward and introduction (vii–x; pp. 1–17)
Week 2	Development and History of Human Rights	Read: Reichert Chapter 1 (pp. 18–44) and weekly readings Essay One Due

table continues

Week	Topic	Reading, Online Reading, and Assignments
Week 3	Voices of Poverty and Social Injustice	Weekly readings Reflection Paper 1 due
Week 4	Universal Declaration of Human Rights	Read: Reichert Chapter 2 (pp. 45–79) and weekly readings Reflection Paper 2 due
Week 5	International Covenant on Civil and Political Rights	Read: Reichert Chapter 3 (pp. 80–102) and weekly readings Reflection Paper 3 due
Week 6	International Covenant on Economic, Social, and Cultural Rights	Read: Reichert Chapter 4 (pp. 103–120) Global Village Project due
Week 7	Populations at Risk for Poverty and Social Injustice	Weekly readings Midterm exam
Week 8		Weekly readings Group Project presentations Reflection Paper 4 due
Week 9	Diversity Within a Human Rights Perspective	Read: Reichert Chapter 5 (pp. 121–143) and Weekly readings Group Project presentations Reflection Paper 5 due
Week 10	Human Rights and Children, Persons With Disabilities, Persons With HIV- AIDS, Gays and Lesbians, Older Persons, and Victims of Racism	Read: Reichert Chapter 6 (pp. 144–168) and weekly readings Group Project presentations Reflection Paper 6 due
Week 11	International Aspects of Human Rights	Read: Reichert Chapter 7 (pp. 169–193) Group Project presentations Reflection Paper 7 due
Week 12	International Aspects of Human Rights	Weekly Readings Reflection Paper 8 due
Week 13	Applying Human Rights to the Social Work Profession	Read: Reichert Chapter 8 (pp. 194–214) Reflection Paper 9 due

table continues

Week	Topic	Reading, Online Reading, and Assignments
Week 14	Applying Human Rights to the Social Work Profession	Read: Reichert Conclusion (215) and Weekly Readings Reflection Paper 10 due
Week 15	Course Wrap-Up	Weekly Readings Final essay due
Finals Week		Final exam

Text and Readings for the Course

Course Text

Reichert, S. (2011). *Social work and human rights: A foundation for policy and practice* (2nd ed.). New York, NY: Columbia University Press.

Required Readings

Unnatural Causes: Is Inequality Making Us Sick? Seven part series on the racial and socioeconomic indicators of health/disease (DVD; available from http://www.unnaturalcauses.org/)

United Nations. (1948). *Universal declaration of human rights*. Available at http://www.un.org/en/documents/udhr/

Course Readings—a series of articles and studies selected by the instructor and others, to be added as the course progresses, listed by week assigned on D2L

Course Assignments, Evaluation, and Grading

Course Components

Beginning in the third week and for most weeks following students are required to compose a 2–4 page reflection on one of the readings from the previous week or on a visit to a local nonprofit program that addresses poverty and social justice issues. The weekly reflections will be graded as satisfactory or unsatisfactory. Students will have one opportunity to rewrite an unsatisfactory reflection. Over the course of the semester at least 10 reflection papers are required. Students may hand in papers due in one week during the following week, but if the papers are late by more than 1 week they will not receive full credit and the Dropbox will not accept them. The first weekly reading reflection will be based on attendance at the Community Action Fair, and there will be a separate handout detailing this assignment.

The remaining weekly reflections should contain the following topical paragraphs:

- What you think the author is saying and why, or what you observed during the visit
- Relation of the reading to some other reading or course topic
- Your reaction to the reading in terms of your passions/interests, views, sense of the facts, and/or experiences
- "Now What?" or what is it that you think should be done or said

Two Essays

Students will write two essays, 3–5 pages each, grades A–F.

The first will relate to your own public story—how do you relate to the topic of poverty and social justice based on your own values, family background, and experiences. The second is a final paper on how you see yourself as a citizen and change agent as a result of this course and other influences. In addition, what is your personal perspective on human rights and social justice—what do you think should be done about it, if anything? What is your personal philosophy of social justice?

Group Project

This project will ask student teams to research, critique, analyze, summarize, and present on a population group that suffers from injustice or human rights abuses. This project will be detailed in a separate handout.

Midterm Exam

The midterm will be based on all course materials and discussion up to the date of the exam.

Final Exam

The final exam will be based on all course materials from the midterm on, including student presented information.

Class Participation

There will be much class discussion including class-wide, small group, and outside class discussions. Attendance and class participation is expected and will be monitored.

Global Village

Students will be assigned a set of coordinates, a gender, and an age. Students will research their context and construct a story of their lives in this context, taking into consideration relevant aspects of human rights and social justice for the setting. Students are encouraged to be creative in how they share their stories.

Extra Credit

Students who attend an event from an approved list of events that relate to the course topic and write a reflection paper based on the event can earn up to three extra credit points. For the most part, the credit awarded will be on a one-to-one basis, so an event that is 2 hours long can be submitted for consideration for two extra credit points.

Course Requirements/Grading

Grading will be based on the following:

- Weekly reading reflections, 20 points
- Initial essay, 10 points
- Global village, 15 points
- Midterm exam, 10 points
- Group project, 15 points

- Final essay, 15 points
- Final exam, 10 points
- Class participation, 5 points
- Extra credit, 3 points

Evaluation

Course Environment

The class environment will be seminar style with some smaller group discussions and exercises. Guest speakers will present a variety of perspectives that will include the voices of those who have or are living in poverty and social justice.

Reference

Council on Social Work Education. (2008). *Educating policy and accreditation standards.* Retrieved from http://www.cswe.org/File/aspx?id=41861

Special Topics: Human Rights Law

Ogden Rogers
University of Wisconsin—River Falls

Course Description

Social work has foundational values in the dignity of the individual and the causes of social and economic justice. How are these values expressed in the global arena? What are human rights?

This course will take a primary documents approach to the exploration of human rights and the international instruments that have been created to enumerate these rights. We will explore the purposes and mechanisms of law and a number of the major documents that constitute international human rights law and international humanitarian law. The course will use Socratic method, case study, and simulation as vehicles of learning jurisprudence from a global human rights perspective.

Course Competencies

Accreditation standards require the baccalaureate social work curriculum to prepare graduates for generalist practice through mastery of a set of competencies, which are measurable through practice behaviors composed of knowledge, values, and skills. Social work students delineate the educational goals and objectives of the social work program through demonstration of specific competencies that serve to inform and aid evaluation of students' preparation for generalist social work practice. These competencies serve as a link between what may be observed or demonstrated in student knowledge, values, and skill performance and the program's curriculum expectations. In a general way, these competencies and accepted practice standards operationalize the educational objectives for students, faculty, and administration and provide a common set of definitions to gauge performance and behavior.

The 10 competencies (Council on Social Work Education, 2008) are as follows:

1. Identify as a professional social worker and conduct oneself accordingly.
2. Apply social work ethical principles to guide professional practice.
3. Apply critical thinking to inform and communicate professional judgments.
4. Engage diversity and difference in practice.
5. Advance human rights and social and economic justice.
6. Engage in research-informed practice and practice-informed research.
7. Apply knowledge of human behavior and the social environment. Engage in policy practice to advance social and economic well-being and to deliver effective social work services.
8. Engage in policy practice to advance social and economic well-being and to deliver effective social work services.
9. Respond to contexts that shape practice.
10. Engage, assess, intervene, and evaluate with individuals, families, groups, organizations, and communities.

After completion of this course, the student is expected to be able to demonstrate (through course activities, assignments, and/or exams) the following outcomes.

Outcomes	Objectives	Competencies	Course Assessment Mechanism
Understand and apply principles of human rights, social and economic justice	Demonstrate understanding of political and social values underpinning social work in an international human rights context. Demonstrate understanding mechanisms of oppression and economic process underpinning poverty and vulnerability	1, 2, 5, 9	Exam questions Written assignments
Understand and apply knowledge of jurisprudence principles that inform policy and international law	Identify & describe basic concepts of legal decision making and compare and contrast their use in different legal systems	3, 5, 8, 9	Exam questions Written assignments
Understand and apply critical thinking skills within the context of professional generalist social work practice with matters concerning professional ethics in an informed international context	Describe the values and ethics of the profession of social work as embodied by the NASW Code of Ethics Identify and analyze ethical dilemmas typical of social work practice. Demonstrate understanding of ethical theories and their relationship to social work and social welfare and human rights law	1, 2, 3, 5	Exam questions Written assignments Class exercises

Course Requirements

Texts

International Committee of the Red Cross. *The Geneva Conventions of 1949 and their additional protocols.*

Reichert, E. (2003). *Social work and human rights: A foundation for policy & practice.* New York, NY: Columbia University Press.

Wronka, J. (2008). *Human rights & social justice: social action & service for the helping & health professions.* Thousand Oaks, CA: SAGE Publications.

This course includes a number of assigned journal articles and international legal instruments that will be made available to you via D2L. Please refer to the content page on D2L for a list of these articles.

Required readings have been assigned for each week of the semester, as shown on the class schedule. Reading assignments should be completed prior to the first class of each week for which they are assigned. You will be expected to be prepared to engage in small and large group activities tied to the content of those chapters. One of the primary purposes of class time will be to help you engage with the reading materials in ways that will encourage you to reflect on the readings and explore their meanings and relevance.

Two examinations will be given during the semester: a midterm and a final. The final examination will be comprehensive.

D2L Discussions

There will be a few random discussions requested on D2L throughout the semester. Participation in discussion is one way of demonstrating professional commitment.

Examinations

There are two examinations: a midterm and a final. The final will be cumulative.

Paper

A 10–20 page paper will be due 2 weeks before end of term. Please use APA format with at least five references. The paper can be focused in one of the following ways:

1. Human rights problem: Pick a problem that surfaces in the world and discuss its nature, efforts at correction, solution, or remedy. Cite applicable human rights law and describe controversies arising from the problems. Describe controversies that arise from the solutions. Discuss modification of either law or enforcement.

2. Human rights policy: Identify a concern of human rights and discuss the pros and cons of the right. Cite the applicable human rights law. Discuss critiques of the law. Make an argument for what should be done.

Grading

Letter grades will be assigned from an arithmetic mean score of the two examinations and a paper (Analysis of a Human Rights Problem or Policy). All measurements have equal statistical weight. Assignments that are not completed will be given a measurement of zero.

Course Schedule

This schedule is a guideline, not a contract. It is subject to change. Readings and small written assignments may be added as the semester progresses. Not all text chapters are assigned in order, so be careful about checking the schedule to see which reading is required for which date.

Week 1: Course & Orientation

- Syllabi
- Introduction to active learning classroom philosophy
- Introduction to D2L website resources
- Introduction to a framework for reading

Week 1–2: Fundamentals of Human Rights Law

- The Concept of Human Rights
- Theories and Foundations of Law

Reading:

- *Exploring the History of Social Work as a Human Rights Profession* by Lynne Healy
- *Viewing Human Rights and Social Work through an International Perspective* by Elisabeth Reichert
- *Humanity: How Does it Influence International Law?* by Robin Coupland
- *Human Rights & Social Justice* by Joseph Wronka *Chaps 1-2*

Week 3: The U.S. Constitution & Bill of Rights

Reading:

- Preamble to Declaration of Independence 7-4-1776
- Constitution of the United States & Amendments 1–10

Week 4: The Universal Declaration of Human Rights

Reading:

- Healy, Forward, Intro, Chapter 2
- Wronka, Chapter 3
- Universal Declaration of Universal Human Rights

Week 5: International Covenant on Civil & Political Rights

Reading:

- Healy, Chapter 3
- Wronka, Chap 4
- *International Covenant on Civil & Political Rights*

Week 6: International Covenant on Economic, Social and Cultural Rights

Reading:

- Healy, Chapters 4, 7
- Wronka, Chap 6
- *International Covenant on Economic, Social and Cultural Rights*

Week 7: Rights of the Child; Midterm Exam

Reading:

- Text, Chapter 6, pp. 162–179
- *UN Declaration of the Rights of the Child*

Week 8: Spring Break

Week 9: Rights of Vulnerable Groups

Reading:

Rights of Women

- Text, Chapter 5
- *Convention on the Elimination of All Forms of Discrimination Against Women*

Rights of Disabled Persons

- Text, Chapter 6
- *International Convention on the Protection and Promotion of the Rights and Dignity of Persons with Disabilities, Americans with Disabilities Act*

Week 10: Refugee Rights

Reading:

Convention Relating to the Status of Refugees

Week 11: Adoption

Reading

Hague Adoption Convention

Weeks 12–13: International Humanitarian Law

Reading

- Social Work and The International Humanitarian Law: Rights, Roles, and Responsibilities-Rogers (2008)
- The Geneva Conventions of 1949, Protocols Additional 1977
- Hague Conference 1907

Week 14: Final Exam

Bibliography

The following works represent monographs and journal articles that support the lectures and the various international instruments that we will read in class.

Addams, J. (1907). *Newer ideas of peace & freedom.* Syracuse, NY: Mason Henry Press.

Androff, D. K. (2010) The problem of contemporary slavery: An international human rights challenge for social work. *International Social Work, 54*(2), 209–222.

Council on Social Work Education. (2008). *Educational policy and accreditation standards.* Retrieved from http://www.cswe.org/File.aspx?id=41861

Coupland, R. (2001). Humanity: How does it influence international law? *International Review of the Red Cross, 83,* 969–989.

Healy, L. (2001). *International social work: Professional action in an interdependent world.* New York, NY: Oxford Press.

Healy, L. (2011). *Exploring the history of social work as a human rights profession. International Social Work 51,* 735–748

Hoffman. S. (1996). *The ethics and politics of humanitarian intervention.* Notre Dame, IN: University of Notre Dame Press.

Ignatieff, M. (1997). *The warrior's honor: Ethnic war and the modern conscience.* New York, NY: Henry Holt.

Lundy, C. (2007). Social and economic justice, human rights and peace—The challenge for social work in Canada and the USA. *International Social Work, 50,* 727.

Murdach, A. (2011). Is social work a human rights profession? *Social Work, 56,* 281–283.

Reichert, E. (2003). Human rights and social work through an international perspective. *Journal of Intergroup Relations, 30*(1), 76–84.

Rogers, O. (2008). Social work and the international humanitarian law: Rights, roles, and responsibilities. *Journal of Social Work Values & Ethics, 5*(2). Retrieved from http://www.socialworker.com/jswve/content/view/90/65/

Skegg. A. (2005). Human rights and social work: A western imposition or empowerment to the people? *International Social Work 48,* 667–672.

Solis, G. (2010). *The law of armed conflict: International humanitarian law in war.* New York, NY: Cambridge University Press.

United Nations High Commissioner for Refugees. (2001). *Protecting refugees: A field guide for NGOs.* New York, NY: United Nations.

Webb, S. A. (2009). Against difference and diversity in social work: The case of human rights. *International Journal of Social Welfare, 18,* 307–316.

Graduate Syllabi

Introduction to Graduate Syllabi

Lynne M. Healy

This section includes syllabi and modules that demonstrate different approaches to teaching human rights in the MSW curriculum. The 2008 version of the Educational Policy and Accreditation Standards (EPAS) includes a competency focused on human rights and social justice. All social work students must achieve at least beginning competence to advocate for human rights. Social work programs are responding by infusing human rights content into required courses and in some cases developing more specialized courses on human rights.

Two of the syllabi in this section, one from Grand Valley State and one from the University of Connecticut, are specialized courses on human rights and social work. These provide an introduction to human rights laws and the United Nations human rights machinery and link these to social work practice and social policy issues. Although not all readers will be able to launch similar courses in their own institutions, the readings and written assignments provide ideas that can be adapted to other courses. A third specialized course offered by George Mason University addresses human rights through travel-study to Costa Rica; this course has an emphasis on gender and human rights.

Human rights provides an important perspective for teaching international social work. A course syllabus on international social work from the University at Buffalo demonstrates the integration of substantial coverage of human rights in an elective on international social work. Readers are also referred to the syllabus for International Social Work, Texas State University, in the section on Undergraduate Syllabi. This course is offered for either graduate or undergraduate credit.

The syllabus for Women, Children, and Families (University of Connecticut) exemplifies using human rights as the overarching theme for teaching about social work with women and children. This course, required for students who elect a focused area of study in women, children, and families, incorporates relevant United Nations treaties and human rights concepts and bridges domestic and global issues.

The required foundation area of social welfare policy and services offers ample opportunities to integrate human rights. The section contains two modules and one syllabus as examples. Modules from Case Western Reserve University and the University of Maryland show how human rights can be taught in two to three sessions of a required social policy course to meet the EPAS competency on human rights and social justice. The full syllabus for Global Perspectives on Social Policy (George Mason University) demonstrates integration of human rights content and an international perspective throughout a policy course.

Human Rights and Social Work

Julia A. Guevara
Grand Valley State University

School of Social Work Mission[1]

The Grand Valley State University School of Social Work prepares its students to attain social work practice and professional leadership; advance the field's knowledge of effective professional practice and education through research and evaluation; enhance and sustain the welfare and well-being of the citizens, organizations and communities of West Michigan, the state, the nation, and the world; and further the goals of the university and of the social work profession in this region and beyond.

All of the school's programs are grounded in the profession's body of knowledge, values, and skills that support and enhance the opportunities, resources, and capacities of people to achieve their full potential; prevent and alleviate personal, interpersonal, organizational, and societal problems; and improve the conditions that limit human development and adversely impact the quality of human life. The school celebrates and affirms the importance of diversity in all of its forms, and it supports the expansion of human rights, cultural competence, empowerment, social and political justice, civic participation, and equality in West Michigan and around the world.

The school's legacy emphases on social justice and on meeting the significant professional workforce needs of an expansive West Michigan social services sector remain strong. A third distinctive feature of the school is its integration and promotion of domestic and international service learning opportunities that prepare of students for 21st century practice in increasingly global economic and social contexts.

Course Description

The course is structured to provide students with a basis for literacy about modern human rights, including core principles, key documents, institutions, and practices. A framework for the analysis of social work/human rights interactions is used and systematically applied, including the effect of social, political, and economic policies and programs on human rights; health and social consequences of human rights violations; and the inextricable linkage between promoting and protecting mental and physical health, community well-being and family functioning, and promoting and protecting human rights.

---

[1] The mission statement is included here as an example of a school of social work that has integrated human rights in its statement.

Council on Social Work Education, *Educational Policy and Accreditation Standards* (EPAS) Competencies and Advanced Practice Behaviors

Competency

Advocate for human rights and social justice (Educational Policy [EP] 2.1.5).[2]

Advanced Practice Behavior

Demonstrate necessary skills to change social institutions to be more humane and responsive.

- Knowledge (1): Students will understand the key historical, political, legal and moral influences that have shaped the idea of "human rights."

- Knowledge (2): Students will be able to explain the concept of a "human right."

- Knowledge (3): Students will identify the major international declarations, treaties, and covenants governing human rights.

- Value (1): Students embrace the inherent value and dignity of all human beings.

- Value (2): Students will be able to articulate the value of advocating for human rights.

Identify weakness in various systems and develop and propose social policies that promote social justice.

- Knowledge (4): Students will identify mechanisms for monitoring and enforcing human rights standards.

- Value (3): Students will recognize the importance of promoting social justice.

Competency

Engage in informed research (EP 2.1.6).

Advanced Practice Behaviors

Design and implement various steps in the research process.

- Knowledge (5): Students will be able to identify the human rights documents used to conduct research, such as the Covenant on Economic, Social and Cultural Rights and the Covenant on the Elimination of Discrimination against Women.

- Value (4): Students will recognize the value in human rights research.

Integrate qualitative and quantitative research in all aspects of advanced generalist practice.

- Knowledge (6): Students will critically examine international human rights issues and the corresponding policies.

- Value (4): Students will recognize the value in human rights research.

---

[2] Educational policies and practice behaviors are taken from the Educational Policy and Accreditation Standards of the Council on Social Work Education (2008), available at http://www.cswe.org/File.aspx?id=41861.

Competency

Engage, assess, intervene, and evaluate with individuals, families, groups, organizations, and communities (EP 2.1.10).

Advanced Practice Behaviors

Engagement

Adapt one's ability to engage diverse clients and client systems.

- Knowledge (7): Students will understand the importance of educating themselves about cultures different from themselves to engage in a culturally competent manner.
- Value (1): Students embrace the inherent value and dignity of all human beings.

Assessment

Show increasing ability to independently conduct assessments as a continuing and dynamic process that guides goal and objective setting with clients and client systems at multiple levels.

- Knowledge (8): Students will be able to be able to analyze the contemporary challenges and trends in human rights theory and practice.
- Value (5): Students will recognize the importance of taking multiple perspectives into account.

Intervention

Differentially use a variety of evidence-based tools and strategies with more depth and breadth to assess client systems at all levels and guide interventions.

- Knowledge (9): Students will know how to construct and advocate effective policy arguments using international human rights norms and discourse.
- Value (5): Students will recognize the importance of taking multiple perspectives into account.

Evaluate the multisystem dimension of client problems and design approaches that affect change at multiple client system levels.

- Knowledge (10): Students will demonstrate the ability to analyze issues of human rights and social and economic justice in different social contexts.
- Value (5): Students will recognize the importance of taking multiple perspectives into account.

Evaluation

Evaluate advanced generalist practice interventions across systems at multiple levels with diverse populations.

- Knowledge (10): Students will demonstrate the ability to analyze issues of human rights and social and economic justice in different social contexts.
- Value (5): Students will recognize the importance of taking multiple perspectives into account.

The Structure of the Course

The course is organized to start with an introduction to basic human rights philosophy, principles, instruments, and institutions and moving toward providing students with an opportunity to gain an overview of current issues and debates in the field with focus on the problems specific to the current political, social, and economic realities around the globe. This course aims moreover to explore many aspects of the diverse and increasingly complex body of international law regarding human rights that has national and international applications at a time when virtually all nations, including some with egregious records of following these laws, proclaim their acceptance of international human rights standards. The course also seeks to analyze the ways in which allegations of human rights violations are dealt with in US domestic courts and the effects of human rights discourse in international politics and relations.

The course is divided into three parts, as follows.

First, the focus will generally be on the Western rights tradition and other sources of rights; several alternative philosophical perspectives to rights will be considered. Second, the course will also cover the International Human Rights movement beginning with its origins, including the key international declarations, agreements, and instruments. The principal focus will be on how rights are enforced and protected in national and international courts and other treaty and political bodies. Also covered are economic and social rights, regional human rights systems, and several national systems for the protection of human rights.

Implicit in this approach is the assumption that protection and preservation of human rights requires legal and other advocacy skills on the part of social workers. Accordingly, the third part of the course requires a focus on students' developing proficiency in the EPAS Competencies and Advanced Practice Behaviors.

Required Readings

There is no textbook for this course. The specific readings for each class session will be identified in the course outline. Following are key human rights reference resources.

International Covenant on Civil and Political Rights. Available at http://www.ohchr.org Click on Human Rights Instruments. There are six parts to this covenant and a total of 53 articles.

International Covenant on Economic, Social and Cultural Rights. Available at http://www.ohchr.org Click on human rights instruments. There are five parts to this covenant and a total of 31 articles.

Universal Declaration of Human Rights. Available at http://www.un.org/en/documents/udhr/

United Nations. http://www.un.org/

United Nations Convention of the Rights of the Child. Available at http://www.ohchr.org/en/professionalinterest/pages/crc.aspx

Convention on the Elimination of Discrimination Against Women. Available at http://www.ohchr.org/Documents/ProfessionalInterest/cedaw.pdf

Human Rights Web. http://www.hrweb.org/

Human Rights Watch. http://hrw.org

Amnesty International. http://amnesty.org/

NASW *Code of Ethics*. Available at http://www.socialworkers.org/pubs/code/code.asp

International Federation of Social Workers/International Association of Schools of Social Work *Statement of Principles*. Available at http://ifsw.org/policies/code-of-ethics/

Reichert, E. (2003*). Social work and human rights: A foundation for policy and practice*. New York, NY: Columbia University Press.

Organization of the Course

Instructional methods used in this course include lecture, large and small group discussion, individual and group exercises, guest speakers, video, field trips, creative demonstration, and reading and written reflections. Guest speakers include agency social work practitioners in the community who work directly with immigrant and refugee groups both documented and undocumented, victims of human trafficking, and women who are prostituted. Students are expected to participate in discussions based on required readings; outside research; and work, field, and/or volunteer experiences. Students are responsible for fully participating in discussion and analysis. A percentage of the grade is based on attendance in class sessions. Absences, lateness, and partial attendance are penalized beginning with the loss of one half grade per incident.

Assignments

Readings and Class Participation

This is an essential component of this course. The expectation is that you will come fully prepared by reading and critically thinking through the concepts offered by the authors and contribute to the discussion. (5 points)

Reflection Papers

On a weekly (more or less) basis beginning with Week 3, students submit their reactions and analytical comments to one of the assigned weekly reading, lecture, or multimedia presentations. Your first response will be from Week 2. Address the key issues, common themes, and so forth. Your analysis should integrate concepts from one of the major covenants, conventions, or from the *Universal Declaration of Human Rights*. In your writing be sure to include your understanding of how social work values and ethics support your analysis. Papers should be no less than two pages, double spaced. (2 points each response unless otherwise indicated; 20 points total)

Creative Expression

Your responsibilities include conveying the essence of one article from the *Universal Declaration of Human Rights* and its interconnectedness to social work and social welfare in your country of choice to a community group. Demonstrate the meaning or intent of the article and relate its importance to the country by creating a 30-second public service announcement by using a digital, Web-based, video, or electronic medium. You are required to provide the instructor access to your work. With the written permission of the student, her or his work may be aired on the public TV cable station. Due over the course of the semester. (20 points)

Research Paper and Presentation

Research and critically examine the literature and current debates relating to one human rights topic in economic, social, cultural, political, and civil rights, such as the rights of the child, women, refugees, immigrants, prisoners, indigenous people, elderly, ethnic, religious and linguistic minorities; and the right to food, adequate housing, health care, education, social services, and so forth; or a particular issue area such as arms (weapons) trading, discrimination, poverty and human rights, enforcement of international human rights laws sexual exploitation of children, human rights and elections, and so forth.

Topic Proposal

Submit a one or two page outline of the topic to be addressed. Include key questions and issues and a minimum of five initial citations. Be sure to discuss your topic with me prior to submitting your proposal. Due Week 6. (10 points)

Use the following framework:

- Introduction
- Overview of key human rights issue including historical, political, legal, and moral influences that shaped this issue
- Analysis of major national instruments or policies that exist to safeguard the identified human rights issue
- Comparison of how these instruments align with the *Universal Declaration of Human Rights* or international covenants, conventions, or other UN declarations
- Mechanisms in place to monitor and enforce these instruments
- Relevant social work values and ethics
- Implications for social work practice
- Recommendations and conclusions

Presentation

Present your research findings. Provide students with an outline of your presentation. (15 points)

Final Paper

A research paper is due at the end of the semester. This should follow the framework for analysis provided in class and should be between 12 and 15 pages, APA style, with a minimum of 10 references. Due on day of presentation. (30 points)

Course Outline

Week 1

Review syllabus and expectations. Overview of the course, human rights, and social work. Questions.

Week 2

Begin discussion of the key historical, political, legal, and moral influences that have shaped the idea of human rights. Video: Amnesty International, animated version of *The Universal Declaration of Human Rights.*

Readings: Reichert; forward, introduction, and Chapter 1; *Universal Declaration of Human Rights*

Week 3

Continue discussion of the key historical, political, legal, and moral influences that have shaped the idea of human rights. Discuss human rights terminology. What is meant by the term *human rights*? What does it mean to have ones' rights protected? Who determines what a human right is? What is social work? Human rights and social work's philosophical values and ideals.

Readings: Select any introductory social work textbook and critically examine the purpose of social work and fundamental social work values. Read Reichert Chapters 2, 7, and 8.

Due: Reflection paper from Week 2

Week 4

What are political and civil rights? How are they different from other human rights? Is the *UN Covenant on Civil and Political Rights* the standard against which human rights violations should be measured? What are the common elements between the two major UN covenants? How are these rights enforced and protected?

Readings: *International Covenant on Civil and Political Rights*; Reichert Chapter 3.

Due: Reflection paper from Week 3 material.

Week 5

What are economic, social, and cultural rights? How are they different from other human rights? Do these rights erode liberty and make people dependent on government handouts? Are they an ill-considered 20th century deviation from the original and civil political rights of the 18th century? The distinction between negative and positive rights; government forbearance versus government performance.

Readings: *International Covenant on Economic, Social and Cultural Rights*; Reichert, Chapter 4

Due: Discuss how these documents are similar and different from each other. This assignment serves as your weekly reflection paper.

Week 6

Hu(man) rights of women and girls. In what ways are these rights "gendered"? A deafening silence on gender and human rights law.

Readings:

- Reichert, Chapter 5
- Youngs, G. (2003). *Private pain/public peace: Women's rights as human rights and Amnesty International's Report on Violence Against Women. Signs, 28*(4), 1209.

- *United Nations Convention of the Rights of the Child*

Due: Reflection paper from Weeks 4 or 5 material.

Week 7

Framework for analysis of human rights and social work. An analysis of women who are prostituted in the United States as a human rights issue as well as a brief overview of women who are incarcerated in the United States.

Reading:

- Prostitution Roundtable Report; available at http://www.nokomisfoundation.org/documents/ WeCanDoBetter.pdf
- United Nations Convention on the Elimination of All Forms of Discrimination Against Women

Guest speakers: Dottie Clune and Jeannie Hosey (planning and communications consultants) and Lucrecia Harvey (Open Door staff)

Due: Reflection paper from Week 6 material

Week 8

Human rights in the United States

Selected readings from http://www.theadvocatesforhumanrights.org/Human_Rights_in_the_United_ States.html

Due: Reflection paper from Week 7 material

Week 9 (midsemester break)

Week 10

Social work and human rights with immigrants and refugees

Reading: Dyer-Ives Foundation. (2003). *New Neighbors, New Opportunities: Immigrants and Refugees in Grand Rapids*. Prepared by Dottie Clune and Jeannie Hosey, project consultants. Available at http:// www.dyer-ives.org/sites/default/files/content_files/New_Neighbors.pdf

Guest Speaker: Donna Abbott, director of the Grand Rapids Branch of Bethany Christian Services

Due: Reflection paper from Week 8 material

Week 11

Vulnerable groups; persons with disabilities and/or HIV/AIDS, gays and lesbians, older persons and victims of racism. Case studies.

Readings:

- United Nations. (1999). *Principles for the Older Person*

- *Universal Declaration of Human Rights*
- United Nations. (1978). *Declaration on Race and Racial Prejudice*
- United Nations. (1975). *Declaration on the Rights of Disabled Persons*
- Reichert, Chapter 6

Due: Reflection paper from Week 10 material.

Week 12

Truth commissions, opened secret police files, declassified congressional reports, trials of leaders of tyranny. How do we handle human rights violations in the United States, and how do we overcome legacies of dictatorships?

Readings:

- South Africa Truth and Reconciliation Commission – apartheid; available at http://www. justice.gov
- Report on the UN Truth Commission on El Salvador – available at http://www.derechos.org/nizkor/salvador/informes.truth.html

Due: Reflection paper from Week 11 material

Week 13

Working in the field of social work and human rights: How to search for employment opportunities, where to search, writing a résumé, and other resources.

Begin student research paper presentations.

Due: Reflection paper from Week 12 material

Week 14

Student research paper presentations.

Week 15

Student research paper presentations.

Week 16

Final exam week, wrap-up.

Bibliography

Amnesty International. (2009). *Report 2009*. New York, NY: Author.

Amnesty International. (2010). *United States of America: Rights for all*. New York, NY: Author.

Basombrio, C. (2000). Looking ahead: New challenges for human rights advocacy, *NACLA Report on the Americas, 34*(1), 7–11.

Brysk, A. (2000*). Globalization: The double-edged sword. NACLA Report on the Americas, 34*(1), 29–33.

Caceres, E. (2000). Building a culture of rights. *NACLA Report on the Americas, 34*(1), 19–24.

Chossudovshy, M. (2000). The globalisation of poverty. In M. Chossudovsky, *The globalization of poverty: Impacts of the IMF and World Bank reforms* (pp. 33–43). Halifax, Nova Scotia: Fernwood Publications.

Danner, M. (1993, December 6). The truth of El Mozote. *The New Yorker.* Available at http://www.webcitation.org/6BvSC8Irn

Estes, R. (1992) Internationalizing social work education. Philadelphia, PA: University of Pennsylvania School of Social Work.

Espiell, H. (1998). Universality of human rights and cultural diversity. *International Social Science Journal, 58,* 525–534.

Hamber, B. (1995, 26 July). *Do sleeping dogs lie?: The psychological implications of the Truth and Reconciliation Commission in South Africa.* Paper presented at the Centre for the Study of Violence and Reconciliation, Seminar No. 5. Braamfontein, Johannesburg, South Africa: Center for the Study of Violence and Reconciliation.

Hamber, B. (Ed.). (1998). *Past imperfect: Dealing with the past in Northern Ireland and societies in transition.* Derry/Londonderry, Northern Ireland: University of Ulster & INCORE.

Hamber, B. (1998). The burdens of truth: An evaluation of the psychological support services and initiatives undertaken by the South African Truth and Reconciliation Commission. *American Imago, 55*(1), 9–28.

Healy, L. (2008) *International social work: Professional action in an interdependent world* (2nd ed.). New York, NY: Oxford University Press.

Healy, L. M., & Link, R. J. (2012). *Handbook of international social work: Human rights, development, and the global profession.* New York: Oxford University Press.

Hokenstad, M. C., & Midgley, J. (Eds.). (2008). *Lessons from abroad: Adapting international social welfare innovations.* Washington, DC: NASW Press.

Ignatieff, M. (2000) *The rights revolution,* Toronto, Canada: Anansi.

McCorquodale, R., & Fairbrother, R. (1999). Globalization and human rights. *Human Rights Quarterly, 21,* 735–766.

Reichert, E. (2006). *Understanding human rights: An exercise book.* Thousand Oaks, CA: SAGE Publications.

Reichert, E. (2007). *Challenges in human rights: A social work perspective.* New York, NY: Columbia University Press.

Schild, V. (2000). Gender equity without social justice: Women's rights in the neoliberal age. *NACLA Report on the Americas, 34*(1), 25–28.

South African Truth and Reconciliation Commission. Retrieved from http://www.justice.gov.za/trc/

United Nations. (1979). Convention on the elimination of all forms of discrimination against women. Available from http://www.ohchr.org/Documents/ProfessionalInterest/cedaw.pdf

United Nations. (1989) Convention on the rights of the child. Retrieved from http://www.ohchr.org/en/professionalinterest/pages/crc.aspx

United Nations. (1948). Declaration on human rights. Retrieved from http://www.unhchr.ch/udhr/lang/eng-print.htm

United Nations Center for Human Rights. (1989). *Teaching human rights.* Geneva, Switzerland: Center for Human Rights.

United Nations Development Program. (2000). *Human rights and human development.* London, UK: Oxford University Press. Read the Overview Summary. Full text of this report is available at http://hdr.undp.org/en/media/hdr_2000_ch0.pdf

United Nations, Office of the High Commissioner for Human Rights. *International covenant on civil and political rights.* Retrieved from http://treaties.un.org/doc/Publication/UNTS/Volume%20999/volume-999-I-14668-English.pdf

United Nations, Office of the High Commissioner for Human Rights. (1966). *International covenant on economic, social and cultural rights.* Retrieved from http://unhchr.ch/html/menu3/b/a_cescr.htm

United Nations Security Council. (1993). *Report on the UN Truth Commission in El Salvador.* Retrieved from http://www.derechos.org/nizkor/salvador/informes/truth.html

Human Rights and Social Work

Kathryn Libal
Lynne M. Healy
University of Connecticut

This course was developed out of faculty interest and expertise and in response to important trends in the social work profession and at the University of Connecticut. It recognizes the increased attention given to human rights in all major documents of the social work profession, globally and nationally. The inclusion of human rights in a core competency in the latest CSWE Education Policy and Accreditation Standards is particularly noted. Our university has given heavy emphasis to human rights education and research since the mid-1990s. The University of Connecticut has a human rights minor and major for undergraduate students; an option for a graduate certificate in human rights for some disciplines; and an active and ongoing program of lectures, research seminars, and visiting scholars in human rights. These are led and coordinated by the University of Connecticut Human Rights Institute. The School of Social Work has been an active partner in these efforts and has sponsored numerous co-curricular programs on human rights.

This elective course, Human Rights and Social Work, is offered in the MSW program and counts toward an International Issues focused area of study, an elective specialization. The course presents human rights as (1) a system of international laws and accountability mechanisms, (2) a set of globally agreed standards, (3) a perspective to guide social work practice at micro and macro levels, (4) a conceptual framework to guide development of social policy, and (5) a framework for ethical decision making in concert with professional ethics. The course was taught for the first time in 2010 and has been approved by the faculty as part of the curriculum. In its current form the course follows a workshop format and is taught on 4 full days in a given semester. This approach affords an opportunity to bring in guest speakers and use film resources, lecture, and small group discussion. Reading assignments between sessions are therefore substantial. Feedback from students confirms the value of working intensively several times over the semester on human rights and social work concerns. The course introduces students to the international human rights regime, linking it to domestic practice and policy concerns. The two major written assignments are designed to further these goals.

Course Description

This course will provide the theoretical, conceptual, and practical foundation for social workers to engage in a human rights-based approach to social work. Students will gain an understanding of the international human rights system, social work's contribution to achieving human rights, and how international human rights principles can be applied to social work practice. We will use a number of cases from varied countries, including the United States, to examine how social workers can both advocate for and respect human rights in their work.

Course Objectives

- To make students aware of the international human rights system, including how human rights treaties operate in international law and the strengths and weaknesses of the treaty-monitoring process for inculcating human rights at local, national, and international levels.

- To provide an understanding of key concepts in human rights, such as civil, political, social, economic and cultural rights; indivisibility and interdependence of rights; cultural relativism versus universalism; rights and/versus responsibilities, the public/private divide in human rights debates; the idea of US exceptionalism.

- To familiarize students with the major UN human rights treaties and the work of the Office of the High Commissioner for Human Rights.

- To increase understanding of how civil society (including social work organizations) plays a critical role in the realization of human rights (through grassroots education, advocacy, and "shadow reporting" processes at the United Nations).

- To develop a basic awareness of human rights and how they relate to social work policies and practices, including an understanding of social work as a human rights profession.

- Discern ways in which social work can contribute to the achievement of human rights, both domestically and internationally.

- Examine how international human rights principles can be applied to social work practice and ethical dilemmas that may arise from such efforts.

- Encourage students to be active as social work professionals advocating for the realization of human rights both domestically and internationally.

Course Outcomes

At the conclusion of the course, students will

A. be able to define and discuss core human rights concepts;

B. demonstrate through class discussions and a course paper a beginning understanding of core human rights treaties and the UN human rights system and practices as they apply domestically and internationally;

C. demonstrate in the course assignments the ability to locate and use key human rights resources;

D. demonstrate the use of a human rights framework to analyze a key social problem or vulnerability that women, children, immigrants and refugees, and other severely disadvantaged groups face;

E. apply a human rights based approach to social work practice through discussions and a final paper on their social work practice; and

F. be able to identify domestic and international issues for social work action on human rights issues.

Reading

Texts

Ife, J. (2008). *Human rights and social work: Towards rights-based practice* (revised ed.). New York, NY: Cambridge University Press.

Kenney, D. N., & Shrag, P. G. (2009). *Asylum denied: A refugee's struggle for safety in America.* Berkeley, CA: University of California Press.

Other readings will be drawn from books on library reserve, journals, and the instructors' collections. When possible, these readings will be posted to the university website.

Course Format

The course will be run as a seminar, with student responsibility for reading and contributing to the discussions. Other resources such as videos and guest speakers will be used. We meet in 4 full day sessions.

We will use the university Web system in several ways, including for accessing readings and additional resources, and supplementary discussions may be conducted via the Web, using a discussion list.

Assignments, Class Participation, and Grading

Class participation and regular reading are part of course expectations and will be taken into consideration in grading. Several written assignments are also required (see below).

Response Paper

In no more than 600 words, write a brief essay reflecting on the reading. Your essay should address the following question: How have the readings shaped or reshaped your understanding of human rights?

Your essay should show integration of ideas from at least three of the readings. You may cite authors simply by name, but if you include a quote, please include the page number from which it is taken.

Response Paper

In no more than 600 words, write a brief essay reflecting on the reading. Your essay should address the following:

- An often cited statement is that since its inception social work has been a human rights profession. Reflecting on the readings for Session 2, assess whether you think this statement accurately portrays the profession in its ideals and practice.

- Your essay should show integration of ideas from at least three of the readings. You may cite authors simply by name, but if you include a quote, please include the page number from which it is taken.

Human Rights Brief

Select a country (not the United States) and a human rights issue of interest. You are to consult at least four sources for human rights reporting, including the relevant treaty report to the United Nations. Other suggestions are committee recommendations, nongovernmental organization (NGO) reports (e.g., Human Rights Watch, Amnesty International, or local NGOs in the country), US Department of State reports, and "shadow reports" that have been submitted by NGOs as part of the human rights

monitoring process at the United Nations. In a well-crafted and researched "Human Rights Brief" (5–6 pages, double-spaced, typed, with appropriate references following APA style) you should do the following:

- Write a concise summary of the human rights issue at stake in the country.

- Outline which aspects of international human rights law are connected with the topic (cite relevant treaties, principles, and specific articles of treaties, and/or general comments that have been written on the issue).

- Summarize the country's position on realization of the human right(s) in question and any evidence from other sources that may challenge the country's portrayal of its human rights compliance.

- Briefly outline how the topic intersects with social work advocacy and/or practice—in other words, how can social workers contribute to the realization of the human right(s) in question?

Essay on Applying Human Rights Concepts and Treaties to Local Realities and Social Work Practice

Choose one of the two following topics to address in a well-written, concise, and well-documented essay (7–8 pages of text, not including title page and reference list; double-spaced, in 11 or 12 point font, with appropriate references following the APA style):

1. Identify a human rights related issue in your practice. Apply at least one of the human rights treaties to the issue, discussing what principles apply and how. Discuss ways in which you would address the issue using a human rights approach. Include both micro and macro actions.

2. Identify a human rights violation in your locality or state. You are to research the issue, applying human rights principles and treaty provisions. Write a brief report on the issue for the treaty committee.

Policy on Attendance

Remember that School of Social Work policy requires you to attend all four sessions. If you know that you will have to miss a day, you must withdraw from the course.

- Participation: 10%

- Response 1: 5%

- Response 2: 5%

- Human rights brief: 40%

- Essay on human rights and social work practice: 40%

Topics and Reading Assignments

All Day Session I

Topics

- Introduction to human rights
- Overview of civil, political, social, and economic rights
- The United Nations human rights system
- Social work as a human rights profession

Read in advance:

Kenney, D. N., & Shrag, P. G. (2009). *Asylum denied: A refugee's struggle for safety in America.* Berkeley, CA: University of California Press. Read pp. 1–198.

Healy, L. (2008). Exploring the history of social work as a human rights profession. *International Social Work, 51,* 735–748.

Ife, J. (2008). *Human rights and social work: Towards rights-based practice.* Cambridge, UK: Cambridge University Press. Read Chapter 1, pp. 4–28.

Wronka, J. (1995). Human rights. In T. Mizrahi & L.E. Davis (Eds.), *The encyclopedia of social work* (pp. 1405–1418). Washington, DC: NASW Press.

United Nations. (1948). *Universal declaration of human rights.* Available from http://www.un.org/en/documents/udhr/

All Day Session II

Topics

- Human rights, values, and social work ethics
- Rights of immigrants, asylum-seekers, and refugees

Read in advance for the topic human rights, values, and social work ethics:

Ife, "Culture and Human Rights," in *Human Rights and Social Work,* pp. 68–88.

IASSW/IFSW Statement of Ethical Principles

NASW (2003). International policy on human rights. In *Social Work Speaks* (6th ed.). Washington, DC: National Association of Social Workers.

International Federation of Social Workers, Policy Statement on Human Rights

Healy, L. (2007). Universalism and cultural relativism in social work ethics. *International Social Work, 51,* 11–26.

Ross, E. (2008). The intersection of cultural practices and ethics in a rights-based society: Implications for South Africa social workers. *International Social Work, 51,* 384–395.

Human Rights Watch. (2011). United States. In *World Report 2011,* pp. 609–627.

Read in advance for the topic rights of immigrants, asylum-seekers, and refugees:

Convention on the Rights of Migrant Workers and Their Families

Kenney, D. N., & Shrag, P. G. (2009). *Asylum denied: A refugee's struggle for safety in America.* Read pp. 199–327.

Vongkhampra, E. G., Davis, C., & Adem, N. (2010). The resettling process: A case study of a Bantu refugee's journey to the USA. *International Social Work, 1–12.* doi:10.1177/0020872809358397

Padilla, Y. C., Shapiro, E. R., Fernández-Castro, M.D., & Faulkner, M. (2007). Our nation's immigrants in peril: An urgent call to social workers. *Social Work, 53,* 5–8.

NASW Arizona. (2010). Social workers, immigration policies, and state benefits. Available at http://www.naswaz.com/displaycommon.cfm?an=1&subarticlenbr=202

Humphries, B. (2004). An unacceptable role for social work: Implementing immigration policy. *British Journal of Social Work, 34*(1), 93–107.

All Day Session III

Topics

Nondiscrimination and equality as human rights principles

Tackling racism, heterosexism, and ableism as human rights concerns

Read in advance:

International Convention on the Elimination of All Forms of Racial Discrimination

Ife, J. "Respecting Human Rights in Social Work Practice" and "Prospects for Human Rights Practice," in *Human Rights and Social Work*, pp. 188–228.

Tang, K-L. (2010). Using international law against racial discrimination: What works, what doesn't. Unpublished presentation presented at the 2010 Joint World Conference on Social Work and Social Development: The Agenda, June 13, 2010, Hong Kong.

Yogyakarta Principles: Principles on the Application of International Human Rights Law in Relation to Sexual Orientation and Gender Identity. (2007). Available at http://www.yogyakartaprinciples.org/principles_en.pdf

Bailey, G. (2012). Human rights and sexual orientation. In L. M. Healy & R. J. Link (eds.), *Handbook of international social work: Human rights, development and the global profession* (pp. 464–471). New York, NY: Oxford University Press.

Hutchinson, G. S. (2012). Human rights of people with disabilities. In L. M. Healy & R .J. Link (eds.), *Handbook of international social work: Human rights, development and the global profession* (pp. 459–463). New York, NY: Oxford University Press.

Read in advance on the topic of children's rights:

UN Convention on the Rights of the Child

Link, R. (2007). Children's rights as a template for social work practice. In E. Reichert (ed.), *Challenges in human rights: A social work perspective* (pp. 215–238). New York, NY: Columbia University Press.

Maundeni, T. (2010). Challenges faced in the implementation of provisions of the United Nations Convention on the Rights of the Child (CRC) in Botswana. *Journal of Social Development in Africa, 25*(1), 59–84.

Libal, K., Mapp, S. C., Ihrig, S., & Ron, A. (2011). Commentary—the Convention on the Rights of the Child: Children can wait no longer for their rights. *Social Work, 56,* 367–370.

Human Rights Watch. (2010). *My so-called emancipation: From foster care to homelessness for California youth.* New York, NY: Human Rights Watch. Read selected pages.

Lewis, M. (2011). The human rights of children in conflict with the law: Lessons for the US human rights movement. In S. Hertel & K. Libal (Eds.), *Human rights in the United States: Beyond exceptionalism* (pp. 255–273). New York, NY: Cambridge University Press.

All Day Session IV

Topics

- Women's human rights
- Public and private spheres—state accountability for gender-based violence
- Poverty and human rights
- The right to access health care
- A rights-based approach to social work practice, Part 2
- Closing discussion: Is there a broader responsibility to realize human rights? Do our social work responsibilities end at our borders?

Read in advance on the topic of women's human rights:

Convention on the Elimination of All Forms of Discrimination Against Women

Declaration on the Elimination of All Forms of Violence Against Women

Ife, J. "Public and Private Human Rights," in *Human Rights and Social Work,* pp. 52–67.

Reichert, E. (2012). Women and the human rights framework. In L. M. Healy & R. J. Link (eds.), *Handbook of international social work: Human rights, development and the global profession* (pp. 447–451). New York, NY: Oxford University Press.

Morgaine, K. (2011). "How would that help our work?" The intersection of domestic violence and human rights in the United States. *Violence Against Women, 17*(1), 6–27.

Siegel, M. D. (2012). Surviving Castle Rock: The human rights of domestic violence. *Cardozo Journal of Law and Gender, 18,* 727–751.

Pervizat, L. (2003). In the name of honor. *Human Rights Dialogue, 2*(10) (2 pp)

Arat, Z. (2003). A struggle on two fronts. *Human Rights Dialogue, 2*(10) (2 pp)

United Nations. (2006, July 9). Executive summary. In *Ending violence against women: from words to action, study of the secretary general.* New York, NY: Author.

Read in advance on the topic of economic and social rights:

International Covenant on Economic, Social and Cultural Rights

Ife, J. Human rights and human needs, in *Human Rights and Social Work*, pp. 89–103.

Mishra, R. (2005). Social rights as human rights: Globalizing social protection. *International Social Work, 48*(1), 9–20.

International Council on Social Welfare. (2010). Protection floor initiative (SPF-I).

International Labour Organization. (2010). Social protection floor initiative. Geneva, Switzerland: Author. Available at http://www.ilo.org/public/english/protection/spfag/download/background/spfibrochure-en.pdf

Staub-Bernasconi, S. (2007). Economic and social rights: the neglected human rights. In Reichert, *Challenges in Human Rights*, pp. 138–161.

Neubeck, K. (2011). Human rights violations as obstacles to escaping poverty: The case of lone-mother-headed families. In S. Hertel & K. Libal (Eds.), *Human rights in the United States: Beyond exceptionalism* (pp. 234–254). New York, NY: Cambridge University Press.

Committee on Economic, Social and Cultural Rights. (2000). *General comment 14: The right to the highest attainable standard of health.* Geneva, Switzerland: United Nations.

Useful Websites

International Federation of Social Workers: *www.ifsw.org*

International Association of Schools of Social Work: *www.iassw-aiets.org*

Become very familiar with the website of the UN High Commission on Human Rights, which is a clearinghouse for all treaties; general comments; documentation, including country reports and responses; and determinations on individual complaints. Website address: www.ohchr.or

Useful Social Work and Human Rights Journals on Human Rights Topics

Human Rights Quarterly

Human Rights Review

International Social Work

Journal of Human Rights Practice

Journal of International Social Welfare

Social Development Issues

Sustainable Human Development and Human Rights: A Gender Perspective, Costa Rica

Dennis J. Ritchie
George Mason University

Laura Guzmán Stein
Former director of the Center for Research on Women's Studies of the University of Costa Rica

This course focuses on the interrelated themes of human rights (particularly women's and children's rights); sustainable human, social, economic, political, and community development; family, gender-based, and community violence; poverty; and health and social services. Students will critically examine policies and programs related to these themes and their implementation.

Teaching/Learning Methods

This field-based seminar will combine lectures and active learning exercises, reading and written assignments, videos, individual and panel guest presentations, and site visits to governmental and nongovernmental organizations across levels from community-based grass roots to national and international organizations. Examples of the kinds of site visits to be incorporated into this course include the following: the Inter-American Institute for Human Rights; the National Institute for Women; government and nongovernmental agencies responsible for protecting the human rights of children; nongovernmental organizations (NGOs) working at grassroots level to empower and realize the human rights of women and children; rural community organization for prevention of violence, information and communication technologies, organic agriculture, and recycling.

Course Objectives

After completion of this course participants are expected to be capable of doing the following:

- Understand and conceptualize human development from a holistic, systemic, and global perspective
- Understand and articulate human rights, age, and gender perspectives to human development
- Understand and be able to articulate the interrelatedness of human development to concepts of social development, economic development, political development, community development, and sustainable development
- Identify and delineate the major international human rights instruments that relate to sustainable human development
- View global and local poverty and violence as two of the major impediments to human development and human rights
- Critically analyze strategies—policies, programs, and social action—in terms of their ability to promote sustainable human development and human rights
- Demonstrate further understanding of and a commitment to addressing the needs and situation of marginalized and vulnerable populations including women and children.

Course Readings

Required Text

Reichert, E. (Ed.). (2007). *Challenges in human rights: A social work perspective.* New York, NY: Columbia University Press.

Recommended Texts

Langwith, J. (Ed.). (2008). *Human rights: Opposing viewpoints.* Farmington Hills, MI: Greenhaven Press.

Reichert, E. (Ed.). (2006). *Understanding human rights: An exercise book.* Thousand Oaks, CA: SAGE.

Wronka, J. (2008). *Human rights and social justice: Social action and service for the helping and health professions.* Thousand Oaks, CA: SAGE.

All additional required readings for this course will be placed on electronic reserve with the library system and/or will be made available through Internet sites. This will enable students to access the required readings prior to departure to Costa Rica and commencement of the course. Additional readings may be provided to participants while on site in Costa Rica.

Assignments

1. Written critical reflections on predeparture assigned readings to be submitted the first week of the course. (20% of course grade)

2. On-site journal that will include daily critical reflections on assigned readings, videos, individual and panel guest lectures/presentations, active learning exercises, and site visits to governmental and nongovernmental organizations. It will also include a section on cross-cultural experience and learning. (30% of course grade)

3. Written and oral presentations at end of the seminar that present a summary of individual's experience of journaling. For example, she or he will share emerging themes, major learning, and experience of crossing cultures and living and working with the group. (10% of course grade)

4. Final integrative paper. This paper is to incorporate Assignment 3 above while integrating the student's research and critical analytic discussion of one major topic of the course. For undergraduate credit the paper is expected to be between seven and 10 pages in length. For graduate credit the paper is expected to have greater depth and length, 10 to 25 pages. The final integrative paper is due after return home. (40% of course grade)

Outline of Course Topics

- Course introduction and overview
  - Major concepts of human development
    - Holistic ecosystems view
    - Relation to concepts of social development, economic development, sustainable development, political development, and community development.
    - Poverty and violence as two major obstacles to human development

- Human rights
  - Human rights, gender and age perspectives
  - Overview of major international human rights instruments and concepts with close examination of those focusing on women and children
  - Relationship between human development and human rights
  - Is human development and enjoyment of human rights possible in a global neoliberal world?
- The situation of women and children worldwide, in Central America and in the United States
  - Strategies—policies, programs, and other planned change efforts—to promote human development and human rights across all systems levels: policies and programs of governmental organizations and NGOs across levels from community-based grass roots to national and international organizations
  - Course wrap-up: summary and sharing of critical reflections on overall experience and learning

Course Schedule

Please note that this is a tentative schedule that may be slightly revised according to availability of guest lecturers and host organizations.

Saturday, June 2

Depart for San José, Costa Rica; meet at San José airport and check into hotel on arrival; evening welcome dinner and general orientation to course and setting.

Sunday, June 3

Free day to rest and prepare for course and discussion of predeparture readings. Optional: Organized sightseeing day trip to Poas Volcano and Peace Waterfalls Park Nature Center (at student's own expense, but highly rated and recommended by former students).

Monday, June 4

Morning session: Course introduction and foundation; students report and discuss themes and questions from assigned readings. Discussion of major concepts of human development: holistic ecosystems view; relation to concepts of social, economic, sustainable, political, and community development. Professors Dennis Ritchie and Laura Guzmán.

Afternoon session: Measuring Human Development. Lecture by Professors Ritchie and Guzmán about main methodologies to measure human development: Human Development Index, Gender Related Human Development Index, Gender Empowerment Measure, Global Gender Gap. Group discussion on the relation of human development and human rights. Walking tour of University of Costa Rica and the City. Daily debriefing and reflections.

Night: Free.

Tuesday, June 5

Morning session: Visit to Fundacion PANIAMOR, a Costa Rican NGO and leader in the field of children's rights. Lecture by Milena Grillo, director: The Protection of the Rights of the Child in Costa Rica and PANIAMOR's programs.

Afternoon session: Visit to the Inter-American Court and Institute for Human Rights. Lecture on the international and inter-American systems for the protection of human rights (What human rights are; origin; the UN system; the inter-American system; national systems—a comparison between the United States and Costa Rica). Daily debriefing and reflections.

Night: Independent study.

Wednesday, June 6

Morning session: Indigenous communities in Costa Rica. Lecture by Gina Valitutti and Yensy Herrera focusing on the situation of women in the indigenous communities of Talamanca, which the group will visit the following day. The discussion will focus on information about the situation of indigenous communities in the area. Preparation for next day's field trip.

Afternoon session: Lecture on commercial sexual exploitation of children, teens, and adult women and its implications for human rights. Lecture by Laura Porras. In Costa Rica, prostitution of adult women is not a crime, but commercial sexual exploitation of children is considered a crime. The lecture focuses on the causes and risk factors for commercial sexual exploitation. Daily debriefing and reflections.

Night: Free

Thursday, June 7

Morning session: 6.00 a.m. departure for Talamanca and the Bribri indigenous community of Yorkin. Breakfast on the road. This is a 5 to 6 hours trip by bus to the place in which the boat will be taken for Yorkin.

Afternoon session: Arrival to Talamanca around noon. Trip by rivers Telire and Sixaola from Bambu to Yorkin (about 1 hour in the motor-powered canoe). Arrival to the ecological tourism project in Yorkin, where we will be staying overnight. Be aware that this visit involves walking cross-country up and down hill, medium-sized distances, crossing rivers in canoes, and sleeping and eating in a rural shelter.

Night: Stay overnight in Yorkin; dinner in the project, Bribri history and songs.

Friday, June 8

Morning session: Yorkin, Talamanca. Breakfast in the community. Visit to chocolate plantation and the local public school. Explanation of chocolate manufacturing process. Walking tour of medicinal plants cultivation.

Afternoon session: Arrive in Puerto Viejo, a beach town on the Caribbean/Atlantic coast, for the weekend.

Night: Free

Saturday and Sunday, June 9 and 10

Lecture(s) in Puerto Viejo on Afro-Caribbean population, culture, and issues, as well as tourism and development. Students will also have ample free time this weekend to relax and enjoy! Return to San José Sunday evening.

Night: Free

Monday, June 11

Morning session: Sharing and debriefing experiences about the field trip to Yorkin and Puerto Viejo. Professors Dennis Ritchie and Laura Guzmán.

Afternoon session: Lecture by Professor Laura Guzman and group discussion. Human rights of women, discrimination and violence against women, the national survey on violence against women, and research on femicide. A comparative perspective: Costa Rica and the United States. Daily debriefing and reflections.

Night: Free

Tuesday, June 12

Morning session: Visit to National Institute for Women (INAMU) at Granadilla de Curridabat. Lecture by Suiyen Ramirez on the National Policy for Gender Equality and Equity and related programs of INAMU.

Afternoon session: Visit to the Center for Women's Studies Research at the University of Costa Rica.

Night: Lecture and discussion on social work in Costa Rica and Latin America in comparison to the United States. Professors Laura Guzmán, Ana Josefina Guell, and Dennis Ritchie. Daily debriefing and reflections.

Wednesday, June 13

Morning session: Sustainable human development—the case of Costa Rica. Lecture by researchers of the State of the Nation Report Project team. Costa Rican reality and how human development indicators are developed and applied.

Afternoon session: Trafficking in persons in Costa Rica and Central America. Lecture by Ana Hidalgo, project officer at the International Office for Migrations. Daily debriefing and reflections.

Night: Free

Thursday, June 14

Morning session: 8 a.m. Departure for trip to San Luis in Grecia (about 2 hours by bus from San José). Visit to women's cooperative dedicated to production of organic personal care products (shampoos, soaps, body creams, and medicinal products, etc.). Tour of farm, lab, and factory with lunch and exchange with co-op members about their history and experiences.

Afternoon session: Visit to San Ramón women's grassroots organization: MUSADE (NGO working in the area of gender based violence against women and children).

Night: Free.

Friday, June 15

Morning session: Lecture on critical analysis of national Responsible Paternity Law and policy representing how human rights of women and children are interrelated and challenges to implementation.

Afternoon session: Group debriefing and reflections. Student work on preparing presentations on individual reflections on course experience and learning.

Night: Free

Saturday, June 16

Morning session: Free

Afternoon session: Presentations and discussion of individual learning experiences; course wrap-up and evaluations.

Night: Farewell dinner.

Sunday, June 17

Depart for United States

Predeparture core foundation readings and written reflections are due May 25.

Assigned Readings and Source Websites

What is Human Development and What Are the Millennium Development Goals?

- Go to http://hdr.undp.org and links on top of page. Open "Human Development" and read this page.

- Go to links at top of page again and open "Reports (1990–2011)" and read the page.

- Go to links on left side of page and open "About the Reports" and read.

- Go back to links on left side of page and open "Global Reports." Go to links on left of page and open "HDR 2000, Human Rights and Human Development" and read page.

- Open "Summary" link on right side of page. Read "Overview pp. 1–13, "Universal Declaration of Human Rights" pp. 14–15, and "Glossary on Human Rights and Human Development" pp. 16–18.

- Return to "Global Reports" page and open link on left side of page to "HDR 2003," Millennium Development Goals: A compact among nations to end human poverty." Then open link to "Summary" and read at least p. x. (The Millennium Development Goals, Human Development and Human Rights Share a Common Mission) and "Overview," pp. 1–14.

- Return to "Global Reports" and open link to "HDR 2009," (Overcoming Barriers: Human Mobility and Development). Then open link to "Summary" and read it.

- Return to "Global Reports" and open link to "HDR 2010," (20 Years On: Pushing the Frontiers of Human Development). Download "Summary" and read it. Then open link to "Overview" and read it.

- Return to "Global Reports" and open link to "HDR 2011," (Sustainability and Equity: A Better Future for All). Open link to "Summary" and read page.

Human Rights in Development

Go to www.ohchr.org/Documents/Publications/FAQen.pdf and open and read Frequently Asked Questions on a Human Rights-Based Approach to Development Cooperation. Read pp. 1–40.

Social Watch Report 2012— Sustainable Development: The Right to a Future

Go to www.socialwatch.org and on left side of page open link to "Social Watch Report 2012." Then look at table of contents on left side of page and open link to "An overview of the Social Watch Report 2012."

International Human Rights Instruments (Major UN Human Rights Documents)

Go to www.ohchr.org and go to right side of page and open link to "Human rights instruments." Then open and familiarize yourself with the following instruments:

- Universal Declaration of Human Rights
- International Covenant on Civil and Political Rights (recommended)
- International Covenant on Economic, Social and Cultural Rights (recommended)
- Convention on the Elimination of All Forms of Discrimination Against Women
- Convention on the Rights of the Child
- Declaration on the Right to Development
- Peruse the entire list and open and explore other documents, other human rights instruments, according to your interests.

The United States and its Ratification of International Human Rights Treaties

Go to www.hrw.org/en/news/2009/07/24/united-states-ratification-international-human-rights-treaties Open and read.

The State of the World's Children (Annual Reports by UNICEF)

Go to www.unicef.org/sowc Open and read *The State of the World's Children 2010: Child Rights*.

The Global Gender Gap

Go to the World Economic Forum's report at http://www3.weforum.org/docs/WEF_GenderGap_Report_2011.pdf

Open *The Global Gender Gap Report 2011* and familiarize yourself with its content.

Predeparture Writing Assignment

Prior to departing for Costa Rica each student is expected to complete the assigned predeparture core foundation readings and written journal entries regarding these readings that will be turned in to the course instructors.

Instructions for Journaling on Predeparture Readings

Write a minimum of two typed pages of your critical reflections on each of the first four sections of the handout on assigned readings and their websites while responding to the questions below.

- What is human development and what are the Millennium Development Goals? What is the relationship between them?

- Human rights and human development: What is the relationship between the two?

- Explain the importance of the concepts of sustainability and equity for promoting human development. What needs to be done to adequately respond to the current global economic and environmental crises and growing inequities? What is the added value of incorporating and using a human rights framework?

- International human rights instruments: What most struck you and what did you learn about them? Consider the Universal Declaration of Human Rights, Convention on the Elimination of All Forms of Discrimination Against Women, Convention on the Rights of the Child, and Declaration on the Right to Development.

- Overall critical reflections and questions: You may add a final section to your responses by reflecting on all the predeparture readings and writing about what you learned about sustainable development and human rights and what questions you would like to discuss with the instructors and your classmates during the seminar in Costa Rica.

This is an informal writing assignment, so you do not need to worry about proper APA style or even spelling and grammar. The focus is on your critical reflections—critical thinking and questioning—regarding the content of the readings and their fit with other things you have learned about human development and human rights to date.

Course Bibliography for Sustainable Human Development, Gender, and Human Rights

Estes, R. (1999). Informational tools for social workers: Research in the global age. In C. S. Ramanathan & R. J. Link (Eds.), *All our futures: Principles and resources for social work practice in a global era* (pp. 121–137). Belmont, CA: Wadsworth.

Healy, L. M. (2008). *International social work: Professional action in an interdependent world.* New York, NY: Oxford University Press.

Healy, L. M. (2008). Exploring the history of social work as a human rights profession. *International Social Work, 51,* 735–748.

Hodgkins, R., & Newell, P. (2002). *Implementation handbook for the convention on the rights of the child.* New York, NY: UNICEF.

Ife, J. (2001). *Human rights and social work.* Cambridge, UK: Cambridge University Press.

Langwith, J. (Ed.). (2008). *Human rights: Opposing viewpoints.* Farmington Hills, MI: Greenhaven Press.

Midgley, J. (1999). Social development in social work: Learning from global dialogue. In C. S. Ramanathan & R. J. Link (Eds.), *All our futures: Principles and resources for social work practice in a global era* (pp. 121–137). Belmont, CA: Wadsworth.

Prigoff, A. (1999). Global social and economic justice issues. In C. S. Ramanathan & R. J. Link (Eds.), *All our futures: Principles and resources for social work practice in a global era* (pp. 121–137). Belmont, CA: Wadsworth.

Ranis, G., Stewart, F., & Ramirez, A. (2000). Economic growth and human development. *World Development, 28*(2), 197–219.

Reichert, E. (Ed.). (2007). *Challenges in human rights: A social work perspective.* New York, NY: Columbia University Press.

Reichert, E. (2006). *Understanding human rights: An exercise book.* Thousand Oaks, CA: SAGE Publications.

Ritchie, D. J., & Kugelmass, J. W. (2003). The emerging democracy of Lithuania: A society in transition and its children. In J. W. Kugelmass & D. J. Ritchie (Eds.), *Advocating for children and families in an emerging democracy: The post-Soviet experience in Lithuania* (pp.1–26). Greenwich, CT: Information Age.

Ryan, W. (1994). Many cooks, brave men, apples, and oranges: How people think about equality. *American Journal of Community Psychology, 22,* 25–35.

UNICEF. (n.d.). *Human rights for children and women: How UNICEF helps make them a reality.* New York, NY: Author.

UNICEF. (2007). *The state of the world's children 2007: Women and children—The double dividend of gender equality.* New York, NY: Author.

UNICEF. (2008). *The state of the world's children 2008: Women and children—Child survival.* New York, NY: Author.

UNICEF. (2009). *The state of the world's children 2009: Maternal and newborn health.* New York, NY: Author.

UNICEF. (2010). *The state of the world's children 2010: Child rights.* New York, NY: Author.

UNICEF. (2011). *The state of the world's children 2010. Adolescence: An age of opportunity.* New York, NY: Author.

United Nations. (n.d.). *The challenge of gender equity and human rights on the threshold of the twenty-first century.* New York, NY: Author.

United Nations Declaration on the Right to Development. (1986, December 4). Adopted by General Assembly Resolution 41/128.

United Nations Universal Declaration of Human Rights. (1948).

United Nations International Covenant on Civil and Political Rights. (1966).

United Nations International Covenant on Economic, Social and Cultural Rights. (1966).

United Nations Convention on the Elimination of All Forms of Discrimination Against Women. (1979).

United Nations Convention on the Rights of the Child. (1989).

United Nations Development Programme. (2005) *Human development report 2005.* New York, NY: Author.

United Nations Development Programme. (2002) *State of the region report on sustainable human development in Central America.* New York, NY: Author.

United Nations Office of the High Commissioner for Human Rights. (2003). *Human rights and poverty reduction: A conceptual framework.* New York, NY: Author.

Women, Law and Development International & Human Rights Watch. (1997). *The human rights of women: step by step.* Washington, D.C.: Women, Law and Development International.

Wronka, J. (2008). *Human rights and social justice: Social action and service for the helping and health professions.* Thousand Oaks, CA: SAGE.

International Social Work

Filomena M. Critelli
University of Buffalo, The State University of New York

In a globalized world, effective social work practice requires incorporation of an international perspective and an understanding of the connections between global and local issues. This course examines critical global social issues, policies, and social welfare institutions in different regions of the world with special attention to human rights, the process of globalization, and its effect on social welfare and human needs. A key premise of the course is to recognize the value conflicts that influence global and international social interventions. The role of international organizations and nongovernmental organizations (NGOs) in shaping international welfare policy and services is also explored.

Course Objectives

After successful completion of this course students will be able to

1. define key frameworks for international social welfare practice (e.g., social development, globalization, human rights,) and use them to analyze and address social problems such as poverty, exploitation, violence and poor health conditions;

2. explain the economic, political, environmental, and technological dimensions of globalization and their effect on social welfare;

3. describe the roles and functions of key international governmental, nongovernmental/ civil society organizations, and international conventions in promoting social welfare and sustainability;

4. identify data and resources used in analyzing global social conditions in international social welfare;

5. assess the prevalence of social problems and human rights violations affecting vulnerable groups in specific countries and regions;

6. compare and contrast the current state of welfare provision in different world regions and the different approaches to structuring social welfare programs and services.

Required Texts

Healy, L. (2008). *International social work*. New York, NY: Oxford University Press.

Mapp, S. (2008). *Human rights and social justice in a global society: An introduction to international social work*. New York, NY: Oxford University Press.

Rothenberg, P. (2006). *Beyond borders: Thinking critically about global issues*. New York, NY: Worth Publishers.

Additional Resources

International Social Work and Social Welfare Organizations

- **Global Impact (International Social Service Organizations):** www.charity.org
- **International Council on Social Welfare (ICSW):** www.icsw.org
- **International Association of Schools of Social Work (IASSW):** www.iassw-aiets.org
- **Inter-University Consortium for International Development (IUCISD):** www.socialdevelopment.net
- **International Federation of Social Workers (IFSW):** www.ifsw.org
- **European Institute for Social Work:** www.socialeurope.de
- **European Centre for Social Welfare Policy and Research (Vienna):** www.euro.centre.org
- **Latin American Network Information Center (LANIC):** http://lanic.utexas.edu/la/region/socialwork/

U.S. National Organizations

- Council on Social Work Education (CSWE) Katherine A. Kendall Institute for International Education http://www.cswe.org/CentersInitiatives/KAKI/KAKIResources.aspx
- National Association of Social Workers (USA)
- Association for Community Organization and Social Administration (ACOSA)

International Social Work Journals

- *Asia Pacific Journal of Social Work* (National University of Singapore in collaboration with the Asia Pacific Association of Schools of Social Work)
- *Australian Social Work*
- *British Journal of Social Work*
- *Caribbean Journal of Social Work*
- *European Journal of Social Work*
- *Indian Journal of Social Work*
- *International Social Work* (official journal of IFSW, IASSW, and ICSW)
- *Journal of Social Development in Africa* (School of Social Work, Harare, Zimbabwe)
- *Journal of the International Consortium for Social Development*
- *Social Work/Maatskaplike Werk* (South Africa)
- *Social Worker/Travailleur Social* (Canadian Association of Social Workers)

United Nations (UN) Resources

There are many excellent UN resources with important human rights, social welfare, and social development reports, and the UN conventions on human rights.

The general UN website is www.un.org. Each UN organization has its own website. Try www. unicef.org_and www.undp.org_for a start.

Additional Data

- Social security programs throughout the world, Social Security Online, research statistics, and policy analysis: www.ssa.gov

- The International Gay and Lesbian Human Rights Commission: www.iglhrc.org

- International Labour Organization (ILO) www.ilo.org

- eAtlas of the millennium goals

Role of Faculty and Students

The instructor will lecture, facilitate class discussions and experiential exercises, model and encourage open discussion, and foster an environment in which students' values, knowledge, and experiences can be explored and their diverse perspectives can be understood, respected, and critically examined. The instructor will also provide readings, assignment information, and be available for consultation and feedback. Assignments will be returned in a timely manner. The instructor invites students to give feedback and suggestions throughout the course.

Assignments and Grading Criteria

Class Discussion Facilitation on Readings

Students will sign up for and be responsible for generating two thought-provoking discussion questions on two of the week's readings and to facilitate a 20–30 minute discussion. Start with a brief introduction/overview of the important points of the readings. The discussion questions should demonstrate that you have read and thought about the materials and explored key themes that emerged and stimulated your interest. Discussion questions should be e-mailed to the instructor and class members by noon of the day before the class. Late questions will be docked 2 points. The instructor will bring a sign-up sheet to class. You should bring copies of the questions to class to distribute. (10 points)

Short Topical Papers on Country of Choice (35 total points)

Select a country of interest from the Global South (should select one by the second week of class) that will be the focus of your research for the semester. The assignments for the short papers are as follows.

Paper 1: Social Development Profile/Assessment

These items serve as an assessment of the country.

- A brief history of the country

- An outline specifying its major ethnic/racial groups; identify/describe groups facing marginalization/social exclusion

- A demographic profile (e.g., total population, population growth rate, age structure,

percentage urban population, life expectancy, infant mortality rates, maternal mortality rates, fertility rates, HIV rates, or any other indicators of interest to you)

- A poverty profile (e.g., income inequality, poverty levels, access to clean water, per capita health expenditures, adult literacy rate, global poverty ranking, ranking on the human development index)

- A brief economic profile (e.g., GDP, GDP growth rate, major industries, major agricultural products, military expenditures, level of high-technology exports, level of foreign investment, foreign debt)

What do the data tell you about the country and its level of human development? Compare this data to that of another country (or countries) in the region or to the United States. You might also find it helpful to organize the information into tables. The assessment should be no more than five pages long and should demonstrate some analysis of the information you present. (10 points)

Paper 2: Social Welfare Services Profile and Analysis

What types of social assistance (government programs targeting poor and/or vulnerable groups such as public assistance or medical programs) and social insurance programs (government programs providing protection against loss of income due to sickness, old age, or unemployment such as social security programs) does the country offer?

Based on your previous country assessment of social development indicators, evaluate how effectively the formal social welfare system corresponds to the country's social conditions. Does it reach those in need? Are there gaps in coverage among certain segments of citizens? (Keep in mind the number of people involved in the informal and formal economies). No more than five pages, including reference material. (10 points)

Paper 3: Status of Human Rights

Review of information on the country's human rights issues or track record. Using the information gathered, identify and describe the state of human rights in the country. No more than three pages. (5 points)

Paper 4: Status of Women

Summarize data and information on the status of women and gender equality using gender development indicators and other sources. Using the information gathered from gender development indicators and other sources describe the status of women in the country and the key issues confronting women. No more than 3 pages. (5 points)

Paper 5: Social Work/ Social Work Education

A description of the status of social work in the country (school of social work and social work programs structure, type of social work practiced (types of degrees, predominant methods used, focus of curriculum). No more than 3 pages.

NOTE: The amount of available information may vary according to the country in question, especially when considering countries with less developed social work education and programs. (5 points)

Class Presentation

During the last two classes pairs of students will deliver 30 minute presentations that summarize key aspects of their projects with data that compares and contrasts their respective countries regarding the major areas such as social development and key social issues or problems, human rights, gender equality, a brief description of its social assistance or social insurance programs, or any interesting/ innovative programs and the level of development of social work and its practice orientation in that country. Use of tables and other visual methods to convey the information concisely is encouraged (creativity, visuals, and handouts encouraged). The presentation is meant to provide an overview of your work to enable the class to learn about other's countries and maximize class opportunities for comparing and contrasting a range of nations. Select areas that highlight the unique characteristics of your countries. Students will be assigned to their teams by the instructor based on region or other factors of similarity among the countries selected by the class. (15 points)

Final Paper: Issue/Practice in Your Selected Country (30 points)

Students will identify an international issue or problem of interest in their selected countries. The paper will analyze the dimensions of the issue and the approaches by service delivery system and programs in the country or region within its historical, environmental, cultural, religious, political, and economic context specific to the identified issue. The paper should focus on an aspect of one of the six global issue areas identified in class: poverty; child welfare; preventable diseases, especially HIV/AIDS; women's issues; population migration; and environment/climate change.

Each student will develop a 12–15 page paper that addresses the following.

Global and Local Dimensions of the Problem/Issue

Provide a concise statement of the issue or problem in your selected country. Contrast this with background information about the global dimensions of the problem and its occurrence in the one or two countries of the region of your country and the United States. The discussion and assessment of the problem should incorporate human rights, social development, and sustainable development perspectives. Be sure to address the problem's relevance to social welfare and its relationship related to diversity and vulnerable populations.

Interventions and Strategies to Address the Issue/Problem

Provide descriptions of major social work, human services, or NGO activity in the country (key governmental, World Bank, World Health Organization, UNICEF, International Labour Organization, or NGO programs operating in the country that address the issue). Discuss the types of interventions and strategies used (e.g., direct practice approaches, organizing, policy practice) to address the problem in your selected country/region. Assess the importance and effectiveness of the work being done (organizational successes, limitations, failures, and challenges in regard to the problem-solving efforts). Be sure to highlight any innovative, culturally relevant programs or approaches and to assess the appropriateness of the projects given the country's social, cultural, political, and economic conditions. Include website information about such organizations when available.

Cross-National Comparisons/Reflections on Applicability to Local Practice

Summarize the major similarities and differences (from the United States) in the approaches used in your selected country to address the problem. How do the approaches reflect the cultural context of your

selected country? Discuss the applicability of (a) approaches used in the country or region that you think would be useful in local interventions here regarding the problem and (b) approaches used to address the problem in the United States that you think would be useful in the country being compared.

Use at least 10 references, including peer-reviewed journals and research reports from credible international agencies or NGOs. Make every effort to include sources from the region or country in question. Resources that will help in the development and research of the paper will be discussed over the course of the seminar, and many are listed on the syllabus. The paper will be assessed for writing, organization, and integration of course content. Use American Psychological Association format. The bibliography and any appendices you may attach are not part of the body or text of the paper.

Students will submit a one-page (ungraded) preliminary identification of the issue paper to class.

Lessons Learned/Reflections Paper (5 points; due with final paper)

Students are urged to reflect on the material covered over the course of the semester and what was learned or changes in perspective that resulted. Some areas you may want to include are how your thinking changed about this country, conditions in the United States, the state of human rights, or world politics as a result of your research; how this material will affect your approach to social work practice; and what, if anything, especially provoked your thinking or stirred your passion for action.

The final paper due date is scheduled for after the last class so that no one would have to do the final presentation and portfolio on the same day and to allow sufficient time to reflect on the final information gathered. It may be handed in earlier.

Grading

Course grades will be based on the following criteria:

- **Short topical papers:** 35 points
- **Discussion facilitation:** 10 points
- **Social issue/practice paper:** 30 points
- **Class presentation:** 15 points
- **Final reflection paper:** 5 points
- **Class participation:** 5 points

Expectations Regarding Written Work

Students are expected to write papers that conform to guidelines of the *Publication Manual of the American Psychological Association* (APA; 6th ed.). Appropriately cite, using APA style, any references that you use. Papers must conform to other APA guidelines (e.g., double-spaced, gender-neutral language, expressing numbers in figures versus in words, page numbers, headings and subheadings, 1-inch margins on all sides, use of a title page for major scholarly papers). Become familiar with the APA guidelines. Students are expected to hand in papers with correct grammar and spelling, and that are free of typographical errors.

Course Outline

Unit One: Conceptual Framework (Weeks 1–6)

WEEK 1: Introduction to the field of international social work and course framework (globalization, human rights, social development, diversity); review of syllabus

Reading: Healy, Chapter 1: International social work: What is it? Why is it relevant?

WEEK 2: Colonialism and its legacy: Examining the roots of global inequality

Reading:

- Mapp, Chapter 1
- Rothenberg , pp. 37–43, 88–106, 126, and 150–157
- Loewenberg, S. (2007). Anti-Americanism: Is anger at the US growing? *CQ Researcher*, March 2007.

WEEK 3: Overview of globalization/global financial institutions

Reading:

- Healy, Chapter 2, Globalization
- Rothenberg,419–431, 446–460, 158–163, 507–514
- Moghadam, V. (2009). "Global Justice Movements" in V. Moghadam, *Globalization and Social Movements*. (New York, NY: Rowman and Littlefield). Come to class prepared to discuss a movement that piqued your interest or that you feel passionate about.

Recommended:

Achbar, M., & Abbott, J. (Directors). (2003). *The corporation*. Canada: Zeitgeist Films.

Black, S. (Director). (2001). *Life and debt*. United States: New Yorker Films.

Prigoff, A. (2003). *Economic development history: Breton Woods to the present*. In A. Prigoff *Economics for social workers*. New York, NY: Brooks/Cole.

A Better World is Possible! Alternatives to Economic Globalization, Report Summary, 2002. Available from International Forum on Globalization. http://www.ifg.org/alt_eng.pdf

WEEK 4: Social development/poverty

Readings:

- Cox, D., & Pawar, M. (2006). *International social work: Issues, strategies, and programs*. Thousand Oaks, CA: SAGE. Chapters 7 & 8, pp. 161–212.
- Rothenberg 323–339, 398–399
- Midgely, J. (2007). Development, social development and human rights. In E. Reichert (Ed.), *Challenges in human rights* (pp. 97–120). New York, NY: Columbia University Press.
- Healy, Appendices B, C, D.

- Ashoka. (2006). Innovator for the poor: The story of Fazle H. Abed and the founding of BRAC. United States: Ashoka Global Academy.

WEEK 5: Global human rights

Readings:

- Mapp, Chapter 2

- Healy, Chapter 3, Development and Human Rights

- Mapp, Appendix One, United Nations Universal Declaration of Human Rights

- Ife, J. (2007). Cultural relativism and community activism. In E. Reichert (Ed.), *Challenges in human rights* (pp. 77–96). New York, NY: Columbia University Press.

Class members are responsible for viewing and coming to class prepared to discuss at least one of the documents on these sites:

- **Amnesty International:** www.amnesty.org

- **Human Rights Watch:** www.hrw.org

- **United Nations Office of High Commissioner for Human Rights:** http://www.unhchr.ch/

- **U.S. State Department—Human Rights:** http://www.state.gov/g/drl/hr/

- **U.S. State Department, Human Rights Country Report:** www.state.gov/www/global/ human_rights/hrp_reports_mainhp.html

WEEK 6: International social welfare organizations: The United Nations and nongovernmental organizations disaster and relief

Readings:

- Healy, Chapter 5, International Social Welfare Organizations and Their Functions

- Healy, Chapter 10, International Relief and Development Practice

- Rothenberg pp. 598–601. Students should do Internet research on one organization on this list and come to class prepared to describe their work.

Recommended:

Aristede J. (2005). A view of globalization from below. In B. Bigelow & B. Peterson (Eds.) *Rethinking globalization: Teaching for justice in an unjust world* (pp. 9–13). Milwaukee, WI: Rethinking Schools.

Class presentation: Dieuveut Gaity, PhD student, former UNDP worker, "Experiences in UN Disaster Relief in Haiti"

Unit Two: Global Social Issues/Vulnerable Groups (Weeks 7–11)

WEEK 7: Global migration

Readings:

- Mapp, Chapter 3

- Rothenberg, pp. 481–487, 526–539

- Bales, K. (2004). *India: The plowman's lunch in disposable people: New slavery in the global economy.* Berkeley: University of California Press. Read pp. 195–231.

Tentative field visit to International Institute to meet with representatives of various programs for immigrants, refugees, and trafficked persons.

WEEK 8: Global gender issues

This class examines the status of women through the areas of gender violence, trafficking, and poverty/income generation strategies.

Readings:

- Mapp, Chapter 7

- Rothenberg pp. 278–287, 594–597.

- Foerstel, K. (2008, May). Women's rights: Are violence and discrimination against women declining. *Congressional Quarterly*, 53–85.

- Goodey, J. (2004). Sex trafficking in women from Central and East European countries: Promoting a "victim centered" and "woman centered" approach to criminal justice intervention. *Feminist Review, 76,* 26-45.

- The Convention on the Elimination of All Forms of Discrimination against Women (CEDAW): http://www.un.org/womenwatch/daw/cedaw/cedaw.htm

Film clip: Disney, A., & Reticker, G. (Directors). (2008). *Pray the devil back to hell.* United States: Fork Films.

WEEK 9: Children/child welfare

This section examines street children, child slavery, child soldiers, and adoption as issues experienced by children in many countries of the world. The UN Convention on the Rights of the Child is examined.

Readings:

- Mapp, Chapter 4

- Rothenberg, pp. 396–397

- Kombarakaran, F. (2004) Street children of Bombay: Their stresses and strategies of coping. *Children and Youth Services Review, 26,* 853–871.

- UN Convention on the Rights of the Child: www.unicef/org/crc/crc.htm

- Ryan, E. (2006). For the best interests of the children: Why the Hague Convention needs to go farther. *Boston College International and Comparative Law Review, 29,* 353–383.

- Cheung, M., & Delavega, E. (2011). Child savings accounts: Learning from poverty policies in the world. *International Social Work, 55*(1), 71–94.

- Felton, J. (2008, July). Child soldiers: Are more aggressive efforts needed to protect children? *Congressional Quarterly*, 23–52.

Review the websites of one these and come to class prepared to discuss it:

- Coalition to Stop the Use of Child Soldiers: http://www.child-soldiers.org/

- United Nations Children's Fund (UNICEF): www.unicef.org

- International Programme on the Elimination of Child Labour (IPEC) www.ilo.org/ipec

Film clips:

- Nair, M. (Director). (1988) *Salaam Bombay*. United States: Cinecom Pictures.
- Feurherz, D. (Director). (2009). *War child*. United States: Reel U Films

WEEK 10: Health/the global AIDS epidemic

Readings:

- Mapp, Chapter 6
- Rothenberg, pp. 356–367, 517–522
- Selgelid, M. (2008). Improving global health: counting reasons why. *Developing World Bioethics, 8*(2), 115–125.
- Wetzel, J. (2004). Mental health lessons from abroad. In M. C. Hokenstad & J. Midgely (Eds.) *Lessons from abroad*. New York, NY: NASW Press.

Recommended:

United Nations. (2004). *Report on the global HIV/AIDS epidemic*. See http://img.thebody.com/unaids/pdfs/unaids_report_summary2004.pdf

WEEK 11: War and conflict

This section examines political and ethnic violence and contemporary wars and their implications for health and social being.

Readings:

- Mapp, Chapter 5
- Lyons, K. (2006). Loss as a Universal Concept. In Lyons et al. (eds). *International perspectives on social work: Global conditions and local practice*. London, UK: Palgrave.
- Rothenberg, pp. 307–314
- De Jong J.T., Komproe, I.H., Van Ommeren, M., El Masri, M., Avaya, M., Khaled, N. ... Somasundaram, D. (2001). Lifetime events and posttraumatic stress disorder in 4 postconflict Settings. *JAMA, 286*, 555–562.

Film: Quinn, C. (Director). (2007). *God grew tired of us*. United States: Newmarket Films.

WEEK 12: Climate change/environmental sustainability

Readings:

- Von Doussa, J., Corkery, A., & Chartres, R. Human rights and climate change. *Australian International Law Journal, 14*, 161–183.
- Oxfam America. (2008). Adaptation 101: How climate change hurts poor communities—and how we can help. Available from http://www.oxfamamerica.org/publications/adaptation-101
- Rothenberg, 540–541, 580–584

Recommended:

- Bloomberg, M., & Aggarwala, R. (2008). Think locally, act globally. *American Journal of Preventive Medicine. 35*, 414–423.

Unit Three: Social Work as a Global Profession (Weeks 12–14)

WEEK 13: Global social work practice and policies: Similarities, differences and challenges

Readings:

- Healy, L. M. (2001). Chapter 4, Social work around the world today; Chapter 9, Values and ethics for international professional action

- Mapp, Chapter 9, Appendix B

- Gray, M. (2005). Dilemmas of international social work: Paradoxical processes in indigenization, universalism and imperialism. *International Journal of Social Welfare, 14*, 231–238.

Select one of the following based on interest:

- McDonald, C. (2007).Wizards of Oz: The radical tradition in Australian social work. In M. Lavalette & I. Ferguson (Eds.). *International social work and the radical tradition.* London, UK: Venture Press.

- Ramos, B. M., Botton, M. L., & Wright, G. A. (2009). Peru: A focus on individual practice. In C. Tice & D. Long (Eds.), *International social work: Policy and practice.* Hoboken, NJ: Wiley.

- Norward, J. (2007). Social work and social activism in post-democratic South Africa. In M. Lavalette & I. Ferguson (Eds.), *International social work and the radical tradition.* London, UK: Venture Press.

- Midgley, J., & Livermore, M. (2004). Social development: Lessons from the Global South. In M. C. Hokenstad & J. Midgely (Eds.), *Lessons from abroad: Adapting international social welfare innovations* (pp. 117–135). New York, NY: NASW Press.

Student Presentations

WEEK 14: Wrap-up

Readings:

- Healy, Chapter 12, Understanding and influencing global policy

- Healy, Chapter 14, Social work as a force for global change and development

Student Presentations

Social issues paper and reflection paper due.

Women, Children, and Families: Policies and Programs

Robin Spath
University of Connecticut

This three-credit elective is available to all students as well as being the required course for those seeking to complete the Women, Children, and Families substantive area. It focuses on selected policies and programs for women and children, in particular those dealing with income supports, domestic violence, foster care and adoption, and child maltreatment. Particular attention will be paid to how social problems such as poverty, family violence, and poor parenting are conceptualized as women's issues and how the policies that seek to address these problems affect women. Throughout the semester we will consider human rights-based and feminist approaches to policies and programs for women, children, and families. Throughout the course we examine the effects of gender, racism, class, ethnicity, and sexual orientation on policy formation, implementation, and social change.

The course will meet in four sessions from 9 am to 5:00 pm as follows:

- Unit I: Overview: Definitions, Dimensions, and Dilemmas
- Unit II: The Right to Adequate Income
- Unit III: The Right to Protection From Harm
- Unit IV: The Right to Continuity of Nurturing Relationships and Defining Family Membership

Learning Outcomes

After completing this course, students will

A. have a greater understanding of the effects of gender in social problem identification, policy development, and implementation from a national and a global perspective;

B. better understand and appreciate the diversity in contemporary American families with regard to form, culture, and ethnicity;

C. be able to delineate and critically examine selected major policies and programs that support—or fail to support—the integrity, needs, and values of women, children, and families;

D. become more familiar with feminist and human rights perspectives and theories in critiquing social policies and programs, and;

E. be able to identify social policies that consider women principally as family members—mainly mothers—rather than as individuals and explore alternative solutions to these social policies.

Learning Activities

The course includes a variety of learning activities including brief lectures, class discussion, guest speakers, audiovisual materials, and small group exercises. Student preparation for and participation in class discussions is essential. Reading response papers and a policy advocacy project, including written updates, a summary paper, and brief in-class presentation, offer students an opportunity to deepen knowledge about key social issues and develop policy analysis skills. These assignments are based on each student's particular area of practice expertise or interest in the general area of services and programs for families.

Texts

The readings required for this class are on electronic course reserve. Students who have questions about or problems with accessing the site should contact the Learning Resource Center.

Requirements

See below for assignment guidelines.

Student grades for this course will be based on the following:

- Preparing for, attending, and actively participating in all four class sessions, including participating in in-class pop quizzes and exercises (10%)

- Writing short response papers based on the readings (50%)

- Completing an advocacy project and presenting in class on that project (20%) and submitting a brief paper summarizing the project (20%)

Written work should meet graduate standards of writing proficiency and should conform to accepted standards of citation. The format found in the *Publication Manual of the American Psychological Association* (APA; 6th ed.) should be used for all papers unless otherwise noted. Written assignments will be graded based on the following, along with other criteria identified in each assignment:

- Thoroughness and completeness of content

- Clarity and logic of presentation

- Evidence of critical thought

- Quality of writing

Assignments Prior to the First Class

Most special schedule classes that meet for fewer than the 10 weekly sessions will require an assignment due at the first class. Registered students may obtain the preassignment 2 weeks prior to the start date of the semester via e-mail. It is the students' responsibility to obtain the assignment.

Reading Assignments

Unit I: Overview: Definitions, Orientations, and Dilemmas

Abramovitz, M. (2001). Everyone is still on welfare: The role of redistribution in social policy. *Social Work, 46,* 297–308.

Allen, S., Flaherty, C., & Ely, G. (2010). Throwaway moms: Maternal incarceration and the criminalization of poverty. *Affilia: Journal of Women and Social Work, 25*(2), 160–172.

Alzate, M. M. (2009). Sexual and reproductive rights practice in social work. *Affilia: Journal of Women and Social Work, 24*(2), 108–119.

Hyde, C. (2009). Feminist approaches to social policy. In J. Midgley & M. Livermore (Eds.), *The handbook of social policy* (pp. 247–262; 2nd ed.). Los Angeles, CA: SAGE.

Libal, K., Mapp, S., Ihrig, E., & Ron, A. (2011). The United Nations Convention on the Rights of the Child: Children can wait no longer for their rights. *Social Work, 56,* 367–370.

Mama, R. (2010). Needs, rights and the human family: The practicality of the Convention on the Rights of the Child. *Child Welfare, 89*(5), 177–189.

Morell, C. (1987). Cause is function: Toward a feminist model of integration for social work. *Social Service Review, 61*(1), 144–155.

Reichert, E. (2012). Women and the human rights framework. In L. M. Healy & R. J. Link (Eds.), *Handbook of international social work: Human rights, development and the global profession* (pp. 447–451). New York, NY: Oxford University Press.

Schott, L. (2009, March 19). *An introduction to TANF.* Washington, DC: Center on Budget and Policy Priorities. Retrieved from http://www.cbpp.org/files/1-22-02tanf2.pdf

United Nations. (1979). *Convention on the elimination of all forms of discrimination against women.*

United Nations. (1989). *Convention on the rights of the child.*

Unit II: The Right to Adequate Income—Work, Child Care, and Income Assistance

Poverty and Welfare

Biggerstaff, M. A., McGrath Morris, P., & Nichols-Casebolt, A. (2002). Living on the edge: Examination of people attending food pantries and soup kitchens. *Social Work, 47,* 267–277.

Broussard, A. C., Joseph, A. L., & Thompson, M. (2012). Stressors and coping strategies used by single mothers living in poverty. *Affilia: Journal of Women and Social Work, 27,* 190–204.

Cook, J. T. & Frank, D. A. (2008). Food security, poverty, and human development in the United States. *Annals of the New York Academy of Sciences, 1136*(1), 193–209.

Gustafson, K. S. (2011). The criminalization of poverty. In *Cheating welfare: Public assistance and the criminalization of poverty* (pp. 51–70). New York, NY: NYU Press.

Human Rights Watch. (2010). Selected pages from *My so-called emancipation: From foster care to homelessness for California youth.* New York, NY: Human Rights Watch. (Read pages 1–13 and 64–66).

Laakso, J. (2000). Child support policy: Some critical issues and the implications for social work. *Social Work, 45,* 367–370.

National Public Radio. (2008, November 25). [Podcast]. *Day to day: The state of the social safety net.* Available at http://www.npr.org/templates/story/story.php?storyId=97458868

Pressman, S. (2003). Feminist explanations for the feminization of poverty. *Journal of Economic Issues, 37,* 353–361.

Roll, S. & East, J. (2012). Child care as a work support: A socialist feminist policy analysis. *Affilia, 27,* 358–370.

Tillmon, J. (2003). Welfare is a women's issue. In G. Mink & R. Solinger (Eds.), *Welfare: A documentary history of U.S. policy and politics* (pp. 373–379). New York, NY: NYU Press.

WNPR, Connecticut Public Broadcasting Network. (2013, January 3). [Podcast]. *Where we live: Feeding our children.* Available at WNPR/Connecticut Public Broadcasting Network WNPR/Connecticut Public Broadcasting Network http://www.yourpublicmedia.org/node/23566

WNPR, Connecticut Public Broadcasting Network. (2011, February 17). [Podcast]. *Where we live: Joette Katz and DCF's new direction.* Available at http://www.yourpublicmedia.org/node/10569

WNPR, Connecticut Public Broadcasting Network. (2008, February 19). [Podcast]. *Where we live:*

Office of the Child Advocate. Available at http://www.cpbn.org/program/where-we-live/episode/office-child-advocate

Unit III: The Right to Protection From Harm: Child Maltreatment and Family Violence

Child Maltreatment and Juvenile Justice

Goodkind, S. (2005). Gender-specific services in the juvenile justice system: A critical examination. *AFFILIA: Journal of Women and Social Work, 20*(1), 52–70.

Jonson-Reid, M., Drake, B., & Kohl, P.L. (2009). Is the overrepresentation of the poor in child welfare caseloads due to bias or need? *Children and Youth Services Review, 31*, 422–427.

Lewis, M. (2011). The human rights of children in conflict with the law: Lessons for the US human rights movement. In S. Hertel & K. Libal (Eds.), *Human rights in the United States: Beyond exceptionalism* (pp. 255–273). New York, NY: Cambridge University Press.

McGowan, B. G. & Walsh, E. M. (2000) Policy challenges for child welfare in the new century. *Child Welfare, 79*(1), 11–27.

Risley-Curtiss, C., & Heffernan, K. (2003). Gender biases in child welfare. *Affilia, 18*, 395–410.

Stein, J. T. (2000). The adoption and safe families act: Creating a false dichotomy between parents' and childrens' rights. *Families in Society, 81*, 586–592.

Svevo-Cianci, K., & Velazquez, S. C. (2010). Convention on the Rights of the Child special protection measures: Overview of implications and value for children in the United States. *Child Welfare, 89*(5), 139–157.

Women, Families, and Violence

Andrews, A., & Khavinson, J. (2011). From international to domestic approaches: Battling DV in the United States. *Domestic Violence Report, 17*(2), 17–32.

Flaherty, M. P. (2010). Constructing a world beyond intimate partner abuse. *Affilia, 25*, 224–235.

Harcum, J. M. (2002). Razing the castle: Making domestic violence a public issue. *Praxis, 2*, 3240.

Irwin, J. (2008). (Dis)counted stories: Domestic violence and lesbians. *Qualitative Social Work, 7*(2), 199–215.

Johnson, S. P., & Sullivan, C. M. (2008). How child protection workers support or further victimize battered mothers. *AFFILIA: Journal of Women and Social Work, 23*, 242–258.

Josephson, J. (2002). The intersectionality of domestic violence and welfare in the lives of poor women. *Journal of Poverty, 6*(1), 1–20.

Laakso, J. H., & Drevdahl, D. (2006). Women, abuse, and the welfare bureaucracy. *AFFILIA: Journal of Women and Social Work, 21*, 84–96.

Morgaine, K. (2009). "You can't bite the hand . . .": Domestic violence and human rights. *Affilia, 24*, 31–43.

O'Shaughnessy, C. V. . (2010). *The elder justice act: Addressing elder abuse, neglect, and Exploitation*. Washington, DC: National Health Policy Forum. Available at http://www.nhpf.org/library/the-basics/Basics_ElderJustice_11-30-10.pdf

Teaster, P. B., Wangmo, T., & Anetzberger, G. J. (2010). A glass half full: The dubious history of elder abuse policy. *Journal of Elder Abuse & Neglect, 22* (1–2), 6–15.

van Wormer, K. (2009). Restorative justice as social justice for victims of gendered violence: A standpoint feminist perspective. *Social Work, 54,* 107–116.

United Nations Declaration on the Elimination of Violence Against Women. (1979).

Unit IV: Defining Family Membership and the Right to Continuity of Nurturing Relationships

Relationships and Defining Family

United Nations Guidelines for the Alternative Care of Children. (2009).

Lind, A. (2004). Legislating the family: Heterosexist bias in social welfare policy frameworks. *Journal of Sociology and Social Welfare, 31*(4), 21–36.

Speziale, B., & Gopalakrishna, V. (2004). Social support and functioning of nuclear families headed by lesbian couples. *Affilia, 19,* 174–184.

Kinship Care and Family Connections

Cox, C. (2009). Custodial grandparents: Policies affecting care. *Journal of Intergenerational Relationships, 7*(2–3), 177–190.

U.S. Department of Health and Human Services, Administration for Children and Families. (n.d.). Overview: Fostering connections to success and increasing Adoptions Act of 2008, PL 110-351. Available at https://www.childwelfare.gov/systemwide/laws_policies/federal/index.cfm?event=federallegislation.viewlegis&id=121.

Gomes, M., & Ross-Sheriff, F. (2011). The impact of unintended consequences of the 1996 U.S. Immigration Reform Act on women. *Affilia, 26,* 117–124.

Gustavsson, N. S., & MacEachron, A. E. (2010). Sibling connections and reasonable efforts in public child welfare. *Families in Society: The Journal of Contemporary Social Services, 91*(1), 39–44.

Mapp, S. C., & Steinberg, C. (2007). Birth families as permanency resources for children in long-term foster care. *Child Welfare, 86*(1), 29–51.

National Public Radio. (2005, November 1). [Podcast]. *News & notes: Raising grandchildren in communities of color.* Available at http://www.npr.org/templates/story/story.php?storyId=4984113

Creating Permanency for Children and Families

Brooks, D., & Goldberg, S. (2001). Gay and lesbian adoptive and foster care placements: Can they meet the needs of waiting children? *Social Work, 46,* 147–157.

Cushing, G., & Greenblatt, S. B. (2009). Vulnerability to foster care drift after the termination of parental rights. *Research on Social Work Practice, 19,* 694–704.

National Public Radio Podcast Series: *Adoption in America.* http://www.npr.org/templates/story/story.php?storyId=12184872

National Public Radio. (2007, July 23). [Podcast]. *Part 1: Mother, son offer transracial adoption insights.* Available at http://www.npr.org/templates/story/story.php?storyId=12136864

National Public Radio. (2007, July 24). [Podcast]. *Part 2: An adoption gone wrong.* Available at http://www.npr.org/templates/story/story.php?storyId=12185524

National Public Radio. (2007, July 26). [Podcast]. *Part 4: An unexpected message, a family redefined.* Available at http://www.npr.org/templates/story/story.php?storyId=12222885

National Public Radio. (2007, July 27). [Podcast]. *Watching a daughter grow via MySpace*. Available at http://www.npr.org/templates/story/story.php?storyId=12282199

National Public Radio. (2010, April 8). [Podcast]. *After 18, foster kids face a tough road ahead*. Available at http://www.npr.org/templates/story/story.php?storyId=125729965

National Public Radio. (2008, May 27). [Podcast]. *Talk of the nation: Transracial adoption: It's complicated*. Available at http://www.npr.org/blogs/talk/2008/05/transracial_adoption_its_compl.html

Pine, B. A., Spath, R., & Gosteli, S. (2005). Defining and achieving family reunification. In G. P. Mallon & P. M. Hess (Eds.), *Child welfare for the 21st century: A handbook of practices, policies, and programs* (pp. 378–391). New York, NY: Columbia University Press.

Rotabi, K. S., & Bromfield, N. F. (2012). The decline in intercountry adoptions and new practices of global surrogacy: Global exploitation and human rights concerns. *Affilia, 27*, 129–141.

U.S. Government Accountability Office. (2007). *African American children in foster care: Additional HHS assistance needed to help states reduce the proportion in care*. [GAO07-816]. Washington, DC: U.S. Congress. (Read the introduction/summary carefully and review the remainder of the document.)

Wolfgram, S. M. (2008). Openness in adoption: What we know so far—a critical review of the literature. *Social Work, 53*, 133–142.

Assignments

Reading Response Papers. Due at the beginning of Sessions 2, 3, 4

For class Sessions 2, 3, and 4, you will prepare a three- to four-page, double-spaced, typed essay in which you write an analytical response to the key issues and themes raised by the required readings. When writing your essay, consider how the readings provoked new ideas or otherwise challenged you to think about social policy for women, children, and families in the United States. What questions or critical thoughts do the readings raise for you? What interests you about the issues raised and why? Integrate direct reference to at least four of the readings in your response paper. Be sure that it is apparent you are engaging the ideas raised in the readings in depth—show that you are making connections across readings and thinking critically about the implications of the materials for your own work and the course. Do not summarize the readings.

You may cite authors simply by name and date, but if you include a quote, please include the page number from which it is taken. Turn in your essay in hard copy.

This is a substantive part of the course and thus will count for 50% of your overall grade. Papers will be evaluated based on the clarity and insightfulness of the writing and the adequacy of engagement with assigned readings. They are not to be summaries of the arguments, but should reflect your critical reflections. Everyone's papers will be different, engaging key themes and articles based on your interest.

Policy Advocacy Project

Each student will choose to do an advocacy project either individually or in a small group (of no more than three or four). Below is a list of possible options, and you may have in mind others to propose.

1. Organize and conduct a meeting of constituents of a local advocacy group (e.g., Love Makes a Family, CT Juvenile Justice Alliance)

2. Attend and speak or testify at public meetings (e.g., State Board of Education, other state agency board meeting, local school board meeting, city or county council, state court of appeals, legislative committee).

3. Visit a local or state public official and advocate your position on the issue of your choice.

4. Organize a letter writing campaign on an issue of your choice.

5. Organize a political rally or protest.

6. Create a blog or Facebook page to engage on a particular policy issue.

7. Create a short video public service announcement that effectively outlines your policy advocacy issue and consider posting on YouTube.

Students may complete an advocacy project other than one from this list with instructor preapproval.

Due Session II: A brief summary of proposed policy advocacy project; who will be involved in the project; what is the topic of interest; target of the project; possible stakeholders; and, briefly, its connection to social work policy practice (1–2 pages). You could include reference to how it intersects with the NASW *Code of Ethics*, human rights principles, and/or the policy statements held in *Social Work Speaks* (on reserve at the library).

Due Session IV: Detailed written summary of your policy advocacy project/event (4–5 pages).

After completing the advocacy project, each student will write a detailed written summary of the project, including the following.

- Which policy advocacy approach was selected and why this was the best strategy for enacting change.

- Summary of the policy advocacy project (e.g., students/organizations they worked with, what they did, what changes were suggested, how they supported their position).

- Description of the outcome of the policy advocacy project.

- Plans for future advocacy.

Topic selection for advocacy project (instructor must approve your choice in advance): Select a social problem or need of children, families, and/or women that interests you from the list below.

I. Right to Adequate Income

- Child support

- Maternity/family leave

- Child care (including Head Start and Care4Kids)

- Work and gender discrimination

- TANF or SNAP reform (again)

- Wage discrimination

- Health insurance for families

- Support/access for kinship caregivers

II. Right to Protection from Harm

- Domestic violence
- Sexual assault
- Child neglect
- Physical abuse of children
- Sexual abuse of children
- Elder abuse
- Substance abuse during pregnancy
- Hate crimes
- Juvenile or adult detention and reform for children and women

III. Right to Continuity of Nurturing Relationships and Defining Family Membership

- Adolescent emancipation from foster care
- Kinship care
- Reunification and/or permanency planning for children in care
- Transracial adoption
- Open adoption
- Gay/lesbian foster care/adoption
- Teen-aged pregnancy programs
- Single parent families
- Reproductive rights/abortion

Social Policy Service and Delivery: Module Incorporating Human Rights

M. C. "Terry" Hokenstad
Case Western Reserve University

This first semester foundation policy course examines the American social welfare system in a global context. It surveys the philosophical, historical, and socioeconomic foundations of social welfare and the evolution of social policy and the social work profession in the United States. It then focuses on the problems of poverty and discrimination and analyzes the adequacy and effectiveness of policies and resulting programs designed to address those problems. Consideration is given to the principles of economic and social justice along with other values of the social work profession in this analysis. The connections between social policy and social work practice are also emphasized.

The course then addresses social policy in an interdependent world. Attention is given to cross-national comparisons of social policies designed to prevent and alleviate poverty and social exclusion. Human rights issues and the programs of international organizations designed to promote and protect human rights are discussed. Finally, social work's roles in the field of human rights, both at home and abroad, are considered.

Course Objectives

Value, knowledge, and skill outcomes, from the Mandel School of Applied Social Sciences Ability Based Learning Program are shown in italic after each objective.

By the end of this course, students should be able to

A. understand the functions and structure of social welfare within contemporary American society (*Think Critically*);

B. demonstrate knowledge of how the dynamic interaction of ideas, socioeconomic trends, events, and individuals have influenced the historical development of social welfare policy and the social work profession (*Think Critically, Communicate Effectively, and Advocate for Social Justice*);

C. demonstrate a knowledge of how the dynamic interaction of ideas, socioeconomic trends, events, and individuals have influenced the historical development of social welfare policy and the social work profession (*Think Critically, Communicate Effectively, and Advocate for Social Justice*);

D. analyze and critique the policies and programs designed to address problems of poverty and discrimination in American society (*Think Critically, Communicate Effectively, Value a Diverse World, and Integrate Social Work Values and Ethics*);

E. apply an understanding of social theory, poverty research, and ethical reasoning to the analysis of a substantive piece of social policy (*Think Critically and Communicate Effectively*);

F. identify and use links between social welfare policy and social work practice (*Think Critically, Communicate Effectively, Advocate for Social Justice, and Integrate Social Work Values and Ethics*);

G. appreciate and understand the value of cross-national comparisons in the critique of social policies and programs (*Think Critically and Value a Diverse World*);

H. appreciate and understand the global context of human rights issues and actions (*Think Critically and Value a Diverse World*); and

I. understand the forms and mechanisms of discrimination and social exclusion and apply strategies of advocacy and social changes that advance social and economic justice (*Think Critically and Advocate for Social Justice*).

Course Outline

- **Module I:** Social Welfare: Contemporary Issues and Contextual Influences
- **Module II:** Policy Analysis and Social Action
- **Module III:** Social Policy in an Interdependent World

Module III: Social Policy in an Interdependent World

Content

- Globalization and the Future of Social Policy
  - Realities of global interdependence
  - Social and sustainable development
  - Human services and the service society
  - What role for social work?
- Lessons From Abroad: Adapting International Social Welfare Innovations
  - Comparative framework of policy analysis
    - Societal context
    - Social policy examination
    - Social policy comparison
      - Cross national similarities and differences
      - Differential effects
  - Examples
    - Scandinavian poverty prevention policies
    - British personal social service programs
- International Organizations and Humanitarian Programs
  - The United Nations (UN)
    - The Economic and Social Council
    - Humanitarian programs in the UN family
- International Nongovernmental Organizations

- Human rights issues and responses
  - » Human rights violations in a global society
    - Human slavery in the United States and around the world
    - Violations of civil and political rights
    - Violations of economic and social rights
  - » The International Bill of Human Rights
    - Universal Declaration of Human Rights (1948)
    - International Covenants on Human Rights (1966)
  - » Human diversity and human rights
    - Declaration and International Convention on the Elimination of all Forms of Racial Discrimination (1963–1968)
    - Convention on the Elimination of all Forms of Discrimination Against Women (1981)
  - » Social work's role in promoting and protecting human rights
    - Human rights and social work ethics
    - Human rights and vulnerable populations
    - Human rights dilemmas for social workers
- Human Migration in the 21st Century
  - Immigrants: legal and illegal
    - » The immigration process
    - » Transferable human capital
    - » Implications for human services
  - The state of the world's refugees
    - » Defending refugee rights
    - » Return and reintegration
    - » Statelessness and citizenship
    - » Social work's role in immigrant relocation and refugee resettlement
- Adjustment to receiving country
  - Social and health services
  - Advocacy to prevent marginalization

Readings

Karger & Stoesz. (2012). *American social welfare policy.* Boston, MA: Pearson. (Chapter 18)

van Wormer, K. (2003). *Social welfare: A world view.* Chicago, IL: Nelson Hall. (Chapters 10 and 11)

Hokenstad, M. C., & Midgley, J. (2004). *Lessons from Abroad: Adapting international social welfare innovations.* Washington, DC: NASW Press.

Reichert, E. (2006). *Understanding human rights: An exercise book.* Thousand Oaks, CA: SAGE.

Human Rights and Social Policy: International and Global Perspectives

Jody Olsen
University of Maryland

The global human rights and social policy module is designed for use in foundation year social welfare and social policy courses.

Students are introduced to four key areas:

- Social policy as social action sanctioned by society and how societies' beliefs and values affect policies

- Global interdependence and its influence on society and social policy

- Roles of international agencies and organizations on influencing global, regional, and national social policy, and human rights

- Social work intervention opportunities and methods for globally framed social policy reform

Learning Objectives

1. An understanding of the relationship of stated social policies to society values and behaviors and variability of policies within societies based on these values and beliefs

2. Knowledge of the range of social policy priorities internationally as manifested in different societies

3. Knowledge of international organizations affecting global social policies and their strategies for affecting change

4. Opportunities for social policy intervention in international settings locally, regionally, and globally

Estimated Time for Module

The content could be covered in two course sessions or be integrated into components of three policy class sessions (relationship of social policies and societal values, beliefs, and behaviors; key international human rights and global policy organizations; roles for social work in global policy development and human rights advocacy).

The content is covered in lectures, class discussion, and small group discussions/exercises.

Suggested Locations in Social Welfare and Social Policy Foundation Year Courses

Learning Objectives 1 and 2 can be integrated into an introduction to social welfare course, specifically definitions of social welfare and social policy, selectivity versus universality, globalization and social policy, and social policy and social science.

Learning Objectives 3 and 4 can be integrated into definitions and dimensions of poverty and inequality, specifically, concepts and dimensions of poverty; and social trends and alternatives programs, specifically globalization, organizations affecting social policies, and alternative programs.

Educational Policy and Accreditation Standards (EPAS) Competencies

- Educational Policy (EP) 2.1.7—Apply knowledge of human behavior and the social environment.

  - Social workers are knowledgeable about .... the ways social systems promote or deter people in maintaining or achieving health and well-being, ...understanding biological, social, cultural, psychological, and spiritual development.

- EP 2.1.5—Advance human rights and social and economic justice.

  - Each person, regardless of position in society, has basic human rights, such as ....an adequate standard of living, health care, and education. Social workers recognize the global interconnections of oppression. Social work incorporates social justice practices in organizations, institutions, and society to ensure that these basic human rights are distributed equitably and without prejudice. (Council on Social Work Education, 2008)

NOTE: The permanent link containing the Power Point described here and other information is available on the CSWE Katherine A. Kendall Institute (KAKI) website (http://www.cswe.org/CentersInitiatives/KAKI/KAKIResources/63419.aspx).

PowerPoint Presentation

Slide 1: Title page

Slide 2: Learning objectives

Slide 3: Module use in social welfare and policy courses

Slide 4: Connections to EPAS Competencies: EP 2.1.7 – Apply knowledge of human behavior and the social environment; EP 2.1.5 – Advance human rights and social and economic justice

Slide 5: Global learning important for social work global action

- Emphasizes within three points why understanding global perspectives of social work issues affect an understanding of work at home and gives impetus for getting more engaged in global social work related issues.

Slide 6: What is social policy?

- Three different definitions of social policy are given, emphasizing that policy is societally driven, that policy sets action in code, and that policy action helps manage social problems and meet human needs. Policy defines action to meet problems and needs.

Slide 7: What are human rights?

- Three perspectives on human rights are given, with focus on the United Nations (UN) Universal Declaration of Human Rights (UDHR). These perspectives emphasize that *human rights* means "all human beings are born free and equal in dignity and rights." (UDHR, 1948)

Slide 8: Understanding Global and International Social Policies can Affect Social Work Practice

- Social policies are the societal actions that can (but do not always) strengthen human rights. The role policies should play in regard to human rights is a reason why social workers can and should be involved in global social policies.

Slide 9: Discussion Questions

- These questions are designed to reinforce the reasons students should study global social issues, how knowing about these issues adds value and commitment to work in local settings, why knowing about these global issues helps refocus professional work, and how the UDHR can and should influence work even at the local level.

  - How does knowing our own nation's foreign policies affect our local social work profession?

  - How does knowing the policies of other nations and regions of the world affect our own work?

  - What is the difference between human rights and national and global social policies?

  - How might we focus our professional work differently knowing global human rights themes and national responses to them?

  - How does promoting basic human rights affect social policy advocacy, even at a local level?

Slide 10: Societal Norms Influence Social Policies

- This introduces the idea that local, national, and international social policies are drawn from societal norms. Policies are a representation of the culture of those framing the policies.

Slides 11–13: Values and Beliefs Affect Social Policies

- These slides frame out the components of cultural norms from which policies are created and codified. Brief examples are given of what each component means. For example, "How does society determine what is a need, who in a society decides that need?" (for example, do all girls need to go to school, who decides that question?).

- These three slides, 11 components in total, should be presented as a class discussion. Students should be challenged to give additional examples of the components, and in doing so challenged to bring in international examples from their own or family members' experiences. For example, the components of social context of culture (individualism vs. collectivism) offers many opportunities for students to explore examples of societal policies such as individual rights versus the rights of husbands over families, individual deportation versus family considerations, and so forth.

Slide 14: Discussion Questions

- These suggested questions are an extension of discussions above. Questions also ask students why knowing societal values is important to affecting policies.

  - What are examples of how societal values and beliefs affect policies? Draw from your experiences both in the United States and from other countries with which you might be familiar.

  - Why is it important to know how these norms shape policies?

  - How might your actions to change policies be affected by knowing the underlying societal norms?

Slide 15: Examples of Key Global Social Policy Players

- This lists the significant global policy organization players, each of which is discussed in more detail in subsequent slides. This is an opportunity to ask students which organizations they know and what they might know about them. Answers will suggest how much time needs to be given to the subsequent slides.

Slide 16–19: UN Programs: General Assembly, UNICEF, UN Development Programme, World Food Programme, UN Refugee Agency, and International Labour Organisation

- These are only snapshots and focus on the UN organizations most linked to global social policies underlying human rights. They are mentioned because of the unique role the UN plays in defining human rights and the policies needed to support these rights.

Slides 20–24:

- Slide 20 introduces the UN globally recognized human rights documents: the UDHR and the Millennium Development Goals (MDGs). These are introduced at this point because, as part of the UN Charter, these documents have been endorsed by 188 member countries and have become key themes of the other multilateral and international nongovernmental organizations (NGOs). These documents drive the themes around which social workers can engage globally.

- The UDHR (Slide 21) introduces the 30 articles. These articles are accessible at www.ohchr.org. They are the foundation for policy action on a national, regional, and global scale.

Slide 22: UN Human Rights Council

- This slide talks about the UN Human Rights Council as the organization "responsible for strengthening the promotion and protection of human rights around the globe" (UNHRC, 2006). It leads the effort many multilateral, bilateral, and independent international nongovernmental organizations (NGOs) do to support and monitor human rights.

Slides 23–24: UN MDGs

- These slides show the eight goals (in place since 2000, with a completion date of 2015), and the description of what these goals are to accomplish. The MDGs are action oriented; reinforces human rights; and frames national, regional, and global policies. The other multinational, bi-national, and international NGOs take many of their development cues from the MDGs. Through the implementation of the MDGs students can engage in global policy issues.

Slides 20–24 should generate opportunities for further discussion among students.

- UDHR: Why these 30 human rights articles? Why have they retained their global power over the years? Who should be responsible for advocating for them, including here in the United States? Why is the United States relatively unfamiliar with them? Is the United States honoring them? A similar set of questions can be asked of the MDGs. How do the goals link to the UDHR? Why are they relatively unfamiliar here in the United States? Are we meeting these goals?

Slides 25–26: Multinational Organizations

- These two slides give a thumbnail sketch of other key multinational organizations: World Bank, International Monetary Fund, and the Organization of Economic Cooperation and Development. These are mentioned because they play significant roles in supporting the

UN's work supporting the UDHR and the MDGs and offer additional opportunities for social workers to affect policy globally.

Slides 27–28: NGOs

- These slides give a thumbnail sketch of the role international NGOs play and their work supporting the UDHR and MDGs. No particular NGO is named, but example logos of seven organizations show the range of the organizations. Students can be asked about their knowledge of these organizations, roles they play, and how social workers can influence policy through the work of these organizations. Hopefully, many NGOs should be familiar to students.

Slide 29: Discussion Questions

- These questions highlight the information from the previous slides, nudging students to think about their own roles with these organizations and how they can integrate the UDHR and MDGs into work in the United States. By urging students to think about how the UDHR and MDGs can be viewed in social work in the United States, students will continue to clarify the answer to the opening slide, "Why is knowing global social policy important?" This discussion broadens thinking about why and how U.S. policies can and should be integrated into a global framework so the United States can better meet its own needs and affect change in other nations and regions of the world.

  - What is the importance of the UN in global social policies and in protecting human rights? How can international social work support UN agencies in furthering human rights agendas?

  - In what ways, locally and/or globally, can social workers influence the work of multilateral government organizations?

  - In what ways can social workers influence the work of international NGOS, both those providing development support (helping meet MDGs) and those advocating basic human rights?

Slide 30: Social Workers Can Take Action to Influence Global Policy

- This reinforces the importance of action here in the United States (knowing the U.S. foreign policy positions and their global effects, for example) as well as international action.

Slide 31: Taking Action: Stages of Global Policy-Making Process

- This slide outlines the three stages, with quick examples, of Setting Agenda, Formulating Policy, and Implementing Policy.

Slide 32: Small Group Activity and Discussion

- Hopefully, this exercise brings the four core elements of the module together:

  1. Knowing global policy positively affects social work at home and internationally; human rights are affirmed through effective policies.

  2. Policy is rooted in societal values, beliefs, and behaviors that must be understood in order to affect policy.

  3. Key international organizations are leaders in advocating human rights and affecting policies that support these rights.

4. Social workers can and should become involved in these issues.

- Each small group takes a very brief policy "case study" and responds to questions based on the four core elements of the module. With five case studies offered, reporting back gives students an opportunity to experience implications of very different policies and different regions of the world (including the United States).

- Attached to the slides is a description of the case studies (included below). Each group should have copies of both the UDHR and MDGs.

Slide 33: Summary

- Restates the four points noted above.

Slides 34-37:

- List of resources from which the material has been drawn and additional resources students can draw from in preparing for the class discussions.

Case Studies: Examples of Social Policies for Small Group Discussion

For each of the following policy examples, discuss and answer the following questions:

What do you think are specific values, beliefs, and behaviors that might have been underlying factors affecting this policy? Who do you think might have decided the policy? Who might be the enforcers of the policy? What role do those affected by the policy have in its development?

How does the policy relate to the UDHR? Which rights does the policy support or not support?

How could you, through professional social work interaction with intermediate groups or organizations, influence the policy and its effects on the society members it intends to affect?

United States

Deportation is defined by the U.S. Citizenship and Immigration Services (n.d.) as "The formal removal of an alien from the United States when the alien has been found removable for violating the immigration laws."

Classes of Deportable Aliens

Any alien in the United States may be subject to deportation or removal if he or she

- is an inadmissible alien according to immigration laws in effect at the time of entry to the United States or adjustment of nonimmigrant status,

- is present in the United States in violation of the Immigration and Nationality Act or any other U.S. law,

- violated nonimmigrant status or a condition of entry into the United States,

- terminated a conditional permanent residence,

- encouraged or aided any other alien to enter the United States illegally,

- engaged in marriage fraud to gain admission to the United States,

- was convicted of certain criminal offenses,

- failed to register or falsified documents relating to entry into the United States,

- engaged in any activity that endangers public safety or creates a risk for national security, or

- engaged in unlawful voting.

Impact

Please access the following report from Human Rights Watch (2009, April 15) for class discussion:. *US: Deportation Splits Families*. Retrieved from http://www.hrw.org/news/2009/04/15/us-deportation-splits-families

France

This example pertains to the controversy surrounding the ban on wearing the full veil in France. Please access the following report to be read for this class discussion.

Library of Congress. (n.d.). France: Highlights of parliamentary report on the wearing of the full veil (BURQA). Retrieved from http://www.loc.gov/law/help/france-veil.php

Nigeria (West Africa)

This example is from Nigeria's experience with promoting girls' education. Please refer to the following news article for the purpose of class discussion.

United Nations Girls' Education Inititative. (2008, May 27). *Information by country: Nigeria: Newsline.* Retrieved from http://www.ungei.org/news/nigeria_1809.html

Malawi (Southern Africa)

For this class discussion, please read the following material (specifically, the section on maternity and family planning in Malawi, Africa).

Ripple Africa. (n.d.) General information about healthcare in Malawi. Retrieved from http://www.rippleafrica.org/healthcare-in-malawi-africa/healthcare-in-malawi-africa.

Philippines

This case vignette is about violence against women legislation in the Philippines. Please read the following excerpt for the purpose of class discussion.

Philippine Commission on Women. (n.d.). Violence against women. Retreived from http://pcw.gov.ph/focus-areas/violence-against-women

Suggested Readings and References

Council on Social Work Education. (2008). *Educational policy and accreditation standards.* Retrieved from http://www.cswe.org/File.aspx?id=41861

Deacon, B., Hulse, M., & Stubbs, P. (1997). *Global social policy: International organizations and the future of welfare.* London, UK: SAGE.

Dear, R. (1995). Social welfare policy. In R. Edwards (Ed.), *Encyclopedia of social work.* (19th ed., pp 2226-2237). Washington, DC: NASW Press.

Epstein, W. M. (2002). *American policy making: Welfare as ritual.* Boulder, CO: Rowman & Littlefield Publishers.

Farmer, P. (2002). Rethinking health and human rights: Time for a paradigm shift. *Journal of Law, Medicine & Ethics, 30*, 655-666.

Healy, L. M. (2008). *International social work*. New York, NY: Oxford University Press.

Human Rights Watch. (2009). *Forced apart (by the numbers): Non-citizens deported mostly for nonviolent offenses*. New York, NY: Author.

Iatridis, D. (1995). Policy practice. In R. Edwards (Ed.), *Encyclopedia of social work*. (19th ed., pp. 1855–1866). Washington, DC: NASW Press.

Law Library of Congress. (2012). France: Highlights of parliamentary report on wearing of the full veil (BURQA). Retrieved from http://www.loc.gov/law/help/france-veil.php

Mapp, S. C. (2008). *Human rights and social justice in a global perspective*. New York, NY: Oxford University Press.

Midgley, J. (1997). *Social welfare in a global context*. Thousand Oaks, CA: SAGE.

Ripple Africa. (2012). Healthcare in Malawi Africa. Retrieved from http://www.rippleafrica.org/healthcare-in-malawi-africa/healthcare-in-malawi-africa

Toomey, S. T., & Chung, L. C. (2012). *Understanding intercultural communication*. New York, NY: Oxford University Press. pp. 38–63.

OECD. (2013). About the OECD: Members and Partners. Retrieved from OECD at http://www.oecd.org/about/membersandpartners/

United Nations. (1948). *Universal declaration of human rights*. G.A. Res. 217A (III), UN GAOR, Res. 71, UN Doc. A/810. New York, NY: Author.

United Nations. (1948). Universal declaration of human rights general assembly resolution 217A (III), UN Doc. New York: United Nations.

United Nations. (1986). *Resolutions and Decisions adopted by the General Assembly during its Thirteenth Special Session*. United Nations Special Session on Africa (pp. 1–15). New York, NY: Author.

United Nations Girls' Education Initiative. (2008). Promoting girls' education: The experience of Nigeria. Retrieved from http://www.ungei.org/news/nigeria_1809.html

Additional Suggested Readings and References

The 2011 Human Development Report, which features the 2011 Human Development Index (HDI) the Inequality-Adjusted HDI, the Gender Inequality Index, and the Multidimensional Poverty Index. http://hdr.undp.org/en/reports/global/hdr2011/

The Millennium Development Goals and the Road to 2015, Building on Progress and Responding to Crisis, The World Bank (2010): http://issuu.com/world.bank.publications/docs/9780821385876?mode=a_p

Perspectives on Global Development 2012, Social Cohesion in a Shifting World, Executive Summary, OECD (2011): http://www.oecd.org/dataoecd/47/54/49067839.pdf

Selected Topics in Social Work and Social Change: Global and Human Rights Perspectives on Social Policy

Dennis J. Ritchie
George Mason University

Viewing professional social work and policy practice from a holistic human rights and global perspective, this course examines how the social construct of human rights can serve as a useful, powerful, conceptual framework for persons involved in social work practice and education who are committed to effecting planned social change to promote human development and realizing social and economic justice in our world across all levels from the micro through macro and local through global. Students will become familiar with major concepts underlying international social work, current major global social issues, the history of the human rights field, core principles, the international framework of human rights instruments and its relationship to international social work and social work in the United States, and current issues and debates about human rights, especially whether rights should be culturally determined. The role of the United Nations, governmental and nongovernmental organizations, communities and individuals will be examined. Emerging issues including women and children, older persons, persons with disabilities, members of the LGBTQI community, and other marginalized vulnerable populations; economic/social/cultural rights such as to food, housing, health care, and education; meaningful participation and empowerment; and social and economic equality and equity will be emphasized. The course will critically examine the meaning and benefits of transforming social work and policy practice to a focus on a holistic and human rights-based approach rather than a needs-based approach to human development and human services.

Required Text

Wronka, J. (2008). *Human rights and social justice: Social action and service for the helping and health professions*. Thousand Oaks, CA: SAGE.

Recommended Texts

Healy, L. M. (2008). *International social work: Professional action in an interdependent world*. New York, NY: Oxford University Press.

Healy, L. M., & Link, R. J. (Eds.). (2012). *Handbook of international social work: Human rights, development, and the global profession*. New York, NY: Oxford University Press.

Langwith, J. (Ed.). (2008). *Human rights: Opposing viewpoints*. Farmington Hills, MI: Greenhaven Press.

Reichert, E. (Ed.). (2007). *Challenges in human rights: A social work perspective*. New York, NY: Columbia University Press.

Additionally, other readings will be assigned throughout this course and provided as reserve reading or available through the Internet. Students will also identify valuable print and Internet resources.

Course Objectives

On completion of this course, students are expected to have further refined their ability to do the following:

- Explain the meaning of human rights and controversies in defining and realizing them

- Place human rights in historical context

- Identify and explain the major components comprising the framework of international human right instruments with the Universal Declaration of Human Rights (UDHR) as the foundation

- Understand and explain sustainable human development from an international human rights perspective and framework

- Delineate the relationship between various vulnerable population groups and a human rights framework

- View social work as human rights work while employing a holistic conception of human rights and human development

- Critically reflect on and analyze the NASW Code of Ethics and other professional social work documents from a human rights framework reflecting international human rights instruments and the UDHR, in particular

- Explain the implications of applying a human rights framework in every social work curriculum area and to social work and policy practice as a whole

- Critically analyze and present social work case studies and position papers representing a particular population group, thematic issue, and field of social work practice covering the current state of human rights including current violations, concerns, controversies, and needed responses while making a case for the value of using a human rights framework

- Delineate, explain, and apply major concepts underlying international social work and current major global social issues

- Increase self-awareness, particularly regarding one's own value system and personal and professional actions, and how congruent it all is or is not with a human rights perspective and commitment to social and economic justice

- Communicate effectively in writing and orally 1-to-1, in small groups, and in large group settings while exhibiting human rights principles and a humanistic orientation

Instructor's Expectations

The course design necessitates each of us assuming responsibility for what happens in this course as we purposefully work together collaboratively to build our own human rights culture and inclusive, participatory teaching-learning-action community. The instructor expects each person to

- attend and actively participate in all class sessions (please note that since the instructor's philosophy of education and conceptualization of the teaching–learning process emphasizes active learning and dialogue, rather than a lecture format, laptops are not to be used in class except when granted by special permission of the instructor);

- be assertive and ensure that the course is a positive learning-teaching-action experience for yourself and others;

- complete all reading, writing, oral, and mixed media assignments on time;
- evaluate her or his own performance and learning and provide feedback to classmates and to the instructor through completion of a course evaluation and other more informal means; and
- take the initiative to seek clarification of materials or expectations that are unclear.

Course Grading

- Critical reflections paper on core foundation readings, 20%
- Paper on holocaust museum visit and reflections, 15%
- Weekly critical reflections journal, 20%
- Final project/case study oral presentation, 20%
- Final project/case study written paper, 20%
- Final integrative summary and reflection on course, 5%

Degree of active course participation can influence final grade positively or negatively.

Assignments and Evaluation

The nature of assignments and evaluations, including grading, will be discussed as a group at the beginning of the course. Each student will develop an individualized course contract specifying selected weighting for each assignment, means of monitoring progress, evaluation, and grading.

Discussion will focus on the following:

- *Critical reflections paper on core foundation readings for course*: Handouts on assignment and expectations are attached to this syllabus and will be reviewed as a class during the course introduction session. (20%–25% of course grade)

- *Paper on visit to U.S. Holocaust Memorial Museum*: Each student will tour the museum and then write a four to six page typed double-spaced paper. Content will include personal reflections (cognitive and affective) on the experience and what was learned about the Holocaust and its relation to human rights through this experience and from searching the museum's websites: www.ushmm.org (History: Introduction to the Holocaust; Related articles; What is genocide?) Open link to Confront Genocide and explore and read the variety of links on this site. (15%–25% of course grade)

- *Weekly critical reflections journal.* The journal consists of weekly critical reflections on assigned readings and class sessions; you are expected to demonstrate that you have completed all readings and are attempting to integrate this material and content from class sessions into your developing understanding of human rights and personal–professional perspective as a social worker. After completing each Wronka chapter, select and respond to any three "Questions for Discussion" at the end of the chapter and also be prepared to discuss them in class. Reflections on other readings should focus on major concepts/learning and questions from the reading and how it relates to your developing understanding of human rights and personal–professional perspective as a social worker. The weekly journal entry will be collected at the end of each Tuesday class session, and at least five will be given letter grades. (15%–35% of course grade)

- *Final project/policy case study of a selected human rights concern*: Students will use the Internet to research and identify a current human rights concern that they will then focus on and conduct further research to critically analyze and describe the phenomenon. They will analytically describe the current situation, its history, and needed responses to resolve the concern. A global as well as national and/or local view of the issue(s), policies, programs, and services must be presented. Potential topics include aging; child abuse and neglect (preventive and out of home placements); child labor and work; children in and of the streets; community violence; drugs and substance abuse; employment, unemployment, and decent work; environmental degradation and preservation; global pandemic of HIV/AIDS; mental health; migration and refugees; human trafficking; indigenous peoples and cultural survival; status of women; gender-based violence; equality for LGBTQI persons; racial equality; equality for persons with disabilities; natural and human-created disasters; and terrorism and counterterrorism. Students may work on topics individually or in groups.

  - *Oral and/or mixed media presentation*: Students as individuals or a group will present their case studies to the rest of the class during a class session. Mixed methods and an active learning approach are encouraged, for example, a combination of lecture, class exercises, audio visual media (e.g., photovoice or videos as social change strategy), guest presenters, and Internet resources. (10%–25% of course grade)

  - *Written paper on case study*: Each student will write an individual paper on her or his case study. This paper will be between six and 10 typed double-spaced pages. It will present a critical analysis and description of the identified concern including the current situation, its history, and needed responses to resolve the concern. This paper will include citation of references identified through the student's research. It is expected to be well-written: clear and concise and free of errors in spelling and grammar. (25%–35% of course grade)

- *Final integrative summary and reflection on course*: Each student will submit a brief (at least two typed pages) final integrative summary and reflection on the overall course experience focusing on major learning, what you liked and disliked, and any ideas on how you will build on this course experience. (0%–5% of course grade)

- Students will engage in active learning, speaking and writing throughout the semester. Writing will take the form of formal and informal, graded and nongraded exercises.

NOTE: Always keep a copy of every paper you hand in.

Class Schedule

Week 1	
Session 1	Course Intro and Planning: Introductions and personal-professional interests, practicum, and experiences with human rights; discussion of goals for the course; translation into course syllabus and creating a climate of human rights within our course and classroom. Review and revise course syllabus and plan through student participation in planning process; review key course-related websites (e.g., resources include: www.humanrightsculture.org, 2) WITNESS Video Advocacy Planning Toolkit: See It, Film It, Change It at www.ushrnetwork.org/resources-media/witness-video-advocacy-planning-toolkit); and articles on photovoice at http://heb.sagepub.com/content/24/3/369.
Week 2	Reading due: Course core foundation readings (See list of readings) Individualized course contract draft due
Session 2	Discuss UN World Programme for Human Rights Education and Training; finalize course syllabus as a collaborative partnership Videos: http://hdr.undp.org/en/mediacentre/videos/humandev/ (concept of human development) http://www.youthforhumanrights.org/what-are-human-rights.html http://www.youtube.com/user/worldwewant2015 (Millennium Development Goals)
Week 3	Critical reflections paper on core foundation readings due Reading due: Research and selection of topic and methodology for human rights case study/final project Revise individualized course contract
Session 3	Discuss core foundation readings and critical reflections papers
Week 4	Work on Holocaust Memorial Museum paper Reading due: Healy, L. M. (2008). Exploring the history of social work as a human rights profession. *International Social Work, 51*, 735–748.
	No class session: Complete Holocaust assignment
Week 5	Holocaust Memorial Museum paper due Due: Case study topic, preliminary outline, & optional outline
Session 4	Share and discuss Holocaust Museum papers; discuss final Project/policy case study of a selected human rights concern: oral/mixed media and written presentations
Week 6	Reading due: Wronka, Chapters 1 & 2 Journal #1 entry due

Week 7	Reading due: Wronka, Chapter 3
	Journal #2 entry due
Session 6	Advanced generalist/public health model and whole population approaches to human rights and Justice; schedule student case presentations.
Week 8	NO CLASS – SPRING BREAK
Week 9	Reading due: Wronka, Chapter 4
	Journal #3 entry due
Session 7	At-risk, social action, and service strategies across levels and creating a human rights culture
Week 10	Reading due: Wronka, Chapter 5
	Journal #4 entry due
Session 8	A human rights and justice approach to research – action projects for social work
Week 11	Reading due: Wronka, Chapter 6
	Journal #5 entry due
Session 9	Concluding reflections on Wronka text; the state of human rights: begin student presentations of case studies/final projects
Week 12	Journal #6 entry (or peer feedback form) due on student presentations
Session 10	The state of human rights continued: student presentations of case studies
Week 13	Journal #7 entry (or peer feedback form) due
	Student presentations
	Assignment: work on final case study papers & on final integrative reflection paper
Session 11	The state of human rights continued: student presentations of case studies
Week 14	Journal #8 entry (or peer feedback form) due
	Student Presentations
	Work on final papers
Session 12	The state of human rights continued: student presentations of case studies
Week 15	Final term paper due
	Final integrative summary and reflection due
Session 13	Course summary and wrap-up; final course evaluations

Global and Human Rights Perspectives on Social Policy

Some Suggestions for Journal Entries

After identifying key concepts and issues presented in the reading or class session, focus on discussing some combination of the following:

- What most struck you in each reading or presentation and why? What did you like and not like?

- What you learned from this reading or presentation and how, in what ways, it contributes to your understanding of human rights and is relevant to your current or future work. What are the implications for your personal–professional development?

- Major questions, issues, and concerns you have about the content that were raised for you or by you.

- Select and address Questions for Discussion at the end of each Wronka chapter.

- Synthesis of key concepts and emerging themes that are appearing in the course readings, class sessions, and your journal entries.

Course Core Foundation Readings

Assigned Readings and Their Websites

What is Human Development and What are the Millennium Development Goals?

- Go to http://hdr.undp.org and links on top of page.

- Open "Human Development" and read this page.

- Go to links at top of page again and open "Reports (1990–2011)" and read the page.

- Go to links on left side of page and open "About the Reports" and read.

- Go back to links on left side of page and open "Global Reports." Go to links on left of page and open "HDR 2000, Human Rights and Human Development" and read page.

- Open "Summary" link on right side of page. Read "Overview" pp. 1–13, "Universal Declaration of Human Rights" pp. 14–15, and "Glossary on Human Rights and Human Development" pp. 16–18.

- Return to "Global Reports" page and open link on left side of page to "HDR 2003, Millennium Development Goals: A compact among nations to end human poverty." Then open link to "Summary" and read at least p. x. (The Millennium Development Goals, human development and human rights share a common mission) and "Overview," pp. 1–14.

- Recommended Reading (not required): Return to "Global Reports" and open link to "HDR 2009" (Overcoming barriers: Human mobility and development). Then open link to "Summary" and read it.

- Return to "Global Reports" and open link to "HDR 2010" (20 years on: Pushing the frontiers of human development). Download "Summary" and read it. Then open link to "Overview" and read it.

- Return to "Global Reports" and open link to "HDR 2011" (Sustainability and equity: A better future for all). Open link to "Summary" read it.

Human Rights, Poverty, and Inequalities and Post-2015 and the MDGs

- Go to www.worldwewant2015.org

- Open link to "Review and submit your feedback on the draft, unedited report – open until 31 January 2013." Download report titled *Draft* Report on the Global Thematic Consultation on Inequalities, Co-led by UNICEF and UN Women and read pages 6–56. (*NOTE:* This page is closed. It was used in the course and is included as an example of assigning students to review draft reports that are open for comment.)

- Go to www.worldwewant2015.org/education2015, read page and check out links to "Key Resources" on left side of page.

- Go to www.worldwewant2015.org/node/282631 and check out resources and discussion regarding LGBTQI community and Inequalities Post-2015.

- Note that the worldwewant2015 website covers many varieties of inequalities, vulnerable, marginalized and socially excluded populations. Go to www.worldwewant2015.org/inequalities and then go to link for "Official Background Papers" and download and read Discrimination, Inequality & Poverty: A Human Rights Perspective, by Evans & Klasing

- Additional Recommended Reading (not required): Pogge, T. (2005).World poverty and human rights. *Ethics & International Affairs, 19*(1), 1–7. Available at (http://www.carnegiecouncil.org/publications/journal/19_1/symposium/5109.html/_res/id=sa_File1/5109_eia19-1_pogge01.pdf)

Human Rights in Development

- Go to www.ohchr.org/Documents/Publications/FAQen.pdf Open and read frequently asked questions on a human rights-based approach to development cooperation. Read pp. 1–40.

- Social Watch Report 2012—*Sustainable Development: The Right to a Future.*

- Go to www.socialwatch.org and on left side of page open link to "Social Watch Report 2012." Then look at Table of Contents on left side of page and open link to and read "An Overview of the Social Watch Report 2012," pages 1–20.

International Human Rights Instruments (Major UN Human Rights Documents)

Go to http://www2.ohchr.org/english/law. Then open and familiarize yourself with the following instruments:

- Universal Declaration of Human Rights

- International Covenant on Civil and Political Rights (recommended)

- International Covenant on Economic, Social and Cultural Rights (recommended)

- Convention on the Elimination of All Forms of Discrimination Against Women

- Convention on the Rights of the Child

- Declaration on the Right to Development

Peruse the entire list and open and explore other documents, other human rights instruments, according to your interests.

The United States and its Ratification of International Human Rights Treaties

Go to www.hrw.org/en/news/2009/07/24/united-states-ratification-international-human-rights-treaties
Open and read.

Instructions for Critical Reflections Paper on Core Foundation Readings

The five items below refer to the handout on assigned readings and their websites. Write your critical reflections on these readings by responding to each of the following items and their corresponding questions:

1. What is human development and what are the Millennium Development Goals? What is the relationship between them? (minimum of two typed pages)

2. Human rights and human development: What is the relationship between the two? (minimum of two typed pages)

3. Explain the importance of the concepts of *sustainability* and *equity* for promoting human development. What needs to be done to adequately respond to the current global economic and environmental crises and growing inequities? What is the added value of incorporating and using a human rights framework? (minimum of two typed pages)

4. International human rights instruments: What most struck you and what did you learn about them? Consider the Universal Declaration of Human Rights, Convention on the Elimination of All Forms of Discrimination Against Women, Convention on the Rights of the Child, and Declaration on the Right to Development and any other declarations or conventions you are particularly interested in. (minimum of one typed page)

5. Overall critical reflections and questions: Add a final section to your responses by reflecting on all the core foundation readings and write on what you learned about sustainable development and human rights and what questions you would like to discuss with the instructor and your classmates during this advanced policy seminar. (minimum of one typed page)

This is an informal writing assignment so you do not need to worry about proper APA style or even spelling and grammar. The focus is on your critical reflections—critical thinking and questioning—regarding the content of the readings and their fit with other things you have learned about human development and human rights to date.

Teaching Content on Human Rights: Exercises and Supplementary Materials

Introduction to Exercises and Supplementary Materials

Uma A. Segal

Supplementary materials that are found here provide a range of unique tools to help enhance courses at the graduate and undergraduate levels. These materials include teaching vignettes, classroom exercises, and self-assessment scales. Descriptions of major projects and assignments with their several components allow students to assess and integrate knowledge enhanced through courses. Additionally, a module focusing on health care, a challenging "Rules of War" exercise, and a final exam can all be used as models for instructors as they design their own projects.

This section begins with exercises that help students focus on macro issues, provide an overview of human rights, and make linkages with social work. These are followed by several application case vignettes and activities that help students recognize the range of situations in which human rights are violated while engaging them in discussions of several struggles involved in resolving ethical and practical dilemmas. Exercises here explore human rights violations from a global perspective reflecting societal and cultural differences as well as those in country specific contexts. A book titled *The Maid Narratives* can be used to delve further into human rights violations based not only on gender but also on race.

Once students have an understanding of and appreciation for the relevance of human rights in social work, they may be compelled to participate in lobbying efforts, human rights campaigns, and the organization of conferences. Activities next immerse students in human rights experiences that help them develop the skills to create a campaign or organize a conference that has relevance beyond the activity itself. Their knowledge of human rights can be further developed as they disseminate information, and, in the process, they will gain practice skills in planning, organizing, and implementing a program. The section concludes with evaluation tools such as a final exam on human rights law and standardized instruments to assess human rights teaching and learning in social work.

Individually, each of these activities provides instructors a number of interesting exercises that will introduce students to the field of human rights and challenge them to think critically. Their understanding of the significance of context will be enhanced as they participate in simulations of situations that may be entirely different from those they have either encountered or envisioned. As they navigate these exercises, they will be required to explore their own values and perspectives and will hone their skills of delving below the surface in their assessments. The exercises and activities in this section are expected to greatly enhance the classroom experience for students, and many are so designed that they can be used effectively in human rights courses as well as in other foundation and elective social work classes.

Social Work & Human Rights: Making the Connection

Jane McPherson
Florida State University

Social Work and Human Rights: Making the Connection is a group discussion exercise designed for BSW or MSW level social work students. It increases familiarity with the Universal Declaration of Human Rights (UDHR) and can be used to illustrate and spark discussion about the many ways that human rights are part and parcel of social work practice.

Guidance for Instructors

Students may work in teams or small groups. Discussion works best if each group works on articles from different points in the UDHR (e.g., Articles 1, 9, 17, 25). Beyond introducing the UDHR, it may be helpful to have a group discussion of needs beforehand. I give each group a copy of Maslow's hierarchy to work with, although I encourage them to be specific and use their own words.

Guidance for Students

To fill in the "human needs" column, ask yourself which human needs are implied by the rights presented in the article. To fill in the "client population or practice area" column, think of a social work client who might be having a problem with the rights presented in the article. In which practice areas would this issue be most likely to surface?

Principles of Interrelatedness, Interdependence, Indivisibility

Shirley Gatenio Gabel
Fordham University

This exercise facilitates discussion of the articles of the Universal Declaration of Human Rights (UDHR) and the principles of interrelatedness, interdependence, and indivisibility in human rights.

Time: 20 minutes

Materials needed: Each article of the UDHR is separately written on a large card.

Exercise

1. The facilitator distributes the cards face down to the students. Each student receives one card. If there are fewer participants than the 32 articles, the facilitator may want to distribute the cards so that political, economic, social, civil, and cultural rights are represented.

2. Participants read the cards. The facilitator asks one of the participants to read his or her card aloud. After the reading the facilitator removes the card from the participant, announcing that the right specified in the UDHR article has been taken away. The facilitator asks the participants how the rights written on their cards will be affected by the absence of the right removed.

3. Repeat this process for three other articles.

4. Participants discuss what they have learned about the rights and their interrelatedness, interdependence, and indivisibility.

Global Village

Donald D. Mowry
University of Wisconsin—Eau Claire

One way to gain a valuable perspective on our world is to examine how people in different countries are affected by global issues and trends. The activity described here provides an opportunity for class members to simulate being a global village that is in many ways representative of 7 billion people who currently inhabit the earth.

The activity originates in several efforts to describe the world as a global village of 100 people. This idea suggests that it is very difficult to comprehend data about the world's population as a whole, but if one created a global village of 100 people, the numbers would make more sense. For example, if the world were a global village of 100 people, about 20 of those people would live in China, 13 of them would live in Africa, and about 5 would live in the United States. About 13 would be malnourished and about 15 would live on $1.00 a day or less.

We will review the Miniature Earth Project (http://www.miniature-earth.com) website in class.

In this activity each student will be asked to take the role of one individual from a specific country but will in turn represent millions of people who have a similar background. The activity is set up so that the class has a proportionate number of people from the various continents and countries of the world, with half of the class being female and half male, and ages and residence (urban or rural) also being representative.

To begin this activity each student in this class will be assigned a role in the global village and will then use various Internet and other resources to more fully describe the characteristics of the person he or she represents in the global village. The basic characteristics that each student should describe are the following:

- Name
- Age
- Sex
- City and country of residence
- Ethnicity
- Religion
- Life expectancy
- Language
- Annual income (purchasing power parity)
- Occupation
- Nature of communication with others
- Nature of transportation used
- Beliefs associated with this person's religion
- Other relevant information about this person

Once basic characteristics have been identified and described, each global villager can examine how she or he might be influenced by global issues such as population changes, global warming, conflicts, globalization, human rights issues, global poverty, international aid efforts, and technological change currently and in the future. Weekly readings may illuminate and help round out the characteristics and day-to-day life of the global villager.

Country	Sex	Age	Area / City	Latitude	Longitude	Student Assigned
China	Female	32	rural	30° N	105° E	
India	Male	6	rural	20° N	75° E	
United States	Female	73	Alabama	32° N	85° W	
Indonesia	Female	1	Jakarta	6° S	106° E	
Brazil	Male	23	rural	10° S	60° W	
China	Male	5	Shanghai	31° N	119° E	
Pakistan	Male	28	rural	28° N	68° E	
India	Female	15	Mumbai	21° N	70° E	
Germany	Male	60	Hamburg	53° N	9° E	
Russia	Female	25	rural	60° N	60° E	
China	Female	44	rural	40° N	85° E	
Nigeria	Female	4	Lagos	6° N	3° E	
Japan	Male	75	Tokyo	35° N	139° E	
Bangladesh	Female	31	rural	23° N	90° E	
India	Female	48	rural	17° N	82° E	
China	Male	17	Beijing	39° N	116° E	
South Africa	Male	12	township	30° S	20° E	
Mexico	Female	55	Mexico City	19° N	99° W	
Uganda	Male	26	rural	4° N	34° E	
Australia	Male	35	Sydney	33° S	151° E	
China	Male	52	rural	44° N	85° E	
India	Female	33	rural	15° N	76° E	
Iraq	Female	3	Anbar Province	32° N	41° E	
Argentina	Male	18	rural	20° S	68° W	
Philippines	Female	50	Manila	14° N	120° E	
China	Female	23	rural	45° N	88° E	

Country	Sex	Age	Area / City	Latitude	Longitude	Student Assigned
Afghanistan	Female	32	rural	37° N	64° E	
Vietnam	Male	10	Hanoi	21° N	105° E	
India	Male	60	rural	20° N	82° E	
Egypt	Female	16	Cairo	30° N	31° E	
China	Male	72	rural	41° N	105° E	
United States	Male	11	New Orleans	30° N	90° W	
Ethiopia	Female	54	rural	12° N	39° E	
Turkey	Male	37	Istanbul	41° N	29° E	

Global Village Resources

Your global village assignment includes assuming the role of a person and describing his or her life. Include the geographic location of the village and geographic challenges; a brief cultural and ethnic overview; political history and current situation; economic status of the person; status of his or her children (using the Convention on the Rights of the Child: http://www.childrensrights.ie/index. php?q=childrens-rights-ireland/un-convention-rights-child), status of women's rights in the village (using the Declaration on the Eradication of Discrimination Against Women: http://www.unhcr. org/refworld/docid/3b00f05938.html); status of human rights (using the Universal Declaration of Human Rights: http://www.un.org/en/documents/udhr/); health; and progress of the village toward the UN Millennium Development Goals (http://www.un.org/millenniumgoals/). The paper and presentation should be balanced and draw from different perspectives, such as sources that are both supportive and critical of poverty eradication efforts of major players such as the World Bank and the International Monetary Fund. A variety of sources can be used for the paper, including the following:

- Personal contacts with persons from the country
- Experts on the country or region
- Reading model ethnographies
- Viewing selected films
- Conducting electronic searches
- Other resources (guest lecturers, articles, videos)

Personal Contacts

The increasingly global nature of societies lends itself to excellent opportunities for us to have face-to-face encounters with persons of different cultures right in Eau Claire. Please devote some time to finding and contacting members of your destination country to learn more about the challenges and history of the country. Most of these people will probably be eager to spend some time with you to give you a personal perspective on their homeland.

Contacting Experts

Experts can be found in a variety of settings. Normally we think of academics, and there may be experts on campus who can speak knowledgeably about certain political, economic, and social aspects of countries or continents. In addition, when a group of people is forced to leave as refugees, these *diaspora* communities are an often overlooked but excellent source of information.

For academics, look for campuses that sponsor regional study programs in your area, such as Latin American studies or African studies and then see what information, resources, and links you can find on the websites.

Another tactic is to locate individual experts and request specific, brief information. You can use the strategy above to locate individual faculty within institutes or area studies programs, or you can try something like the *Worldwide Email Directory of Anthropologists* and search by geographic location or region or research interest.

Reading Ethnographies

It would be wonderful if we could take an extended period of time to live among the people of your target country and gain an in-depth perspective on their social world and culture. Short of that, you can search for an account, or ethnography, of someone else who has done so.

Here are some ideas to get you started:

- Nepal: http://www.pilgrimsbooks.com/ethnography.html

- Haiti: When the Hands Are Many: Community Organization and Social Change in Rural Haiti, Jennie M. Smith (http://www.google.com/url?sa=t&rct=j&q=&esrc=s&frm=1&source=web&cd =2&ved=0CDMQFjAB&url=http%3A%2F%2Fwww.clas.ufl.edu%2Fusers%2Fmurray%2Frese arch%2FBook_Reviews%2FMurray.review.When.the.Hands.are.Many.doc&ei=bZNBUqy8F4_ Y9ASd4ICoBw&usg=AFQjCNEOvnVcwymnO4VdIDW0aM8oet94sA&bvm=bv.52434380,d. eWU)

- Democratic insecurities: *Violence, Trauma, and Intervention in Haiti,* Erica Caple James (http:// www.ucpress.edu/book.php?isbn=9780520260542)

Viewing Selected Films

Increasingly rich resources are available in ethnographic films, documentaries, commercial movies, and even YouTube.

Campus Documentaries available with link to Films on Demand—go to Library Page, select gray tab labeled "Books and Media," and then select Films on Demand. Be sure to use the pull-down menu to switch between searching by titles or segments—the default is segments.

Example of a documentary: *Unfinished Country: Haiti's Struggle for Democracy; Dreams of Democracy.*

Examples of commercial movies: *Out of Africa* (Kenya), *The Year of Living Dangerously* (Indonesia), *Slumdog Millionaire* (Mumbai, India), *Hotel Rwanda*

Electronic Searches

Be sure to include the sources listed on the course library page; do not just surf the net! Remember to use keywords and don't forget that you can use quotation marks for phrases (e.g., "boy soldiers") and

Boolean operators such as *and, or,* and *not.* So the search African history will give you everything that has *African* and everything that has the word *history.* "African history" AND "Rwanda" will have a much narrower focus and may be more helpful.

Helpful databases, websites, and so forth:

- Institute for Development Studies: A good place to start (download and then go to the section on poverty for the 5 recommended resources plus the ELDIS Poverty Resource guide): http://www.ids.ac.uk/go/agoodplacetostart

- U.S. State Department background notes: www.state.gov/r/pa/ei/bgn

- Country Studies: http://lcweb2.loc.gov/frd/cs/cshome.html

- Virtual Library: www.vlib.org (Look for *regional studies, international affairs, social and behavioral studies, economic studies*)

- World Factbook: https://www.cia.gov/library/publications/the-world-factbook/index.html

- National Geographic: http://travel.nationalgeographic.com/travel/countries/?source=NavTravCount

- United Nations News Centre: www.un.org/News/dh/infocus

- Country development gateways: http://www.developmentgateway.org/programs/country-gateways/country-gateway-network.html

- Human Rights Watch: www.hrw.org

- *New Internationalist*: http://www.newint.org/

- *The Economist*: www.economist.com

- Foreign policy: www.foreignpolicy.com

- World Bank world development indicators: www.data.worldbank.org

- Millennium Development Goals Report 2010: http://www.un.org/millenniumgoals/pdf/MDG%20Report%202010%20En%20r15%20-low%20res%2020100615%20-.pdf

International Online Media Sources

Try to use as many of the following international online media sources as possible. A good strategy might be to search for materials on your global villager on two or three different sources every few days; that way, you will gain exposure to all of them and you may find some very helpful material for your final report.

- *New York Times* (NYTimes)
- BBC (British Broadcasting Corporation)
- Al Jazeera
- *The Economist*
- National Public Radio (NPR)
- *China Daily*
- The World (from Public Radio International and BBC)
- Google News

- *Hindustan Times*
- All Africa
- Global Issues.org
- *Christian Science Monitor*
- *The Globalist*
- United Nations Global Issues website

Mapping Human Rights in Communities

Shirley Gatenio Gabel
Fordham University

The purpose of this exercise is to understand how social and economic factors interact with human rights by having participants map major rights-bearing institutions in different types of communities. The exercise will take approximately 1 hour. The following materials are needed: copies of the Universal Declaration of Human Rights, the Convention on the Rights of the Child, the Convention on the Elimination of all Forms of Discrimination Against Women, or other applicable United Nations human rights document, plus town maps or poster size paper, markers, stickies, or highlighters.

Exercise

Participants are divided into groups of three to five persons, each group representing a different community such as a poor or wealthy community, racially/ethnically segregated community, disabled, or immigrant community, preferably all within a larger community. The participants should be given maps of diversified communities or narratives of communities describing and locating the major institutions of the community (schools, religious institutions, recreation and senior centers, child care facilities, hospitals, post office, fire department, government offices, police stations, clinics, social service agencies, parks, shopping area, etc.) and residential areas for a particular population. Participants will draw the location of housing and the major institutions in the community on the map or poster.

After mapping out their communities, participants should conduct an analysis of the human rights the institutions support using the human rights document. For example, which institution supports freedom of religion? Thought? Use stickies to identify the rights or articles, for example, that each institution supports.

Each group should present their map to the class and address the following questions:

- Were rights-based institutions highly concentrated in certain areas? If they were, what might contribute to this?

- What kinds of rights (social, economic, cultural, political, civil) were represented by rights-based institutions in the community?

- Were there any rights they were not represented by any institutions?

- What were some of the differences between the subcommunities regarding the location of rights-based institutions?

- Were there any obstacles (transportation, cost, discrimination, practices) to accessing the rights-based institutions? Did this differ among the subcommunities represented by the different groups?

- How did social, economic, political, and cultural factors affect the realization of rights in the different communities?

Student work will be evaluated according to the following criteria:

- Introductory paragraph(s) describing the purpose of the paper, with the appropriate amount of background and context, the importance of the paper, and major finding (5 points).

- Brief description of socioeconomic and political country context (15 points).

- Identification of the two articles in a selected country and the country's interpretation of the articles (10 points).

- Dissemination of the articles within the country—by whom and using what methods, including who is left out (15 points).

- Relationship of chosen articles to other articles in the convention (10 points).

- Evaluation of each country's efforts to implement the convention (20 points).

- Recommendations, including roles of social workers (15 points).

- American Psychological Association (6th edition) format, citing, editing, and general writing (10 points).

Universal Declaration of Human Rights (UDHR) Articles: Human Rights and Social Work Applied to the Topic of Health Care Reform

Karen E. Martin
University of Kentucky

Slide 1—UDHR Article 25

All people have the right to a standard of living adequate for the health and well-being of themselves and of their families, including food, clothing, housing, medical care, and necessary social services, and the right to security in the event of unemployment, sickness, disability, widowhood, old age, or other lack of livelihood in circumstances beyond their control.

Mothers and children are entitled to special care and assistance. All children, whether born in or out of wedlock, shall enjoy the same social protection.

Slide 2—Universal Health Care Initiatives: When Did It All Begin?

Slides 3 and 4—Compulsory Health Care

- By 1912 Germany, Austria, Hungary, Norway, Britain, and Russia had all created national health insurance programs.

- Jane Addams and other social workers played a leading role in Roosevelt's campaign (1912) that advocated for national health insurance coverage.

- U.S. involvement in World War I (1914–1918) ruined chances for this country to copy Germany's program.

- The Bolshevik Revolution (1917) caused the so-called Red Scare.

- These events have forever tied national health insurance to a "communist system," making it repugnant to many Americans.

Slide 5—Baby Steps

- Jeanette Rankin, former social worker and first female member of Congress, introduced the Sheppard Towner Infancy and Maternity Act in 1921.

- 20 million pieces of literature

- 100,000 conferences

- Thousands of prenatal care centers

- Millions of home visits from 1922–1929: "You can no more win a war than you can win an earthquake," Jeannette Rankin.

Slide 6—The Truman Years

- On November 19, 1945, only 7 months into his presidency, Harry S. Truman sent a presidential message to the United States Congress proposing a new national health care program. The most controversial aspect of the plan was the proposed national health insurance plan.

- The American Medical Association (AMA) launched a spirited attack against the bill, capitalizing on fears of communism in the public mind. The AMA characterized the bill as "socialized medicine," and in a forerunner of the rhetoric of the McCarthy era, called Truman White House staffers "followers of the Moscow party line."

Slide 7—Operation Coffee Cup

- Operation Coffee Cup was a campaign conducted by the AMA during the late 1950s and early 1960s in opposition to the Democrats' plans to extend health insurance for the elderly in a program now known as Medicare.

- As part of the plan, doctors' wives would organize coffee meetings in an attempt to convince acquaintances to write letters to Congress opposing the program.

- The operation received support from a 1961 LP recording, *Ronald Reagan Speaks Out Against Socialized Medicine*. The recording outlined arguments against what he called socialized medicine.

- The record was to be played at coffee meetings.

Slide 8—Partial Success

- Prior to 1965 nearly half of older adults had no health insurance and many others had inadequate coverage. Medicare was enacted to help ensure that virtually all citizens age 65 or older would have health care coverage.

- Medicaid and Medicare were signed into law by President Lyndon Johnson on July 30, 1965.

- President Harry Truman was the first Medicare enrollee.

Slide 9 and 10—Failures

- Senator Edward Kennedy (D-MA) proposed a single-payer system called the Health Security Act in 1971.

- By 1974 President Richard Nixon advocated what was then considered a conservative compromise reform to insure all Americans in his proposed Comprehensive Health Insurance Act. Both efforts failed.

- In 1993 President Bill Clinton proposed the Health Security Act, which included an individual mandate to purchase coverage and an employer mandate to cover workers, along with subsidies for those who could not afford to enroll in a plan.

- Infamously, a coalition of health insurance and drug companies instigated a public outreach and mass media campaign.

- The campaign generated more than 450,000 contacts to members of Congress, articulating opposition to the Health Security Act, leading to the death of the plan in committee before any congressional votes.

Slide 11—Today

- Baby Boomers causing a strain on the U.S. health care system

Slide 12—Well, At Least We Have Medicare

Medicare is a health insurance program for

- A. people age 65 or older (universal eligibility),
- B. people younger than age 65 with certain disabilities, and
- C. people of all ages with end stage renal disease (permanent kidney failure requiring dialysis or a kidney transplant).

Slide 13—But What About Private Insurance?

With almost 20 years inside the industry, former health insurance vice president Wendell Potter saw for-profit insurers hijack the U.S. health care system and put profits before patients. He spoke with journalist Bill Moyers about how those companies are standing in the way of health care reform: http://www.pbs.org/moyers/journal/07312009/watch.html

Slide 14—New Initiative

- The Administration for Community Living was developed by combining the federal Administration on Aging, Office on Disability, and Administration on Developmental Disabilities into a single agency that supports crosscutting initiatives and efforts focused on the unique needs of individual groups, such as children with developmental disabilities or seniors with dementia.

- This agency works to increase access to community supports and achieve full community participation for people with disabilities and seniors.

Slide 15—What is Happening Now?

- Health care reform: debates, elements, and the Supreme Court

Slide 16—The Under- and Uninsured

- The number of people who lacked health insurance in 2010 climbed to 49.9 million, up from 49 million in 2009, the Census Bureau said in September 2011.

Slide 17—Costs for Families

- According to a report by Milliman (http://www.milliman.com/news-events/?t=p&bnid=138), a global consulting and actuarial firm, the total cost of health care for the average family of four has doubled in fewer than 9 years.

Slide 18—Health Care Disparities

Lack of health insurance is a major factor in health care disparities. Who lacks insurance coverage?

- Approximately 20% of African Americans
- Approximately 33% of Hispanics
- 28% of persons age 18–24
- 26% of persons age 25–34

Slide 19—Consequences

The uninsured are

A. 7 times more likely to forgo health care,

B. twice as likely to skip medical tests, and

C. twice as likely not to fill a prescription.

All of which leads to poorer health and greater medical expenditures in the long term.

Slide 20—Persons Denied for Preexisting Conditions

Slide 21—Profits are Up for For-Profit Insurers

Slide 22—Some Are in Favor of Health Care Reform Because…

- Health care has become too expensive.
- Too many people are uninsured.
- The current system is unfair to those who have medical conditions requiring expensive treatment.
- The system is unsustainable.

Slide 23—Some Oppose Health Care Reform Because…

- The mandate clause is unconstitutional and is seen as an abuse of power.
- They prefer tax credits with which individuals could purchase their own health coverage.
- Incentives are being offered to insurers to offer coverage to people with preexisting conditions.
- The American people don't want this or need it because America is #1 in medical care.
- It is too much change and the process should be incremental

Slide 24—What Are the Goals of Health Care Reform?

The Affordable Health Care Act (ACA) was signed into law by President Barack Obama on March 23, 2010. Its goals are to

A. expand health insurance coverage,

B. improve coverage for those with health insurance,

C. improve access to and quality of care, and

D. control rising health care costs.

Slide 25—Expansion of Coverage

- Expand Medicaid to ALL individuals under age 65 with incomes up to 133% of the poverty level with no assets testing

- Create new health insurance exchanges in which individuals and small employers can purchase coverage

- Provide premium subsidies to eligible individuals and families with incomes up to 400% of the poverty level through the exchanges

Slide 26—Essential Benefits

The essential health benefits must include at least the following general categories (sometimes referred to as "minimum essential coverage"):

- Ambulatory patient services

- Emergency services

- Hospitalization

- Maternity and newborn care

- Mental health and substance use disorder services, including behavioral health treatment

- Prescription drugs

- Rehabilitative services and devices

- Laboratory services

- Preventative and wellness services and chronic disease management

- Pediatric services, including oral and vision care

Slide 27—Individual Mandate

- Individuals will be required to have health coverage that meets minimum standards in 2014

- Individual mandate spreads costs among whole population

- Mandate enforced through the tax system

- Penalty for not having insurance: greater of $695 (up to $2,085 for a family) or 2.5% of family income

- Exemptions for certain groups and if people cannot find affordable health insurance

Slide 28—What Is NOT in the Bill?

- Passage providing physician reimbursement for one time consultation on end of life options was removed.

- Health insurance reform will not use tax dollars to fund abortions.

- The new law does not extend coverage to illegal immigrants.

Slide 29—Some Uninsured Will Remain

The Congressional Budget Office estimates that 23 million Americans will be uninsured in 2019.

- Who are they?
  - Immigrants who are not legal residents
  - People eligible for Medicaid but not enrolled
  - People who are exempt from the mandate (most because they can't find affordable coverage)
  - People who choose to pay the penalty in lieu of getting coverage
  - Many remaining uninsured will be low income

Slide 30—ACA Goes to the Supreme Court

- Do courts have jurisdiction to decide the constitutionality of the ACA's individual mandate provision now?

- If so, is the ACA's individual mandate provision constitutional?

- If unconstitutional, is the individual mandate provision severable?

- Is the ACA's Medicaid expansion constitutional?

Slide 31—What's At Stake?

- Individual mandate
- Medicaid eligibility expansion
- Entire ACA, including
  - Health insurance market reforms
  - Health insurance exchanges
  - Employer responsibility provisions
  - Tax subsidies for premiums and cost sharing
  - Medicare benefits expansion, payment reductions
  - Delivery system reforms (ACOs, etc.)
  - Public Health and Prevention Fund
  - Health care workforce expansions
  - Transparency and program integrity provisions

Slide 32—Public Opinion

Slide 33—What is Missing in the Debate?

- Single payer option

- True universal health care

- Expansion of Medicare for all

- Handout: *Funding a National Single Payer System* (G. Friedman, 2012, available at http://www. healthcare-now.org/wp-content/uploads/2008/09/0312friedman.pdf)

Slide 34—And What About the Rest of the World?

Dr. Paul Farmer: "I believe in health care as a human right" (http://www.youtube.com/watch?v=xJpZn UjtorI&feature=player_embedded)

Human Rights for Women and Children Paper Assignment

Shirley Gatenio Gabel
Marciana Popescu
Fordham University

Students will be expected to do individual research for the paper using the basic concept presented and discussed in class. Suggested sources for country interpretations and progress on implementing the conventions may be found at Office of the High Commissioner for Human Rights, UN Women Progress Reports, UNICEF, HR Watch, Amnesty International, Women's Refugee Commission, Save the Children, and country reports on human rights.

Your essay should be typed, in a font of 11 pt or larger, double-spaced, with 1 inch margins. Your paper should be edited, and sources should be cited using APA (6th edition) format. The paper should be approximately 12–16 double-spaced pages.

Choose either Question A or B, but not both.

A. The Convention on the Elimination of all Forms of Discrimination Against Women (CEDAW)

CEDAW calls for comment to ensure understanding and action, in terms of the states that have ratified and of women on their own and in combination with others. After this, a plan of action is critical, and its implementation should be regularly assessed.

1. Select a country that has ratified CEDAW and that you would like to study further.

    A. Briefly describe the location of the country, its economy, relevant history, and the current socioeconomic and political situation in the country.

    B. What prominent issues are currently confronting the country that may affect its interpretation and ability to implement CEDAW?

2. Chose two articles from CEDAW (choosing from Articles 2, 5, 6, 7, 11, 12, 15, and 16) and discuss the following as it relates to the country of your focus.

    A. Explain how these articles are being interpreted in the country you have chosen to evaluate.

    B. Why it is important to have rights proclaimed by the convention widely known to both women and men?

    C. Whose responsibility is it to make the rights widely known and why?

    D. How are the rights being implemented in the country you have selected to focus on?

    E. What other articles must be realized for the articles you have chosen to be more fully realized? How are the other CEDAW articles related to the articles you have chosen?

    F. What aspects of the three articles need to be addressed in the country of your focus? How are these articles being violated?

3. What are your recommendations for the next steps needed for the fuller realization of the two articles in the country of your focus? How could social workers facilitate the enhancement of human rights?

B. The Convention on the Rights of the Child (CRC)

CRC created a common legal framework of universal standards for the protection of children's rights. It increased governmental accountability and calls for international cooperation. Yet an integrated strategy for CRC implementation is lacking in most of the ratifying states.

CRC proclaims that "States [that is, the governments of the member nations of the United Nations] should make the Convention's rights widely known to both adults and children." In the words of Gabriela Mistral: "We are guilty of many errors and many faults but our worst crime is abandoning the children, neglecting the fountain of life. Many things can wait, the children cannot. Right now is the time their bones are being formed, their senses are being developed. To them we cannot answer 'tomorrow,' their name is 'today.'"

1. Select a country that has ratified the CRC that you would like to study further.

    A. Briefly describe the location of the country and its economy, relevant history, and current socioeconomic and political situation.

    B. What prominent issues are currently confronting the country that may affect its interpretation and ability to implement the CRC?

2. Chose two articles from the CRC (choosing from Articles 13, 16, 20, 23, 24, 29, 30, 32, and 34) and discuss the following as it relates to the country of your focus.

    A. Explain how these articles are being interpreted in the country you have chosen to evaluate.

    B. Why it is important to have rights proclaimed by the convention widely known to both adults and children?

    C. Whose responsibility is it to make the rights widely known and why?

    D. How are the rights being implemented in the country you have selected to focus on?

    E. What other articles must be realized for the articles you have chosen to be more fully realized? How are other CRC articles related to the articles you have chosen?

    F. What aspects of the three articles need to be addressed in the country of your focus? How are these articles being violated?

3. What are your recommendations for the next steps needed for the fuller realization of the two articles in the country of your focus? How could social workers facilitate the enhancement of human rights?

Student work will be evaluated according to the following criteria:

*   Introductory paragraph(s) describing the purpose of paper with the appropriate amount of background and context, the importance of your paper, and major findings (5 points).

*   Brief description of socioeconomic and political country context (15 points).

*   Identification of the two articles in a selected country and the country's interpretation of the articles (10 points).

*   Dissemination of the articles within the country by whom and using which methods, including who is left out (15 points).

*   Relationship of chosen articles to other articles in the convention (10 points).

- Evaluation of each country's efforts to implement the convention (20 points).

- Recommendations, including roles of social workers (15 points).

- APA (6th edition) format, citing, editing, and general writing (10 points).

Teaching Content on Human Rights: Case Vignettes and Discussion Exercises

Human Rights and Social Work Case Vignettes

M. C. "Terry" Hokenstad
Case Western Reserve University

The following vignettes from specific real-life cases illustrate how human rights issues emerge and need to be identified in learning and in social work practice. These vignettes were drawn from the following helpful resource:

United Nations. (1994). *Human rights and social work: A manual for schools of social work and the social work profession.* (Professional Training Series No. 1). New York, NY: Author.

Case No. 1: The Story of Simba

Simba is a 10-year old boy living the life of a street child in a large African city. He is not actually homeless, but lives with his mother and eight other relatives in a two-room rented house in the high-density suburbs. Simba's father often beats him, especially when the father returns home drunk.

Early each morning Simba walks the 5 km to the city center, where he joins the other boys to make money guarding cars in a part of the city that is their territory. Simba prefers this life; certainly it is preferable to staying at home, and he would not go to school anyway. Even without paying the school fees, his mother could not supply his clothes or buy the necessary books. Together with the other boys Simba sniffs glue; it has the effect of taking away his hunger pains, and the dizzy feeling makes him forget problems.

Occasionally the police harass the boys, and Simba has been rounded up and taken to the social welfare authorities more than once. Last time the authorities sent him to a probation hostel for "assessment." He did not like it. He was beaten up by some of the older boys, so he ran away and returned home. Then, once again, he returned to his group of friends on the street. When business is good he makes a few dollars; and after he has bought himself a Coke and some breakfast there will be a little money left for his family.

Questions

1. Which human rights issues are raised by this case?
2. What would be your response as a social worker working for the city welfare authorities?

Case No. 2: Gemma's Story

Justina and Ricardo are farmers living 80 km from the nearest city. Their 10-month-old daughter Gemma became seriously ill with diarrhea, and they took her to a nearby private health clinic. Like many impoverished people, they were turned away by the staff because it was obvious that they could not pay the fees.

The next day Justina took the feverish Gemma and made the long trip to the city on public transport, borrowing money from neighbors for the fare. By this time, Gemma was having convulsions because of the fever, and would not even accept water.

At the small, understaffed government hospital Justina was told that there were no beds available, and to come back the next morning. Having no relatives in the city, and no money to take a room, she found shelter at the public market for the night. That evening, as Justina huddled with her baby on a table, Gemma died.

Questions

1. Which and whose human rights were violated in this case?

2. What would be your role as a social worker in the private clinic or government hospital?

Case No. 3: Ganga's Story

Dowry is customary in many parts of the world, as are arranged marriages involving minors. Ganga, a 15-year old girl from the country, was married to a man from the city, and the dowry as well as the expense of the wedding put her father, a poor farmer, in heavy debt.

The marriage was not a happy one. Physical abuse became frequent when the husband was convinced that no further dowry or presents could be collected from his in-laws. He also made it clear that he did not wish to have children. After finding out that his wife had complained to one of the neighbors, he gagged her, poured kerosene on her, and lit a match. At the last minute, before calling the police, he pretended to save her and burnt his hand in the process. He told the police that Ganga had tried to commit suicide, and this was corroborated by his wife's statement to the magistrate at the hospital, where she remained for 2 days.

Shortly before her death, Ganga told a social worker of the real events of her married life as described above, also disclosing that her husband had been married before and that his wife had disappeared. However, before this information could be submitted to the magistrate and the police, Ganga died and her previous statement was upheld. Thus, no proceedings could be started against her husband.

Questions

1. Which human rights were violated in this case?

2. What action can be taken by a social worker to prevent the occurrence of dowry deaths?

Case No. 4: Displacing the Villagers

A development project proposes to bring irrigation and hydroelectric power to a rural area. This will benefit many farmers and other people, but by submerging existing villages it will displace many economically and socially disadvantaged persons. In response to criticism from social activists, the government claims that the project will raise many people's living standards and help modernization. You see that this will be at the cost of the village communities.

Questions

1. Which human rights are raised in this case?

2. As a social worker working in the villages, what do you try to do?

Human Rights Dilemmas

M. C. "Terry" Hokenstad
Case Western Reserve University

1. You believe that people have a right to work, but the only cash crop in the area where you are a social development worker is a narcotic drug. When his crop is exported it contributes to drug trafficking and additional problems in many countries.

   How do you respond to this dilemma?

2. As a social worker in a clinic you are aware of traditional practices of cutting the sexual organs of pubertal girls (clitorectomy). A woman seeks advice on behalf of her younger sister. The parents indicate that this is a part of the culture and is not the business of professionals in the clinic.

   What is your responsibility in this situation?

3. A development project proposes to bring irrigation and hydroelectric power to a rural area. This will benefit many farmers and other people but, by submerging existing villages, it will displace many economically and socially disadvantaged groups. In response to criticism from social activists, the government claims that the project will raise many people's living standards and help modernization. You see that this will be at the cost of the village communities.

   As a social worker working in the villages, what do you try to do?

   These dilemmas were drawn from *Human rights and social work: A manual for schools of social work and the social work profession* (United Nations, 1994); available from http://www. ohchr.org/Documents/Publications/training1en.pdf

The Heightened Vulnerability of Adolescent Girls

Shirley Gatenio Gabel
Fordham University

The purpose of this exercise is to understand the intersection between different human rights conventions (i.e., the Convention on the Elimination of All Forms of Discrimination Against Women [CEDAW] and the Convention on the Rights of the Child [CRC]), the interrelatedness of rights, roles of duty bearers and rights holders, and the challenges of rights implementation. The exercise takes approximately 60–90 minutes.

Materials Needed

- Case vignettes taken from N. Kristoff & S. WuDunn, *Half the Sky* (Knopf, 2010). Recommended are the stories of Srey Momm and Srey Neth, Muhktar, and Mahabouba. You can also use other sources. It is recommended that the instructor prepare a summary of the vignette.

- Copies of the CRC and CEDAW

- Board or large poster paper

Exercise

If the instructor summarizes the story of the adolescent girl, this exercise can be conducted in class in groups. Otherwise, it may be assigned as an out-of-class exercise

1. Participants read the prepared vignette.

2. Participants should answer the following questions:

    - What rights as specified in the CRC and CEDAW have been violated?

    - Who violated those rights?

    - Should the girl(s) be regarded as children or as adult women? Why?

    - What are the obligations of the state to the girls/women to ensure the fulfillment of their rights in the situation described?

        » Who are the duty bearers in this situation and what are their responsibilities (e.g., national government, teachers, police, parents)?

    - In what ways has the state failed to fulfill its obligations to protect the rights of girl/woman in the situation?

3. Convene the participants.

    - On the board, make two columns: CRC and CEDAW. Have participants contribute the specific CRC and CEDAW articles that were violated. For example:

CRC	CEDAW
Health	
Article 24…	Article 12…
Protection	
Article 19	Article 2
Article 24	Article 5
Article 34	Article 6
Participation	
Article 12	Article 7
Article 13	Article 8

- Discuss who bears responsibility for the rights that have been violated.

- Discuss the convergence of women's and children's rights in the situation described. Should the persons violated be regarded as adults or children and why? How would framing it as a children's or women's issue affect the interpretation of the situation and possible subsequent action?

- Participants should identify the duty bearers in the situation for fulfilling the rights of the adolescent girl and identify overlapping and conflicting responsibilities.

Discussion Cases/Vignettes for Human Rights and Social Work

Kathryn Libal
Lynne M. Healy
University of Connecticut

These discussion vignettes have been used in SWEL 5385: Human Rights and Social Work at the University of Connecticut. Please note that all of the cases were authored by the course instructors. Some of the cases have been previously published in works by the author, but the discussion questions have been created specifically for course use.

Discussion Case: The Intersection of Children's Rights and Immigrant Rights

(Based on a case developed by Ada Sanchez and originally published in L. M. Healy (2008) *International Social Work: Professional Action in an Interdependent World* [New York, NY: Oxford University Press, 2008; pp. 291–292]).

A child welfare supervisor, who is an immigrant from Peru, discussed this case. It is a real case and took place in Connecticut. The words are those of the social work supervisor.

A 6-year-old Mexican girl was referred by her school to our Child Protection Agency as at risk of medical neglect. The child had a rash; although her mother had been advised by the school nurse to take the child to a doctor, she had not done so. The social worker tried to interview the child, but the child seemed afraid and would not answer questions. The social worker then visited the mother with an interpreter and provided a list of doctors. The mother promised to take the child the next day; however, when the social worker visited the mother a week later, she had not followed through. The social worker told me in supervision that she was planning to recommend that protective services follow up to investigate the parents for medical and emotional neglect. During her visits the social worker had become concerned that the mother was always sleeping, could never find her medical or social security cards, and provided very little information. In addition, the social worker suspected the child could be developmentally delayed, because she would not look at the social worker and said very little. I decided to accompany the social worker on a home visit. As soon as the mother opened the door and her mouth, I realized she was from Mexico. Everything suddenly made sense to me. The mother and father were illegal immigrants. The mother worked third shift so she could be home with her child and the father could work during the day. They had no health care insurance and no money to pay for medical care. The mother was putting money aside so that she could take the child to a private doctor. The child was quite intelligent but knew she was forbidden to talk about her family situation.

Discussion Questions

- What is your analysis of the situation of this immigrant family?
- What human rights issues are raised by this case situation?
- As a human rights social worker, how would you shape your role if you were the social worker or social work supervisor?
- What should the social work supervisor do to help this family?

- What do you think would have happened if the supervisor were not an immigrant?

- What policy changes would you recommend at the local, national, and global levels?

Discussion Case: Introducing Policy Change for Children's Rights

Country X has ratified the CRC. This country has a deep cultural tradition of emphasis on parental rights. Children are expected to be seen but not heard. Corporal punishment—sometimes quite severe—is widely, indeed almost universally, accepted. School personnel and staff in other children's institutions may also discipline children physically.

Country X is a relatively small country, with a population about the size of Connecticut's population. It is a fairly poor country, with limited employment opportunities, a high rate of out-migration, and high international debt. It does have an important university that includes both a BSW and an MSW program.

You have been appointed as a consulting team to the Office on Children. How will you advise the office to proceed to introduce children's rights into policy and practice in Country X? What issues will you address first, and who will you engage in the process?

Discussion Case: Applying Human Rights Principles to Social Work Practice With Youth "Aging Out" of the U.S. Foster Care System

In preparation for this case, review the Human Rights Watch report titled *My So-Called Emancipation: From Foster Care to Homelessness for California Youth* (Human Rights Watch, 2010, http://www.hrw. org/reports/2010/05/12/my-so-called-emancipation-0).

You recently took a job at a local child advocacy organization recognized for its ability to build grassroots support for child welfare initiatives. Your organization has become increasingly concerned with the spread of the practice of dropping off youths "in state care" who have aged out of group home facilities at local homeless shelters.

Several youths have shared their stories with legal and social work interns who have been asked to research the details of such cases (see HRW report cited above). Your job is to help develop a campaign at the local and state levels that addresses this troubling practice, and you have been encouraged by several advocates to consider the human rights implications of failing to adequately prepare youths to make this transition after reaching adulthood.

After briefly reviewing the narrative testimonies, consider the following questions:

- What are the human rights principles at stake? Are the human rights of these youths being violated? If so, which rights?

- What are the obligations of social workers as agents of the state (government) in this case?

- What steps would you take to develop an effective campaign to secure the rights of youths aging out of the foster care system?

- Who would be the stakeholders you engage? How? Why?

- What difference might a human rights frame make?

Discussion Case: Cultural Relativism, Universalism, and Gender-Based Violence

This discussion was based on a case published in L. Healy, "Universalism and Cultural Relativism in Social Work Ethics," *International Social Work, 20*(1), 2007, 11–26.

Mrs. Nguyen, a Vietnamese refugee, came to the local welfare agency in the North American community in which she had been resettled. She was originally referred to the social worker for being in noncompliance with welfare work requirements. Mrs. Nguyen had not responded to notices from the welfare office nor had she attended training sessions required to maintain her welfare benefits. In an interview with the welfare office family caseworker, Mrs. Nguyen revealed that her husband had been keeping her a virtual prisoner in their apartment. In addition, she had been frequently beaten and verbally abused. She told the worker that she could not comply with the welfare department orders because she was not allowed to leave home. The caseworker referred Mrs. Nguyen to the local shelter for battered women and warned her that staying with her husband under these conditions was likely to result in the cut-off of all welfare support to her and her children. It could even result in the children being removed from the home, if they were left without sufficient support.

As events unfolded, Mrs. Nguyen decided to go to the shelter and made arrangements for her two children to be collected from school and taken to the shelter with her. On learning what had happened, Mrs. Nguyen's husband was furious. He engaged the help of the local Vietnamese Mutual Assistance Association, and together they accused the welfare agency and the shelter of destroying Vietnamese families in violation of cultural values and principles.

Discussion Questions

- Analyze the human rights issues in this case, using the UDHR and CEDAW.
- What rights are embedded in the issues in this case?
- Who are the relevant rights-holders, and do their rights conflict?

Discussion Case: When Religious Values and Human Rights Values Collide

The following discussion was based on a case written by L. M. Healy. A version of the case was discussed in L. M. Healy (2010), "Ethics in Social Work Management: Contesting the Encroachment of Managerialism in the Social Services," which was published in D. Zavirsek, B. Rommelspacher, and S. Staub-Bernasconi, *Ethical Dilemmas in Social Work: International Perspective* (Ljubljana: Faculty of Social Work, University of Ljubljana).

This case involves administrators and staff of a local Catholic Family Service agency operated by the Catholic diocese. The agency was located in a U.S. state where rights to civil unions for gay and lesbian couples were being debated in the state legislature. The proposal to establish legal civil unions was being strongly opposed by the Catholic Church. The local diocese office issued a directive to all of its agencies asking them to participate in active opposition to civil unions and gay marriage and to oppose the bill under debate. In response, the social work manager asked staff, including social workers, to appear at the legislature to oppose the bill. Some did so, standing outside the legislative office building with signs to oppose the equal rights bill under consideration. The case was brought to the instructor's attention by a gay social work student intern at the family service agency, who went to the legislature to support the bill. He told of his feelings of rejection and isolation at seeing his fellow social workers standing in active opposition to his human rights.

Discussion Questions

- What articles of the Universal Declaration of Human Rights, if any, are involved in this case?

- What social work ethical principles are involved in the case?

- Should universalism in human rights take precedence over religious values?

- How does social work address conflicts between personal, religious, and professional values?

- How might these dilemmas be addressed using human rights principles?

Discussion Exercise: What Difference Does a Human Rights Frame for Violence Against Women Make?

In a small group, review state- and federal-level definitions of violence against women. Note that for the state in question, such legal definitions may be categorized as family violence. How are the legal definitions between state and federal laws similar and how do they differ?

Examine the United Nations Declaration on the Elimination of Violence Against Women (DEVAW). Does DEVAW frame gender-based violence differently from state and federal definitions that you examined? How might a thorough understanding of DEVAW help reshape U.S. policies and judicial approaches to violence against women? Be prepared to share your ideas with the class.

Preamble to LivLand Exercise

Ogden Rogers
University of Wisconsin–River Falls

Preamble: The State of _____

Congress of the LivLand begun and held at the City of River Falls, on Tuesday the 26th of January, two thousand and twelve. The Conventions of a number of the states, having at the time of their adopting the Constitution expressed a desire, to prevent misconstruction or abuse of its powers, that further declaratory and restrictive clauses should be added: And as extending the ground of public confidence in the government, will best ensure the beneficent starts of its institution.

RESOLVED by the representatives of LivLand, in Congress assembled, two thirds of both Houses concurring, that the following Articles be accepted as amendments to the Constitution of LivLand.

1. _____

2. _____

3. _____

4. _____

5. _____

6. _____

7. _____

8. _____

9. _____

10. _____

Exercise on Children's Rights

Christina Chiarelli-Helminiak
University of Connecticut

Children's rights are often confused with what is good for children (Guggenheim, 2005). This small group activity provides students the opportunity to think critically about the difference between rights and what is perceived as good for children.

Students are divided into small groups. Each group is provided with a sheet of chart board paper and markers. Instruct the students to divide the sheet in half, writing *Children's Rights* on one side and *Good for Children* on the other. Provide students with an example for each column, such as *protection* as a right and *age appropriate toys* as good for children. Allow the groups 10–15 minutes to generate their own lists of children's rights and what is good for children.

Bring the class back together. Ask each group to present its list to the whole class. If you have sticky chart board paper, each list can be cut in half with all of the *Children's Rights* halves being stuck on one side of the wall and *Good for Children* halves on the other side.

After the groups have presented their lists, ask students for feedback on what has been presented as a children's right versus something that is good for children. Engage the class in a discussion using the following questions:

- What is the difference between children's rights and what is good for children?
- What is missing from the *Children's Rights* lists when examining the Convention on the Rights of the Child?
- Are there any items listed as *Good for Children* that you think are not necessarily good for children?
- Are there any items on the *Good for Children* list that you think should be identified as children's rights?
- How might things perceived as good for children differ in various countries?
- What shapes our views about what is good for children? What about for children's rights?

Reference

Guggenheim, M. (2005). *What's wrong with children's rights*. Cambridge, MA: Harvard University Press.

The Maid Narratives

Katherine van Wormer
University of Northern Iowa

Here is an unusual angle of the human rights focus in social work. Approximately 10 of the White narrators, some anonymous, were social work educators who grew up during the days of segregation. The form of racism described in all the narratives was especially noxious.

As we think about human rights history, an often overlooked group is the women who worked as domestic servants in the segregated South. We should note that it was such workers who in Montgomery, AL, engaged collectively in the first successful Civil Rights struggle, the Montgomery bus boycott, in 1955–1956. This is where the young Martin Luther King got his start. *The Maid Narratives* is a book dedicated to women who worked as maids in the Deep South and who showed resilience and resistance in the face of mass oppression.

The Maid Narratives: Black Domestics and White Families in the Jim Crow South contains narratives from women of the Great Migration from Mississippi and Louisiana to Iowa and by southern White women who grew up with maids in their homes (for information about the book, see http://lsupress.org/books/detail/the-maid-narratives/ and The Maid Narratives Facebook page.

An article about one of the book's narrators can be found at http://www.desmoinesregister.com/article/20121008/LIFE/310090017/Des-Moines-woman-recalls-life-maid.

Incorporating a National Human Rights Campaign Into Social Work Teaching

Jane McPherson
Florida State University

Step 1. Choose a Campaign and Choose a Class

Choosing a campaign and choosing a class in which to include it are linked actions. The campaign should address either the content or the process of the class. For example, a child welfare class might engage students in the Child Rights Campaign (http://www.childrightscampaign.org/), which is working toward U.S. ratification of the Convention on the Rights of the Child. Or the campaign could be to get involved with one of several activist projects at the Children's Defense Fund (http://www.childrensdefense.org/programscampaigns/). A course on social work with women might get involved in the National Organization of Women's work to ratify the Convention on the Elimination of all Forms of Discrimination against Women (http://www.now.org/ratifywomen/act.html) or support initiatives against gendered violence. An international social work class could get involved with the Conflict-Free Campus Initiative (http://www.raisehopeforcongo.org/content/conflict-free-campus-initiative), which is promoting conflict-free minerals, or with Amnesty International's campaigns (http://www.amnesty.org/en/activism-center). A domestic social policy class could ally itself with organizations lobbying for national legislative change. There are myriad options. Instructors concerned that some students might be alienated by a specific cause can give students a choice among campaigns or allow students to find a campaign of personal interest to them.

In spring and summer 2012 I incorporated One Million Bones (www.onemillionbones.org) into my BSW-level macro practice class. One Million Bones is a national arts-activism project that educates about genocide and mass violence, and advocates for intervention to prevent violence and assist survivors. Specifically, One Million Bones puts clay in the hands of participants and invites them to sculpt replicas of human bones while learning about human rights concepts and crises. Through a partnership with Students Rebuild (www.studentsrebuild.org), One Million Bones also provides a $1 donation to survivors of violence for each bone made. Finally, the bones are made to be seen: One Million Bones creates large-scale installations with these bones across the United States. The largest installation—1,000,000 bones—was installed on the National Mall on June 9th, 2013. Here is a video link to our One Million Bones project that shows my students making bones and creating installations in our community (http://youtube/7Zhd8bt4xG0).

The usual macro practice syllabus requires students to pick an agency or organization, complete an organizational assessment, and work in teams to organize an event or intervention at the agency. I used One Million Bones as the central activity of the course, so students chose an agency or organization where they wanted to make bones. They made an assessment of the organization (including identifying key informants) and scheduled and carried out a bone-making event at the location. In this way, the One Million Bones campaign fit easily into the usual syllabus for teaching macro practice.

Step 2: Give Students the Tools They Need to be Successful

We made bones in class beginning on Day 1. I gave attention to making sure that students were educated about One Million Bones, as well as the issues it raises: genocide, racism, life in the Democratic Republic of Congo, conflict minerals, and so forth. It was important that they felt comfortable with the process of making bones—and the content of One Million Bones—before they went out into the community as teachers and activists.

I prepared a checklist of everything that the students would need for their events. This was a strategy to give them confidence, teach them about organizing events, and also to give them the greatest chance of success.

I prepared PowerPoint presentations the students could show/adapt and provided them with video links that could help them. Students were required to consider the age and experience of their audiences as they determined which materials might be appropriate. For example, when engaging children in the project, it was more appropriate to show them photographs of children that might be helped by their bone-making than to explain the dynamics of genocide or show graphic images of violence.

Step 3: Connect the Human Rights Campaign to a Social Work Mission

I also integrated human rights content into the standard macro practice curriculum, using human rights as a central theme and One Million Bones as a central activity. Traditional social work issues (e.g., poverty, health care, discrimination, and violence) were presented in macro context with an attention to human rights concerns, and links were made between civil rights violations familiar to U.S. citizens (e.g., discrimination on the basis of race, gender, religion, ethnicity, and sexuality) and human rights violations such as crimes against humanity, mass rape, and genocide. Relevant human rights documents, such as the Universal Declaration of Human Rights (United Nations, 1948b) and the Convention Against Genocide (United Nations, 1948a) were also introduced.

Step 4. Run the Campaign in Your Classroom

As students were engaging the community, I ran the campaign in the classroom. I gave students constant feedback about the difference they are making in the world. With One Million Bones, we had a class tally of events held, bones made, and dollars raised. In a different campaign, this might be signatures collected, petitions signed, or letters written.

In the course of two semesters my students provided human rights education at more than 20 events in the community—at organizations including the Senior Center, a Jewish temple, Walmart, and an art center. They made bones with hotline volunteers, at-risk youths, young adults with disabilities, summer campers, and students in local elementary and high schools. One group of students even organized an event under a local tree that has been connected to four lynching deaths of Black men between 1897 and 1937. Overall, the students made more than 6,000 bones and therefore raised more than $6,000 for survivors of mass violence.

Benefits to Students

Students were proud of their accomplishments in the real world. As one student wrote on her final evaluation,

> The most meaningful part of this project for me was my personal donation to this project. I was truly proud of myself for all the bones I personally sculpted. I didn't do it for recognition or a "pat on the back," I did it out of the goodness of my heart, and, for a second, I thought if this was my family I would want someone to lend a hand and help them through their rough times; this is why I loved this project.

Students were empowered. This student comment was typical: "One Million Bones has taught me that doing something small is the best place to start. A bunch of people doing something small can end up making a huge difference."

Human rights events in the community are newsworthy; therefore, about 30% of the students had the opportunity to be on radio, television, or in the newspaper. Here are press pieces that feature student participants on television (http://www.youtube.com/watch?v=cX8wyU1ZS7g) and in a newspaper article (http://csw.fsu.edu/articles/onemillionbones/).

Students who participated in this project increased their exposure to human rights by 36%, as measured by the Human Rights Exposure in Social Work scale (McPherson & Abell, 2012).

References

McPherson, J., & Abell, N. (2012). Human rights engagement and exposure in social work: New scales to challenge social work education. *Research in Social Work Practice, 22*, 704-713. doi:10.1177/1049731512454196

United Nations. (1948a). *Convention against genocide.* New York, NY: Author.

United Nations. (1948b). *Universal declaration of human rights.* New York, NY: Author.

The Truth Commission Assignment

Melissa Affronti
Nicole Trabold
Nazareth College and State University of New York

To whom it may concern:

The Greater Rochester Collaborative Master of Social Work Program Advanced Social Policy class is looking for individuals who would be willing to share stories about human rights violations. These stories will be collected in preparation for a Truth Commission scheduled for October 2008. The Commission will be part of a poverty conference planned by the Social Action Welfare Alliance, a local human rights advocacy group. A truth commission is an opportunity for community members and/or professionals to tell the stories of human rights violations that are occurring in our society. Invited commissioners, people who are leaders in social change, then report their ideas on how these violations can be prevented. To have a successful truth commission, it is necessary to collect the real, heartfelt stories of downsizing, welfare cuts, housing evictions, and denial of health care benefits and current economic struggles that leave families without food, clothing, and shelter. This event provides an opportunity for an organized public forum that allows for the analysis of the causes, consequences, and potential solutions to these human rights abuses. The time commitment for this project is relatively short and will entail meeting with a student to create a testimony of the human rights violations experienced and demonstrate the economic hardships members of the Rochester Community are facing. The hope of this project is to create a collective voice and advocate for changes in policy that have been instrumental in these human rights violations.

Best regards,

Melissa Affronti, PhD, LMSW
Nicole Trabold, PhD, LMSW
Advanced Social Policy Instructors
State University of New York, Brockport and Nazareth College

Truth Commission Assignment

This is a multifaceted assignment that will pull together several areas of social work skill development. First, it will allow the student to learn about several human rights violations that occur with at-risk populations. Second, the student will be able to make the connection between human rights violations and policy. Third, the student will analyze a policy based on the human rights violations and will make recommendations for policy change. Finally, by collecting and presenting client stories the student will make a direct contribution to a local poverty conference and may influence systems change. The Social Welfare Action Alliance, the local human rights advocacy group organizing the fall poverty conference, will make a small presentation during the first class on truth commissions and will attend the final class during which students will present testimony.

Part I

The student will collect evidence of human rights violations from people with whom he or she works to provide services or with an agency that has agreed to take part in this project. The student will complete a human rights violations form that includes a summary page. The student will also work with the person whose rights have been violated to write a testimony of his or her experiences. A format for the testimony will be distributed to the class. (Reports form completion will count for 10 points; testimony will count for 15 points.)

Part II

The student will select one policy (local, state, or federal) or a section of a policy that is connected to the human rights violations. The student will write a 10–12 page policy analysis paper using the following outline.

1. Provide a copy of the relevant policy or section of the policy found at the federal, state, or local level. *(2 points)*

2. Provide a brief history of this law including:

   A. Why it was introduced; that is, which political, economic, and social circumstances led to the formation of this policy? *(3 points)*

   B. Which special interest groups supported or were against passing the bill? *(3 points)*

   C. Which problems are supposed to be addressed by this public policy? *(3 points)*

3. How does the policy construct and distribute social power? *(4 points)*

4. What appear to be the cultural and social values inherent in this policy? *(5 points)*

5. What are three specific changes (*9 points*) you would recommend for this policy and why? Please include examples of how the current social *(3 points)*, political *(3 points)*, and economic context *(3 points)* of this policy would be changed as a result of your recommendations.

Part III

The student will present the testimony during the final class and provide a plan for how the testimony can be reported during the conference (e.g., poster, personal testimony from client). Members from the Social Welfare Action Alliance will attend the final class. *(Total: 5 points)*

Truth Commission Assignment Checklist and Format: Parts A and C

1. Choose one person, family, couple for the focus your testimony of Economic Human Rights Violations

2. Collect their stories by conducting interviews, preferably face to face. You should take as much time as necessary for acquiring the needed information. You may need to build trust and rapport before you can fully document and understand the economic human rights violation.

3. Complete Appendix C of the *Guide to Organizing a Truth Commission*

   A. This should include information regarding the specific economic human rights being violated – please refer to Appendix C for examples of violations for each article.

B. Make sure that the confidentiality waiver on the bottom of Appendix C is signed and any qualifications are documented.

C. This is worth 10 points of your final grade. The grade will be based on thoroughness and critical thought. The summary must be at least two pages and must not exceed four pages doubled-spaced. Please type the testimony directly into Appendix C.

4. Prepare for the presentation (the presentation should not exceed 15 minutes).

    * You will need to plan how this information will be presented on the last day of class.

        » Will the individual/family/couple be present, will they present the testimony, will you present the testimony, and so forth?

        » This should be a process that you all decide on and something that makes sense for what you are presenting.

        » Please provide a brief summary/outline of your presentation format. Will you be speaking? Will you have visuals or handouts? What led to these decisions? Please also include a brief outline of the content. This is worth 5 points of your final grade. The grade for the presentation will be based on overall professionalism, clarity, and organization.

5. Create testimony; this is what will be presented on the last day of class.

    * You will want to create a final product that outlines the economic human rights violations and how you plan to present this information.

        » The testimony can be done by/with the individual, family, or couple that you are working with.

        » This process should include some of the following: narrative, pictures, video, artwork, poem, music/song.

        » You will need enough content for a presentation that will not exceed 15 minutes but will not be less than 5 minutes.

        » The most important things are to accurately recount the violations that are presented to you and that the individual/family/couple is/are comfortable with what is being presented about them.

        » Be creative and enjoy this process.

        » This is worth 15 points. The grade for the testimony will be based on thoroughness, clarity, and the documentation/link to human rights violations.

Attending will be students and instructors of both sections of the Social Work Policy class, he social work program director, Social Welfare Action Alliance members, truth commissioners, and representatives from community organizations.

The event will be filmed by local Indymedia (http://rochester.indymedia.org). Releases for filming will be distributed with the guide to organizing a truth commission as people enter the event. Releases will be collected prior to the opening comments.

Agenda

- Opening comments (Social work program director)
- Introductions (Joint Policy instructors)
- Violations of economic human rights (People whose rights have been violated and students
- Truth commissioners will comment and answer the following questions:

    1. What does this testimony tell us (your Questions 4 a-c)?

    2. Which visions and strategies are best to address these problems (your Question 4c)?

        » Are these economic human rights violations?

        » Could they have been prevented?

        » Who is responsible?

        » What's the solution to these economic human rights violations?

Rules of War

Ogden Rogers
University of Wisconsin—River Falls

The former Marxist state of Grouchostan split into two different countries at the end of the Cold War: Sylvania to the north and Fredonia to the south.

Sylvans enjoyed their mountainous and forested region that hosted numerous mining opportunities for a number of rich mineral deposits. Rivers and streams provided for a modest industrial power base. They maintain a capital city of Harpo in the central Northeast.

Fredons occupied a land of rolling plains and generally favorable weather that made for a strong agricultural economy. Their capital city is Gummo in the central southeast, but they enjoy Groucho as a major economic and cultural hub.

At the base of the hills of Sylvania lay a mixed forested/agricultural land divided on both sides by a split in a major river. This rich area was known as Ambivila, with its major city of Groucho, which was the capital of the former Grouchostan. The population was a mix of ethnic Fredons and Sylvans, and it has been contested since the fall of Grouchostan. It is presently controlled by Fredonia.

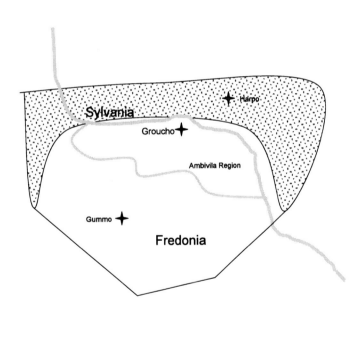

Under Soviet controlled Gouchostan, the primary language was Russian, which is now the common language of both groups. The differences between the Sylvans and the Fredons appear subtle, but are intensely held.

Sylvania has an orientation to Slavic culture and has adopted a civil law-based constitution. Sylvans tend to shake right hands in greeting and hold the fork in the right hand when eating.

Fredons have an old history of western colonization prior to Soviet occupation. There has long been a bilingual English–Slavic tradition. Although they shake right hands in greeting, Fredons eat with the fork in the left hand, English-style, and have adopted a common-law legal system.

In recent weeks the government in Harpo has complained that minority Sylvans in Groucho are being harassed by the local Fredons. They have massed artillery and infantry on the northern edge of the River Zeppo and have indicated that they intend to move into and occupy Groucho for the protection of all its citizens. Fredonia has issued a statement that no aggressive motion across the northern branch of the Zeppo will be tolerated.

The Sylvan president has communicated to the Fredonian government that its aggression toward ethnic Sylvans will not be tolerated and that if they come to armed conflict, he would like to propose some rules to protect the basics of humanity.

Assignment

You group will be either a Fredonian or Sylvanian military legal commission. Your task is to construct some basic rules of combat that can be proposed to both sides for agreement before aggression begins.

Establish a preamble and develop at least 10–15 articles to be proposed to the "other side."

Violations Scenarios

Fredonian forces have battled Sylvanians all afternoon to gain a bridge into Groucho. The infantry has tried several attacks and was repulsed. There are many wounded and dead soldiers lying on the bridge.

A Fredonian ambulance pulls onto to the bridge in an apparent attempt to rescue the wounded, and Sylvans cease fire. The ambulance speeds up approaching the Sylvan positions and as it does, soldiers fire from their position in the ambulance at Sylvan forces. Sylvans fire back at the ambulance. The ambulance overturns in the skirmish, and several Fredonian soldiers are captured.

The Sylvan soldiers want to kill them on the way to the detention center, but a Sylvan platoon commander orders them to stand down.

Are there any Fredonian violations? Are there any Sylvanian violations?

If so, cite applicable convention and articles. What actions can be taken? By whom? Under what authority?

Human Rights Law Exam

Ogden Rogers
University of Wisconsin—River Falls

Human Rights Law Final Exam

Student Name_____

Student ID Number_____

Instructions

1. Be sure you are using a #2 pencil.

2. Put only your name and student ID number on the answer sheet and fill in the appropriate circles completely.

3. Select the best answer and only one answer for each question.

4. When finished, turn in both the examination and answer sheet.

5. Never eat in a place called Mom's or play cards with a man named Doc.

Exam Questions

1. Which one of the following international legal instruments does not have a preamble basis in the United Nations Charter?

   A. International Covenant of Civil and Political Rights

   B. UN Declaration on the Rights of the Child

   C. The Geneva Conventions

   D. International Covenant Economic, Social, and Cultural Rights

   E. The UN Declaration of Human Rights

2. Which legal theory is based on a premise that all law is a social contract?

   A. Natural law theory

   B. Legal positivism

   C. Legal realism

   D. Critical legal studies

3. The legal tradition that tends to bind judges to making decisions based on analogy of prior court decisions:

   A. Natural law

   B. Common law

   C. Civil law

   D. Canon law

4. The 9th Amendment case successfully brought before the U.S. Supreme Court who felt he was denied a right to counsel:

   A. *Gideon v. Wainwright* (Florida)

   B. *Roe v. Wade*

   C. *Kideon v. Washington*

   D. *Tarrasoff v. California Board of Regents*

5. International law instruments have a hierarchical system. What is the correct order of instruments from broadest to the most narrow?

   A. Charter, declaration, treaty, covenant, convention, statute, protocols

   B. Protocols, statute, convention, covenant, treaty, declaration, charter

   C. Convention, treaty, declaration, statute, protocols, covenant, charter

   D. Treaty, declaration, covenant, charter, protocols, convention, statute

6. That portion of a legal instrument that provides the rationale for the document's creation:

   A. Signature

   B. Articles

   C. Preamble

   D. Procedures

7. A person who seeks asylum in a new country fearing persecution in his or her country of origin and who has been granted protected status in a new country:

   A. Detainee

   B. Retained person

   C. Asylee

   D. Refugee

   E. Internee

8. Basic legal brocard that supports the idea behind the prior decision theory of common law:

   A. *Veritas et justitia*

   B. *Pacta sunt servanda*

   C. *Bona fide*

   D. *Stare decisis*

9. Process whereby a nation agrees to be bound by an international treaty after the instrument has already gone into force:

   A. Ratification

   B. Accession

   C. Reservation

   D. Derogation

10. Amendment to the U.S. Constitution that protects the right to remain silent and not bear witness against self

    A. 1st

    B. 3rd

    C. 5th

    D. 6th

11. Articles 22–27 (Column IV) of the Universal Declaration of Human Rights focus on

    A. Collective and social rights

    B. Individual civil and political rights

    C. Rights of due process and fair trial

    D. Freedom from torture and assault on human dignity

12. Which international legal instrument codifies the Universal Declaration of Human Rights "Column IV" rights?

    A. UN Declaration on the Rights of the Child

    B. The Geneva Conventions

    C. The Hague Adoption Conventions

    D. The International Convention on Civil and Political Rights

    E. The International Convention on Economic, Social and Cultural Rights

13. Which legal theory acknowledges that law is constructed by fallible humans and allows other types of evidence such as science to support legal arguments?

    A. Natural law theory

    B. Legal positivism

    C. Legal realism

    D. Critical legal studies

14. Basic legal brocard that supports the idea behind the contract theory of international law:

    A. *Veritas et justitia*

    B. *Pacta sunt servanda*

    C. *Bona fide*

    D. *Stare decisis*

15. Which legal theory holds that law exists independently of people and is discoverable by reason?

    A. Natural law theory

    B. Legal positivism

    C. Legal realism

    D. Critical legal studies

16. Which of the following is a nonbinding international legal instrument?

    A. UN Declaration on the Rights of the Child

    B. The Geneva Conventions

    C. The Hague Adoption Conventions

    D. The International Convention on Civil and Political Rights

    E. The International Convention on Economic, Social, and Cultural Rights

17. Many human rights instruments allow derogation under what following circumstances?

    A. priority to one's national citizens

    B. priority to women and children

    C. priority to public order and safety

    D. priority to religious concerns

18. The legal tradition that bases law on the principle in the Qur'an and the teachings of Mohammad:

    A. Natural law

    B. *Jus gentium*

    C. Sharia law

    D. Canon law

19. Which legal theory holds that law is essentially made by the powerful to serve their needs?

    A. Natural law theory

    B. Legal positivism

    C. Legal realism

    D. Critical legal studies

20. The "first generation" of human rights tend to focus on:

    A. Individual civil and political rights

    B. social, cultural, and economic rights

    C. collective peace, sustainable development, and ecological rights

    D. protection of the most vulnerable in armed conflict

21. Process whereby a nation agrees to be bound by an international treaty before the instrument has gone into force:

    A. Ratification

    B. Accession

    C. Reservation

    D. Derogation

22. The principal in international legal instruments that realizes that developing nations may not have the resources to make all human rights guarantees available but must make a good faith effort over time:

    A. Proportionality

    B. Progressive implementation

    C. Distinction

    D. Nondiscrimination

23. The legal tradition that requires all law to be positive in construction and publicly published:

    A. Natural law

    B. Common law

    C. Civil law

    D. Canon law

24. Which one of the below would represent an example of substantive law in a legal instrument?

    A. Preamble

    B. Signature

    C. Articles

    D. Date of entry into force

25. Which system of law uses lawyers to act as advocates for different sides of an argument to "fight out" the truth?

    A. Common law

    B. Civil law

    C. Natural law

    D. Positive law

26. "Normative law" is said to be based on

    A. What is ideal, rather than real

    B. What is real, rather than ideal

    C. What has already been decided

    D. What is only agreed to in a legislature

27. American social reformer instrumental in developing the Universal Declaration of Human Rights

    A. Eleanor Roosevelt

    B. Thomas Paine

    C. James Madison

    D. Thomas Jefferson

28. Which of the legal instruments below is binding law?

    A. Declaration of Independence of the United States

    B. Constitution of the United States

    C. Universal Declaration of Human Rights

    D. Declaration on the Rights of the Child

23. Activity by a state that is considered so horrible that it "shocks the sensibility of humanity" is captured in the

    A. The Nonderogation Clause

    B. The Martens Clause

    C. The Due Process Clause

    D. The Santa Clause

30. Which of the below is the name of an obligation on a person or a state that is created by a law?

    A. Right

    B. Freedom

    C. Duty

    D. Privilege

31. Amendment to the U.S. Constitution that protects right to a speedy public trial and right to confront accusers

    A. 1st

    B. 3rd

    C. 4th

    D. 6th

32. Basic legal brocard that argues the reciprocity agreements found in international law:

    A. *Quid pro quo*

    B. *Nullem crimins*

    C. *Bona fide*

    D. *Stare decisis*

33. Which one of the below would represent an example of defining an aspect of jurisdiction in a legal instrument?

    A. Preamble

    B. Procedures

    C. Articles

    D. Date of entry into force

34. Principle in the Geneva Conventions that limits combatants to firing only on legitimate military targets:

    A. Proportionality

    B. Indicative use

    C. Distinction

    D. Military necessity

35. One of the below would be an example of empirical critique of poor positive law

    A. The U.S. Bill of Rights

    B. The Constitution of the United States

    C. Legal slavery in the United States prior to the Emancipation Proclamation

    D. The Civil Rights Act

36. The "second generation" of human rights tend to focus on

    A. Individual civil and political rights

    B. Social, cultural, and economic rights

    C. Collective peace, sustainable development, and ecological rights

    D. Protection of the most vulnerable in armed conflict

37. Which of the international legal instruments below comes into force with the onset of armed conflict?

    A. UN Declaration on the Rights of the Child

    B. The International Humanitarian Law

    C. The UN Declaration of Human Rights

    D. The International Convention on Civil and Political Rights

    E. The International Convention on Economic, Social, and Cultural Rights

38. The "power of enforcement" in natural law arises in

    A. The use of force to fine or imprison

    B. The conscious

    C. The use of international economic sanctions

    D. Agreement from all the nations of the world

39. Most international human rights instruments are not self-executing and require what kind of law written by a sovereign state?

    A. Common law

    B. Sharia law

    C. Municipal law

    D. Natural law

True-or-False Instructions

Answer each of the questions with only one answer. Fill in only one circle completely for each answer. Follow the following code: True=A; False=B.

		True	False
40.	Customary international law is known as the Law of Nations.	(A)	(B)
41.	International treaties and conventions are not self-executing in the United States.	(A)	(B)
42.	Positive law is ultimately enforced by sanction of force.	(A)	(B)
43.	The Universal Declaration of Human Rights has been criticized by eastern countries as being too "individual rights oriented."	(A)	(B)
44.	*Jus cogens* is law in which derogation is acceptable.	(A)	(B)
45.	Thomas Paine based *The Rights of Man* in positive law philosophy.	(A)	(B)
46.	*Miranda v. Arizona* (USSC 1966) requires police to advise suspects of their 5th Amendment rights.	(A)	(B)
47.	The *U.S. Code* is municipal federal law.	(A)	(B)
48.	The Universal Declaration of Human Rights was developed to be binding law.	(A)	(B)
49.	The Universal Declaration of Human Rights implies that rebellion might be legal.	(A)	(B)
50.	The Americans with Disabilities Act is municipal law.	(A)	(B)
51.	The Geneva Conventions are part of the "supreme law of the land" in the United States.	(A)	(B)
52.	The Universal Declaration of Human Rights asserts legal government must be based on the will of the governed.	(A)	(B)
53.	The *jus gentium* was a code of law developed by Hammurabi.	(A)	(B)
54.	The Code Napoleon is an early example of natural law.	(A)	(B)
55.	Persons *hors de combat* are not legitimate military targets	(A)	(B)

Human Rights Exposure and Engagement: Using Standardized Instruments to Assess Human Rights Teaching and Learning in Social Work

Jane McPherson
Florida State University

The Human Rights Engagement in Social Work (HRESW) and the Human Rights Exposure in Social Work (HRXSW) are the only two scales measuring human rights knowledge, attitudes, and behaviors that have been validated in populations of social work students (McPherson & Abell, 2012).

These scales have multiple uses in the classroom, including the following:

Prior knowledge assessment: If used early in the semester, the scales can be used to assess students' prior exposure to human rights and/or engagement with human rights concepts. Both scales make reference to the Universal Declaration of Human Rights (UDHR), although no prior knowledge is necessary to complete them. Also, they can serve as a good introduction to teaching the UDHR and other human rights concepts for social workers.

Self-evaluation and discussion: The scales can also be used for student self-evaluation, and then used to structure small group and/or class discussion about the UDHR and human rights.

Teaching evaluation: If an instructor asks students to complete the scales at the beginning of the semester and again at the end (pretest/posttest), the scales can be used to measure learning over the course of the semester by comparing the pretest and posttest means. In one classroom students' human rights exposure, as measured by the HRXSW, increased by 36% over the course of the semester (McPherson & Cheatham, in press).

Scoring Instructions

- **HRESW:** For each completed scale, reverse responses for Items 4 and 8 (e.g., a score of 6 should be logged as a score of 2). Next, substituting the new scores for Items 4 and 8, add up the circled responses and divide the total number by 25. This results in an individual score ranging from 1 to 7, with higher scores indicating greater human rights engagement. To get the class mean, calculate an average of the individual scores.

- **HRXSW:** For each completed scale, add up the circled responses and divide the total number by 11. This results in an individual score ranging from 1 to 7, with higher scores indicating greater human rights exposure. To get the class mean, calculate an average of the individual scores.

Reliability

In the validation study (McPherson & Abell, 2012), the HRESW was calculated to have strong reliability (α = .894; *M*=6.02; *SD* = .644), and the reliability of the HRXSW was acceptable (α = .734; *M*=4.46; *SD*=.905) (Cronbach & Meehl, 1955).

References

Cronbach, L. J., & Meehl, P. E. (1955). Construct validity in psychological tests. *Psychological Bulletin, 52,* 281–302.

McPherson, J., & Abell, N. (2012). Human rights engagement and exposure in social work: New scales to challenge social work education. *Research in Social Work Practice, 22,* 704-713. doi:10.1177/1049731512454196

McPherson, J., & Cheatham, L. P. (In press). Measuring human rights impact in social work education: The One Million Bones example. *Journal of Social Work Education.*

This scale measures human rights engagement in social work (HRESW). It addresses (1) your endorsement of human rights ideas, (2) your sense of the relevance of human rights to the social work profession, and (3) your application of human rights in your own social work practice.

Several of the items refer to the Universal Declaration of Human Rights (UDHR), which was passed unanimously by the United States and the other members of the UN General Assembly in 1948. No previous knowledge of the UDHR is necessary to complete this scale. If you don't currently have an active social work practice, please answer those questions in terms of clients you have had in the past or might have in the future. There are no RIGHT or WRONG answers.

Please answer with your true thoughts, beliefs, and opinions according to the following scale:

Strongly Disagree	Disagree	Slightly Disagree	Neither Agree nor Disagree	Slightly Agree	Agree	Agree
1	2	3	4	5	6	7

1	I believe that equal rights for all are the foundation for freedom in the world.	1	2	3	4	5	6	7
2	As a social worker, I pursue social change, particularly on behalf of victims of discrimination and oppression.	1	2	3	4	5	6	7
3	The high rate of incarceration among of Black men in the United States is a human rights issue that is appropriate for social work intervention.	1	2	3	4	5	6	7
4	Sometimes torture is necessary to protect national security.	1	2	3	4	5	6	7
5	It is unethical for social workers to ignore violations of their clients' human rights.	1	2	3	4	5	6	7
6	Domestic violence is an area of social work practice that is motivated by concern for the victim's human rights.	1	2	3	4	5	6	7
7	I would advocate for my client's rights, even if that advocacy put me in a difficult situation.	1	2	3	4	5	6	7
8	Poverty is not a human rights issue.	1	2	3	4	5	6	7
9	I help my clients by educating them about their human rights.	1	2	3	4	5	6	7
10	Everyone has the right to reasonable working hours and periodic holidays with pay.	1	2	3	4	5	6	7
11	It is social work's mission to ensure an adequate standard of living for the health and well-being of the families we work with.	1	2	3	4	5	6	7

12	When I think about my clients' economic needs in terms of human rights, I can reduce the stigma of poverty.	1	2	3	4	5	6	7
13	I believe that everyone has a right to just wages, and supplemented, if necessary, by other means of social protection.	1	2	3	4	5	6	7
14	I am committed to advocating for my clients' human rights.	1	2	3	4	5	6	7
15	Social workers should promote the human right to health care.	1	2	3	4	5	6	7
16	I advocate for my clients' right to high-quality, accessible health care.	1	2	3	4	5	6	7
17	Mothers with young children are entitled to assistance from their governments.	1	2	3	4	5	6	7
18	When my clients lack access to food, clothing, housing, and medical care and necessary social services, it is my responsibility as a social worker to intervene on their behalf.	1	2	3	4	5	6	7
19	Social workers should advocate for their clients to have access to quality education, regardless of their race, income, or neighborhood zone.	1	2	3	4	5	6	7
20	I believe that the right to housing requires adequate shelter, and also the right to live in security, peace, and dignity.	1	2	3	4	5	6	7
21	Respecting clients' freedom of religion is part of social work practice.	1	2	3	4	5	6	7
22	When I work with clients, I acknowledge their inherent human dignity.	1	2	3	4	5	6	7
23	I think that infectious disease is a human rights issue.	1	2	3	4	5	6	7
24	Social workers should partner with their clients in the effort to access and uphold human rights.	1	2	3	4	5	6	7
25	I am a human rights advocate.	1	2	3	4	5	6	7

This scale measures human rights exposure in social work (HRXSW). It addresses your exposure to human rights principles.

Please answer according to the following scale:

Strongly Disagree	Disagree	Slightly Disagree	Neither Agree nor Disagree	Slightly Agree	Agree	Agree
1	2	3	4	5	6	7

1	I have read the Universal Declaration of Human Rights.	1	2	3	4	5	6	7
2	My social work curriculum covered the Universal Declaration of Human Rights.	1	2	3	4	5	6	7
3	My education covered human rights violations that happen in the United States.	1	2	3	4	5	6	7
4	My coursework covered international human rights issues.	1	2	3	4	5	6	7
5	Social work has been a good way for me to learn about human rights.	1	2	3	4	5	6	7

6	I have heard or read about social and cultural rights.	1	2	3	4	5	6	7
7	I hear about human rights from the media on an ongoing basis.	1	2	3	4	5	6	7
8	I learn about human rights issues in my work.	1	2	3	4	5	6	7
9	My friends and family discuss human rights issues with me.	1	2	3	4	5	6	7
10	I am aware that the United Nations has a role in monitoring international human rights.	1	2	3	4	5	6	7
11	I have heard that the National Association of Social Workers endorsed the Universal Declaration of Human Rights.	1	2	3	4	5	6	7

Teaching Content on Human Rights: Media and Bibliography

Introduction

Lynne M. Healy

This section contains entries that provide suggestions for videos that can be used in the classroom to enhance teaching human rights. The first is a playlist on YouTube with a discussion guide. The second is a list of documentary films on human rights issues in the United States. These are of particular importance in helping instructors bring the topic of human rights home to domestic practice and policy concerns. Following the two lists of video resources are two specific recommendations with discussion questions. *The House We Live In* is part of a series on race. This video is recommended for teaching about housing discrimination and the broader issue of racism. It is especially useful in courses on social welfare policy. Another suggested video is *The Corporation,* which introduces human rights and corporate roles and power, subjects less frequently addressed in human rights courses. The final media suggestion is a film that can be used to introduce the topic of human rights and the Universal Declaration of Human Rights. The entry suggests using a social work textbook to enhance and extend the learning from the film.

The volume concludes with a selective bibliography of works that are particularly useful for the teaching of human rights and social work. It reflects the growing contributions of social work authors to the human rights literature and also includes a modest number of works from other disciplines and websites of key human rights organizations.

Human Rights: A Quick Start Supported Through YouTube

Ruthanne L. Hackman
Keuka College

This module consists of a 27-minute playlist on YouTube and discussion. The learning objectives for this module are for students to have a foundational understanding of human rights that they can use in future discussions on policy and social justice issues. This module has been used in diversity courses, but also has utility in social welfare policy and social welfare history courses. Typically, it has been well-received by undergraduate students and could be a resource for graduate students.

Purpose

The purpose of this YouTube playlist is to provide a foundation of working knowledge regarding human rights. After a brief introduction to the topic, the 27-minute playlist is shown in its entirety and followed by a classroom discussion. The video content ranges from misunderstandings about human rights, to the creation and history of human rights, the organizations working on human rights issues, the universality of human rights, and a human rights issue in the United States. Although some of the videos are dated, the information remains relevant. Often, the students become engaged with this discrepancy and are sent to research the current status of one of the issues highlighted in one of the videos. The playlist is posted on the online course management system for the students to access later, as needed. Throughout the course and in other parts of the curriculum, students need to integrate human rights into their assignments.

Learning Objectives

After students watch this playlist and participate in discussion, the learning objectives are assessed at a later date through multiple choice and essay questions on exams. This content also is integrated into papers. Specific pieces of knowledge that students should be able to articulate after the module include the following:

- Human rights did not always exist/were not always recognized
- Human rights cannot be taken away, but may be ignored and violated.
- Human rights are not like civil rights and transcend borders.
- The United Nations is the primary institution for oversight of human rights.
- Human rights can be violated anywhere in the world, including the United States.
- Many organizations fight for human rights.
- The most important person in protecting your human rights is you.

Students also should be able to list 5–10 Articles of the Universal Declaration of Human Rights.

Playlist

Below is the list of YouTube videos in the playlist order with brief annotations. In addition, the following link should start with the first video and share the full playlist: http://www.youtube.com/watch?v=yoBKTANRN9I&feature=share&list=PLCBDEFBDFF87A32D2

Human TV. (Nov. 24, 2008). *What Do Human Rights Mean to You?* http://youtu.be/yoBKTANRN9I (Run time 1:50)

This video presents responses from various people on the street regarding their understanding of human rights. Showing this video first gives the students a sense that common people, like themselves, have little understanding of human rights. It works well as an ice breaker for the topic.

UNICEF. (November 20, 2008). *UNICEF: Archbishop Desmond Tutu on Universal Human Rights.* http://youtu.be/v3R_kBqROOQ (Run time 0:35)

This is a public service announcement by Archbishop Desmond Tutu and produced by UNICEF that highlights the Universal Declaration of Human Rights in relationship to children.

Acluvideos. (September 11, 2008). *Anniversary of the Universal Declaration of Human Rights.* http://youtu.be/B6VO0fsg6r8 (Run time 8:21)

This video produced by the American Civil Liberties Union starts with original footage of Eleanor Roosevelt's address to the United Nations General Assembly. It provides a historical overview of the formation of the Universal Declaration of Human Rights and how it has been used and implemented for 60 years.

Human Rights Action Center. (December 5, 2008). *The Universal Declaration of Human Rights II.* http://youtu.be/aiFIu_z4dM8 (Run time 5:46)

Each of the 30 articles is presented by an artist, advocate, or child. This video was produced by the Human Rights Action Center to celebrate the 60th anniversary of the Universal Declaration of Human Rights. Although the Universal Declaration of Human Rights is a required reading for this course, hearing the articles read by familiar celebrities seems to get students interested in the articles. Typically, by the end of this session students can list 5–10 articles.

Human Rights Action Center. (December 9, 2008). *Universal Declaration of Human Rights in Passports.* http://youtu.be/AVbzsRxB5aU (Run time 1:14).

This video by the Human Rights Action Center highlights the campaign to have the Universal Declaration of Human Rights printed in passports. It highlights the human rights violations against Aung San Suu Kyi of Burma. The postvideo discussion emphasizes how human rights are different from civil rights in that they transcend borders, and it highlights the current status of the Burmese leader.

Amnesty USA. (May 28, 2009). *2009 Global Status of Human Rights.* http://youtu.be/r7Qw9QFHrZc (Run time 5:09).

The video produced by Amnesty International highlights the human rights crisis that is exacerbated by the economic crisis. The video highlights of human rights violations worldwide ranging from war and ethnic discrimination to famine.

media4movements. (April 19, 2009). *United Workers Human Rights Zone March, April 18, 2009.* http://youtu.be/WXoOEiNy1Wk (Run time 1:24)

This video produced by the United Workers shows the demonstration in Baltimore, MD, on April 18, 2009, calling for human rights for the workers of Inner Harbor. The video is in English and Spanish with subtitles. This video is shown to help students understand that human rights violations are committed not only in foreign countries, but that they also can occur in the United States.

Amnesty International. (November 21, 2008). *Fire Up.* http://youtube/6f_bssjf5sA . (Run time 1:48).

This cartoon and video produced by Amnesty International is part of the campaign to celebrate Human Rights Day, December 10. This video provides students with a call to action, which they can choose to address individually or collectively.

nyfael. (September 12, 2009). *Youth For Human Rights—No One Can Take Away Human Rights.* (Run time 1:01; www.youtube.com/watch?v=sGUSufivz9c)

This video produced by Youth for Human Rights explores Article 30. It emphasized that human rights cannot be taken away, although they can be ignored and violated. Likewise, the discussion emphasizes that everyone has human rights and language to use when describing human rights.

Selected Documentary Films Illustrating Human Rights Concerns in the United States

Kathryn Libal
Lynne M. Healy
University of Connecticut

These documentary films provide rich resources for class discussion to illustrate the relevance of human rights work in the United States. Of note, the human rights film advocacy organization, WITNESS, collaborates with local partners to create documentaries to use in policy advocacy and to raise public awareness. WITNESS regularly updates its website and includes resources for advocacy related to a particular film and campaign. Many human rights nongovernmental organizations now devote resources to video production and share short films through YouTube or Vimeo. The National Economic and Social Rights Initiative (www.nesri.org), Human Rights Watch (www.hrw.org), and WITNESS (www.witness.org) provide good examples of this kind of work.

Ain't I a Person *(2011)*

This film created by social work professor Keith Kilty focuses on the experiences and thoughts of several individuals who are poor or near-poor in the United States. It provides contextual background on poverty in the United States, trying to dispel some of the dominant myths of poverty. It intersects well with discussions on economic and social rights in the United States. A study guide is available at http://www.aintiaperson.com/.

An Age for Justice: Confronting Elder Abuse *(2009)*

This short documentary focuses on elder abuse in the United States and the importance of creating legislation that addresses the complexities of abuse often perpetrated by family members and friends. The film is a collaborative effort by the National Council on Aging and WITNESS. It is one of the few documentary resources that explicitly address the intersection of the elderly and human rights in the United States. Available from http://elderjusticenow.org/videos.

Children in No Man's Land *(2008)*

Focusing on the narrative of two children who come to the United States from Mexico, this film addresses the plight of undocumented children seeking reunification with their families. The film speaks powerfully to children's rights, particularly with regard to the right to family, right to an adequate standard of living, and right to education, as well as rights of migrant workers and their families. Additional resources, including advocacy suggestions, available at http://impactofilms.com/cinml/.

Made in L.A. *(2007)*

This film profiles the lives of three Latina immigrants who engage in struggles for the rights of workers in a factory producing clothes for a popular retailer in the United States. It highlights issues relevant to social and economic rights, women's rights, and addresses structural racism in the United States. Available from www.pbs.org/pov/madeinla/.

No Justice Out Here **(2008)**

This short PBS documentary profiles the stunning inadequacies of federal laws and policies related to crimes committed on native lands or reservations in the United States. The film strikingly shows the interrelationship of civil, political, social, economic, and cultural rights. It also intersects with recent human rights monitoring and reporting on lack of services and appropriate programs on reservations to address family violence and violence against women. Access the documentary at http://www.pbs. org/wnet/expose/2008/11/no-justice-out-here.html

Sin by Silence **(2008)**

Sin by Silence chronicles the work of several women imprisoned for killing their husbands or partners in a context of domestic violence and the advocacy organization they formed more than 20 years ago called Convicted Women Against Abuse (CWAA). The film underscores ongoing questions of equality before the law for women who kill their abusive spouses. The documentary's strength is in the focus on the CWAA's prison-based organizing and women's rights mobilization to end violence against women. Curriculum and advocacy materials can be accessed at http://www.sinbysilence.com/film/

Testify! Voices for Human Rights in the U.S. **(2010)**

This short documentary profiled on WITNESS's website showcases several short documentaries that were submitted to WITNESS and the U.S. Human Rights Network prior to the United Nations Human Rights Council Universal Periodic Review of the USA in 2010. Available online at http://www.witness. org/campaigns/all-campaigns/us-human-rights-network.

The Harvest/La Cosecha **(2011)**

Robin Romano's film developed from an idea first covered in his award-winning work, *Stolen Childhoods*. *The Harvest* follows the lives of three migrant worker children and their families as they follow the harvest in a number of Southern states. The film highlights examples that could be addressed in class discussion about ethical dilemmas of supporting children's right to education and right to participate in family life. The film is beautifully shot, and its strength is the depth of engagement with youths' voices about life as a migrant child farm worker in the United States. Additional resources available at http://theharvestfilm.com/.

The New Asylums **(2005)**

This film, produced for Frontline and available from www.pbs.org, documents the incarceration of the mentally ill. Following deinstitutionalization and closure of mental hospitals, an unintended consequence has been that large numbers of mentally ill people are now housed in prisons and jails. For this film Frontline went inside Ohio's prison system to document and discuss the implications of the growing number of mentally ill prisoners. It provides ample opportunities to draw lessons for human rights of the mentally ill. The film is approximately 1 hour in length. Order from www.pbs.org

The Released **(2009)**

The Released is a follow-up film to an earlier PBS film, *The New Asylums*. This documentary, produced for Frontline, follows individuals with mental illness as they are released from a men's prison and attempt to adjust to life in the community. It can be used to explore issues of corrections policy, homelessness, and mental health. Through the stories of the inmates and interviews with professionals, the struggles of the men are poignantly portrayed. This hour-long film has applications to many social work courses and displays the complexities of social policy decisions and their implications for human rights. Order from www.pbs.org.

Tying the Knot *(2004)*

This film skillfully outlines the movement to gain equality of rights to marriage and its benefits in the United States. Though it was filmed in the mid-2000s and now is somewhat dated in terms of legislation passed in a number of states granting the right to same-sex marriage, it is still highly relevant and of superb caliber. Available from www.snagfilms.com/films/title/tying_the_knot/.

Unnatural Causes *(2008)*

This seven-part documentary series is one of the best resources available that explores the intersection between racism, social inequality, and health disparities. Though not framed as a human rights concern, the series illustrates the imperative to address the right to the highest attainable standard of physical and mental health in the United States today. Paired with a discussion of the National Economic and Social Rights Initiative's efforts to highlight health in its advocacy, this resource provides a powerful illustration of health as a human right. Curriculum materials related to the film series are superb and can be accessed at http://www.unnaturalcauses.org/. For NESRI's campaign see www.nesri.org.

Well-Founded Fear *(2000)*

This is one of the most powerful films addressing the rights of asylum-seekers in the United States. It tackles entrenched problems that asylum-seekers face when they do not have adequate legal representation in immigration court. Though it was filmed prior to September 11, 2001, and the ensuing War on Terror, the film remains timely. Curriculum and advocacy resources are available at http://www.pbs.org/pov/wellfoundedfear/.

What I Have Been Through Is not Who I Am *(2012)*

Co-created with End Child Prostitution and Trafficking, this short documentary highlights the voices of exploited and forgotten children, adult survivors, law enforcement officers, and prosecutors throughout the United States to draw attention to a campaign to protect sexually exploited children in the United States from criminalization. The film does not sensationalize the idea of sex trafficking; rather, it underscores that the sexual exploitation of children, regardless of nationality or whether they crossed borders, is a human rights concern.

The House We Live In Documentary and Discussion Questions

Kristen Faye Bean
University of Hawai'i at Manoa

The third video in the *Race: The Power of an Illusion* documentary, titled *The House We Live In,* can be used to examine racism and housing rights. It can be ordered here: http://www.pbs.org/race/000_General/000_00-Home.htm.

The video is a three-part documentary about race in society, science, and history. *The House We Live In* is essential for any social welfare policy course. The video explores the social construction of whiteness in the United States, how racism was imbedded in housing policy and created housing segregation, and how economics incentivizes racism. After students learn about economics and politics during a social welfare policy course, this video is used as a review toward the end of the course. Discussion questions (attached) are used after the video. However, each class tends to focus on different aspects of the video that were shocking or important to their learning. I have found the video to be powerful in changing students' preconceived notions of social construction, economics, and equal opportunities.

Discussion Questions

1. How has social construction of race affected policy?

2. How have policies exacerbated the social construction of race?

3. How have economics and the social construction of race played a role in housing policy?

4. I told you at the beginning of the course that "policy doesn't work." In the case of housing policy in the United States, is this true? If so, who benefited and who was disadvantaged?

5. Is housing a human right? If yes, how might this change our approach to housing policy?

6. We discussed affirmative action last week. These policies and others are intended to make up for institutional racism. Even with these policies, can we create equal opportunities for all?

7. Critical race theorists believe that racism is ubiquitous (present everywhere) and always will be. Critical race theories say that the issue actually is not about race, but about power, and once a certain race has power, people of that race will do everything to maintain it. After seeing this movie, do you believe that this is true?

8. Some say that sexism was the first form of racism. Certain races are feminized to make them appear inferior. How was this demonstrated in the movie?

To broaden the discussion of the film into a more extensive module on human rights and racial discrimination, students can be directed to the International Convention on the Elimination of All Forms of Racial Discrimination (United Nations). The United States has ratified this treaty and submits periodic reports to the treaty body, the Committee on the Elimination of Racial Discrimination (CERD). Suggest that students review the most recent report submitted by the United States, the concluding comments by the CERD, and the alternative or shadow report submitted by the U.S. Human Rights Network. Housing discrimination and segregation are addressed in these reports. All these documents can be found at www.ohchr.org under the 72nd session of the CERD.

Human Rights and "The Corporation"

Karen. E. Martin
University of Kentucky

Using this DVD and supplement material, students will learn the legal developments that created the modern corporation and how the behavior and purpose of corporations has changed over time. The film explains how corporations are required above all to be profitable. Students witness varying types of corporations violating an equally diverse set of Universal Declaration of Human Rights articles. As the actions and beliefs of the corporation are analyzed by personality traits, students observe evil corporate action being efficiently and effectively managed by self-described caring and compassionate chief executive officers.

The documentary is 145-minutes long; thus, the majority of class time is spent watching this film. Typically, it is shown the last class of the semester. Because the concept of human rights is now more familiar to students, they can easily identify corporate actions as human rights violations. Topics of discussion may include ethics, social responsibility, health, and environmental effects due to corporate misdeeds and problems related to globalization.

Students seem to enjoy watching the documentary because of its varied topics and new information. However, much of this new information concerns the corporations very familiar to students. Students engaged in discussions after viewing the film are astounded at the depth, reach, and tactics of many of the multinational companies profiled.

If the DVD is purchased for U.S. educational DVD/VHS packaging, a password is provided to access the U.S. Study Guide, which is billed as being "tailored for teachers to suit courses and disciplines ranging from the natural sciences to the humanities, from politics and law to business" (The Corporation.com, 2012). If purchased in any other format, only a limited online free guide is available.

References

Achbar, M., & Abbott, J. (Directors). (2003). *The corporation*. Vancouver, Canada: Big Picture Media Company. Available from http://www.thecorporation.com/

The Corporation.com (2012). Study guides. Retrieved from http://thecorporation.com/index.cfm?page_id=16

An Introduction to Human Rights

Karen E. Martin
University of Kentucky

This module introduces social work students via lecture, multimedia, and discussion to the term *human rights*, how human rights developed over time, and how they relate to the social work profession. It is intended for BSW or MSW students.

The class begins by showing the video, *The Story of Human Rights,* designed to appeal to young adults. It provides an excellent introduction to the Universal Declaration of Human Rights (UDHR) and what are human rights. Discussion following the video helps students understand how social work from its inception has always been a human rights profession (IFSW, 2008). The first accompanying booklet, *What Are Human Rights,* discusses in succinct language the 30 articles of the UDHR. The other booklet, *The Story of Human Rights,* provides a brief history of the development of the UDHR, names famous persons who have promoted human rights, and again includes the 30 articles of the UDHR. The 173-page Educator's Guide was written for a younger audience than the BSW or MSW student; however, many of the suggested discussion topics and questions can easily be made relevant to college students.

The film and accompanying materials can be effectively used in conjunction with the textbook *Human Rights and Social Justice* (Wronka, 2008). Wronka provides a much more detailed history of human rights development and clarifies how social work and human rights are closely intertwined. He also informs students about the five core notions of human rights. The categorization of articles within the UDHR assists students to better identify certain types of violations. As an in-class exercise, several current events topics can be introduced to the class, and students can then be asked which UDHR articles have been violated. This quiz game approach helps students associate current news with a document written more than 60 years ago, making immediately relevant something that may have originally seemed simply historic. Examples of such topics could include health care reform, immigration, the death penalty, genocide, and human trafficking.

The 10-minute video provides an engaging overview of the UDHR. Students' attention is quickly earned as the audio and graphics make for a memorable and thought-provoking presentation. Following the video, an interactive lecture is delivered that includes a social work perspective on human rights. For many social work students, this will be new knowledge. The textbook provides human rights theories within a social work perspective.

The Education Package available from the Youth for Human Rights Package webpage includes an educator's guide; the documentary, *The Story of Human Rights;* 30 award-winning public service announcements illustrating the 30 human rights; a music video; and two booklets, *What Are Human Rights?* and *The Story of Human Rights.* These are distributed free of charge.

Accompanying the textbook by Wronka (2008) are instructor resources on CD (which include PowerPoint slides for each chapter with notes from the author), a test bank, a sample syllabus, and teaching tips.

References

International Federation of Social Workers (IFSW). (1988). *Human rights*. In International Policy Papers. Retrieved from http://ifsw.org/policies/human-rights-policy/

Wronka, J. (2008). *Human rights and social justice: Social action and service for the helping and health professions*. Thousand Oaks, CA: SAGE Publications.

Youth for Human Rights International. (2010). Education package details. Retrieved from http://www.youthforhumanrights.org/educators/education-package-details.html

Human Rights and Social Work Bibliography of Selected Works

Lynne M. Healy
Kathryn Libal
University of Connecticut

M. C. "Terry" Hokenstad
Case Western Reserve University

Amnesty International, www.amnesty.org; Useful website of a leading human rights nongovernmental organization that includes human rights education resources.

Armaline, W. T., Glasberg, D. S., & Purkayastha, B. (2012). *Human rights in our own backyard: Injustice and resistance in the United States.* Philadelphia, PA: University of Pennsylvania Press.

Benedek, W. (Ed.). (2006). *Understanding human rights: Manual on human rights education.* Belgium: European Training and Research Centre for Human Rights and Democracy.

Clapham, A. (2007). *Human rights: A very short introduction.* New York, NY: Oxford University Press.

Coicaud, J. M., Doyle, M. W., & Gardner, A.-M. (2003). *The globalization of human rights.* Tokyo, Japan: United Nations University Press.

Council on Social Work Education, Katherine A. Kendall Institute for International Social Work Education. http://www.cswe.org/kaki; Offers a database of resources to encourage the infusion of international issues into social work curricula.

Dewees, M., & Roche, S. E. (2001). Teaching about human rights in social work. *Journal of Teaching in Social Work, 21*(1/2), 137–155.

Healy, L. M. (2008). Exploring the history of social work as a human rights profession. *International Social Work, 51,* 735–748.

Healy, L. M. (2007). Universalism and relativism in social work ethics. *International Social Work, 50,* 11–26.

Healy, L. M., & Link, R. J. (2012). *Handbook of international social work: Human rights, development, and the global profession.* (Chapters on women's rights by E. Reichert; children's rights by R. Link; rights of persons with disabilities by G. Strand Hutchinson; human rights and sexual orientation by G. Bailey; theories by S. Staub-Bernasconi, and an overview by J. Wronka). New York, NY: Oxford University Press.

Hertel, S., & Libal, K. (Eds.). (2011). *Human rights in the United States: Beyond exceptionalism.* New York, NY: Cambridge University Press.

Hugman, R. (2008). Ethics in a world of difference. *Ethics & Social Welfare, 2*(2), 118–132.

Human Rights Education Association. http://www.hrea.org The Human Rights Education library contains more than 3,000 full-text guides, curricula, textbooks, and other documents that can be used for formal or informal education about human rights.

Human Rights Watch. http://www.humanrightswatch.org; Good source of information on a wide range of global human rights issues, including significant focus on United States.

Humphries, B. (2004). An unacceptable role for social work: Implementing immigration policy. *British Journal of Social Work, 34*(1), 93–107.

Ife, J. (2012). *Human rights and social work: Towards rights-based practice* (3rd ed.). Cambridge, UK: Cambridge University Press.

Ife, J. (2009). *Human rights from below: Achieving rights through community development.* London, UK: Oxford University Press.

Inter-American Commission on Human Rights. http://www.cidh.oas.org

International Association of Schools of Social Work, Human Rights Committee. Resource file available at http://www.iassw-aiets.org

International Council of Social Welfare. (1969). *Human rights and social welfare. Proceedings of the XIVth International Conference of Social Welfare.* Helsinki, Finland: Author.

International Federation of Social Workers (IFSW). (2004). *Manual on children's rights.* Available at http://www.ifsw.org

International Federation of Social Workers (IFSW). (1996). *Human rights: Policy statement.* Available at http://www.ifsw.org

International Federation of Social Workers European Division e.V. (2010). *Standards in social work practice meeting human rights.* Berlin, Germany: Author. Retrieved from http://cdn.ifsw.org/assets/ifsw_45904-8.pdf

Jewell, J. R., Collins, K. V., Gargotto, L., & Dishon, A. J. (2009). Building the unsettling force: Social workers and the struggle for human rights. *Journal of Community Practice, 17,* 309–322.

Lundy, C. (2011). *Social work, social justice, and human rights: A structural approach to practice* (2nd ed.). Toronto, Canada: University of Toronto Press.

Mapp, S. (2007). *Human rights and social justice in a global perspective: An introduction to international social work.* New York, NY: Oxford University Press.

McPherson, J., & Abel, N. (2012). Human rights engagement and exposure: New scales to challenge social work education. *Research on Social Work Practice* [Online]. doi: 10.1177/1049731512454196

Mishra, R. (2005). Social rights as human rights: Globalizing social protection. *International Social Work, 48*(1), 9–20.

National Economic and Social Rights Initiative. http://www.nesri.org; Founded in 2004, this organization fosters localization of human rights norms and practices in the United States, with a focus on economic and social rights. The site has valuable fact sheets, resources, and short video clips of campaigns, and also profiles its key campaigns on health, education, housing, and work.

Reichert, E. (Ed.). (2007). *Challenges in human rights: A social work perspective.* New York, NY: Columbia University Press.

Reichert, E. (2011). *Social work and human rights: A foundation for policy and practice* (2nd ed.). New York, NY: Columbia University Press.

Reichert, E. (2006). *Understanding human rights: An exercise book.* Thousand Oaks, CA: SAGE Publications.

Sewpaul, V., & Matthias, C. (2013). Child rights in Africa [Special issue]. *International Social Work, 56.*

Smith, R. K. M., & van den Anker, C. (Ed.). (2005). *The essentials of human rights*. London, UK: Hodder Arnold.

Staub-Bernasconi, S. (2012). Human rights and their relevance for social work as theory and practice. In L. M. Healy & R. J. Link, *Handbook of international social work: Human rights, development and the global profession* (pp. 30–36). New York, NY: Oxford University Press.

Steen, J. A., & Mathieson, S. (2005). Human rights education: Is social work behind the curve? *Journal of Teaching in Social Work, 25*(3/4), 143–156.

Steen, J. A. (2006). The roots of human rights advocacy and a call to action. *Social Work, 51*(2), 101–105.

United Nations. (1994). *Human rights and social work: A training manual*. Geneva, Switzerland: UN Centre for Human Rights, International Federation of Social Workers, and International Association of Schools of Social Work. (A revised manual is underway and can be accessed on the International Federation of Social Workers website: http://www.ifsw.org.)

United Nations, Office of the High Commissioner for Human Rights. http://www.ohchr.org; This website is an excellent resource for students and researchers. It contains the full text of all United Nations human rights instruments and updates on human rights issues. Of particular interest for research are the periodic country self-reports and treaty body assessments of compliance with the Convention on the Rights of the Child, the Convention on the Elimination of Discrimination Against Women, and other major treaties.

United Nations. (1998). *Human rights today: A United Nations priority*. New York, NY: United Nations Department of Public Information.

UNESCO. (2011). *Contemporary issues in human rights education*. Paris: Author. Available at http://unesdoc.unesco.org/images/0021/002108/210895e.pdf

Wronka, J. (2008). *Human rights and social justice: Social action and service for the helping and health professions*. Thousand Oaks, CA: SAGE.

Wronka, J. (1995). Human rights. In R. Edwards, (Ed.), *Encyclopedia of social work* (19th ed., pp. 1405–1418). Washington, DC: National Association of Social Workers. (A shorter version is in the 20th edition, 2008.)

Notes on the Editors and Primary Contributors

Lynne M. Healy, MSW, PhD, is Board of Trustees Distinguished Professor at the University of Connecticut School of Social Work and co-director of the Center for International Social Work Studies. She was a visiting professor at the University of the West Indies in Jamaica in 1994 and 1995, a visiting lecturer/consultant at the University of Mauritius, and has lectured at universities and conferences in 25 countries. Her areas of publication include internationalizing social work curriculum, international social work, human rights, human service agency management, and ethics. She has written several articles on human rights and social work, co-edited (with Rosemary Link) the *Handbook of International Social Work: Human Rights, Development and the Global Profession* (Oxford, 2012), and co-edited a 2012 special issue of the *Journal of Social Work Education* on globalization and social work education. Dr. Healy chairs the International Association of Schools of Social Work (IASSW) Human Rights Committee and represents the IASSW on the United Nations NGO Committee for Social Development. She has been involved in numerous Council on Social Work Education (CSWE) commissions and is a current member of the Katherine A. Kendall Advisory Committee. She was honored by CSWE in 2004 with the Individual Award for Advancing Education for International Social Work.

M. C. "Terry" Hokenstad, PhD, is a Distinguished University Professor at Case Western Reserve University and holds the Ralph S. and Dorothy P. Schmitt Professorship in the Mandel School of Applied Social Sciences. He also serves as professor of global health in the School of Medicine. In a career spanning more than four decades, he has given special attention to the internationalization of social work and the challenge of an aging world. Hokenstad has uniquely combined these two areas of expertise in his teaching and writing, as well as in his leadership roles at the United Nations and in national and international organizations such as CSWE and the International Association of Schools of Social Work (IASSW). He has authored and edited numerous books, articles, chapters, and monographs in the fields of comparative social welfare, care of older people, and social work practice and education. In addition, he has served as an editor-in-chief of *International Social Work* and as an editorial board member for a number of other scholarly journals. Hokenstad has received the Significant Lifetime Achievement Award from CSWE and the IASSW Katherine Kendall Award for a Lifetime of Distinguished International Service to Social Work Education.

Amy Restorick Roberts, PhD, completed her doctoral studies at the Mandel School of Applied Social Sciences of Case Western Reserve University. Gerontology is her main research interest, with emphasis in international social work, long-term care services and supports, and quality of life for older adults. She recently joined the faculty of Miami University in the Department of Family Studies and Social Work.

Uma A. Segal, PhD, is professor and director of the baccalaureate social work program at the University of Missouri—St. Louis, and holds a Fellow appointment with the university's international studies and programs. She is visiting professor at the University of Tskuba (Japan), Alliance University (India), and the Universidade do Minho (Portugal). Her current research focuses on immigrant and refugee integration. Her most recent project took her to Brazil to study migration between Brazil and Japan in the last three decades, and she is also embarking on a project funded by the Silberman Award on the health of older immigrants. Segal co-edited (with Doreen Elliott) a four-volume book series titled *Refugees Worldwide* (Praeger Publishers, 2012) and (with Doreen Elliott and Nazneen S. Mayadas) a book, *Immigration Worldwide* (Oxford University Press, 2010). She also wrote *A Framework for Immigration: Asians in the United States* (Columbia University Press, 2002). She has published several peer reviewed journal articles and invited chapters and has presented her research on all continents. From 2004 to 2012 she was editor-in-chief of the *Journal of Immigrant & Refugee Studies,* which she moved into the international and interdisciplinary realm addressing issues of human migration. Segal currently serves on the Katherine A. Kendall Institute Advisory Board and on the Board of Directors of CSWE. She received a Fulbright fellowship (2013–2014) to establish a new school of social work, with a dual international and rural focus, at Alliance University in Bangalore, India.

Joseph Wronka, PhD, is professor of social work at Springfield College, where he has taught human rights, international social work, social policy, and qualitative research for 20 years. A Fulbright senior specialist scholar in the discipline of social work, his areas of specialty are in social justice, poverty, human rights, and phenomenology. He is also permanent representative to the United Nations in Geneva for the International Association of Schools of Social Work. He has extensive teaching and practice experience, including in Europe, Alaska, New York City, and India. The author of four books and numerous articles in popular and scholarly journals, he has presented his work in 13 countries. An accomplished musician, he enjoys playing classical and ethnic pieces on the accordion and piano.